CW00825625

ECOLOGY AND MANAGEMENT OF
Invasive Riverside Plants

LANDSCAPE ECOLOGY SERIES

Ecology and Management of Invasive Riverside Plants
Edited by Louise C. de Waal, Lois E. Child, P. Max Wade and John H. Brock

ECOLOGY AND MANAGEMENT OF
Invasive Riverside Plants

Edited by
LOUISE C. de WAAL, LOIS E. CHILD, P. MAX WADE
International Centre of Landscape Ecology
Loughborough University, UK

and

JOHN H. BROCK
School of Agribusiness and Environmental Resources
Arizona State University, USA

Published for the International Centre of Landscape Ecology

by

JOHN WILEY & SONS

Chichester · New York · Brisbane · Toronto · Singapore

Other Wiley Editorial Offices

John Wiley & Sons, Inc., 605 Third Avenue,
New York, NY 10158–0012, USA

Jacaranda Wiley Ltd, G.P.O. 33 Part Road, Milton
Queensland 4064, Australia

John Wiley & Sons (Canada) Ltd, 22 Worcester Road,
Rexdale, Ontario M9W 1L1, Canada

John Wiley & Sons (SEA) Pte Ltd, 37 Jalan Pemimpin #05-04,
Block B, Union Industrial Building, Singapore 2057

Library of Congress Cataloging-in-Publication Data

Ecology and management of invasive riverside plants / edited by
   L.C. de Waal, L.E. Child, P.M. Wade and J.H. Brock
       p.   cm.—(Landscape ecology series)
   Includes bibliographical references and index
   ISBN 0-471-94257-X
   1. Weeds—Control. 2. Riparian plants—Control. 3. Riparian
plants—Ecology. 4. Plant invasions. I. Wade, P. M. (P. Max)
II. Series.
SB611.E26   1994
639.9'9—dc20   93-30022
                                                       CIP

British Library Cataloguing in Publication Data

A catalogue record for this book is available from the British Library

ISBN 0-471-94257-X

Typeset in 10/12pt Times by Acorn Bookwork, Salisbury, Wilts
Printed and bound in Great Britain by Biddles Ltd, Guildford and Kings Lynn

Contents

List of Contributors

John P. Bailey
Botany Department, University of Leicester, University Road, Leicester LE1 7RH, UK

David J. Beerling
Department of Animal and Plant Sciences, School of Biological Sciences, PO Box 601, University of Sheffield, Sheffield S10 2UQ, UK

John H. Brock
School of Agribusiness and Environmental Resources, Arizona State University, Tempe, Arizona, 85287–3306, USA

Joe M. Caffrey
Central Fisheries Board, Mobhi Boreen, Glasnevin, Dublin 9, Ireland

Ed Darby
International Centre of Landscape Ecology, Department of Geography, Loughborough University of Technology, Loughborough, Leicestershire, LE11 3TU, UK

F. Hugh Dawson
NERC, Institute of Freshwater Ecology, River Laboratory, East Stoke, Wareham, Dorset, UK

Louise C. de Waal
International Centre of Landscape Ecology, Department of Geography, Loughborough University, Loughborough, Leicestershire, LE11 3TU, UK

Felicité S. Dodd
International Centre of Landscape Ecology, Department of Geography, Loughborough University, Loughborough, Leicestershire, LE11 3TU, UK

Simon V. Fowler
International Institute of Biological Control, Silwood Park, Bukhurst Road, Ascot, UK

Richard P. Garnett
Monsanto plc., Thames Tower, Leicester LE1 3TP, UK

Deborah J. Hill
Swansea City Council Planning Department, Swansea, West Glamorgan, UK

Anthony N. G. Holden
International Institute of Biological Control, Silwood Park, Bukhurst Road, Ascot, UK

Harald Lundström
Borgmästaregatan 3, S-23104 Trelleborg, Sweden

John P. Palmer
Richards, Moorehead and Laing Ltd, 3 Clwyd Street, Ruthin, Clwyd, LL15 1HF, UK

Bruce Philp
Scottish Agricultural College, Auchincruive, Ayr, KA6 5HW, UK

Karel Prach
Department of Plant Ecology, Botanical Institute of the Czechoslovak Academy of Sciences, 379 82 Trebon, the Czech Republic

Petr Pyšek
Institute of Applied Ecology, 281 63 Kostelec nad Cernymi lesy, the Czech Republic

Liz Roblin
National Rivers Authority, Glan Tawe, 154 St Helen's Road, Swansea, West Glamorgan, SA1 4DF, UK

Clare Sampson
Bunting Biological Control Ltd., Great Horkesley, Colchester, Essex, CO6 4AJ, UK

David Spencer-Jones
Water Wise Consultancy, Plowmans, Park Road, Forest Row, Sussex, UK

Arnie Stensones
Monsanto plc, Thames Tower, Leicester LE1 3TP, UK

Gordon E. D. Tiley
Scottish Agricultural College, Auchincruive, Ayr, KA6 5HW, UK

Ulla Vogt Andersen
Royal Veterinary and Agricultural University, Department of Botany, Dendrology and Forest Genetics, Botanical Section, Rolighedsvej 23, DK-1958 Frederiksberg, Copenhagen, Denmark

P. Max Wade
International Centre of Landscape Ecology, Department of Geography, Loughborough University, Loughborough, Leicestershire, LE11 3TU, UK

Preface

The Landscape Ecology series seeks to focus on a range of topics which present challenges to the landscape ecologist. It brings together the researcher and the practitioner to present a spectrum of views and knowledge in order to encourage an integrated solution to contemporary issues. The topics included are international and the contributions will draw upon the experiences of experts around the world. Landscape ecology concerns the inter-relationships between the various components of the landscape—flora, fauna, soil, water and air. This focus needs to take into account both the growing body of knowledge concerned with the processes which underlie the landscape, for example ecological, geomorphological and climatological processes, and the experience gained by those managing the landscape such as the engineer, the conservation officer and the administrator.

Plant invasions are not a new phenomenon. Humans have been busy moving plants around from one part of the world to another for centuries and some of these species have become accepted components of the flora, for example *Acer pseudoplatanus* (sycamore) in the British Isles. There are those species which have proved themselves to be unwanted, generating a range of problems, mostly associated with agricultural activities. Some, however, have brought about significant changes in the wider landscape, with the river environment being one component especially prone to invasion by alien plants. Throughout the world the biotic and abiotic characteristics of river habitats are being altered by a relatively small number of invasive plant species. This first volume explores the reasons why the riparian zone of rivers is prone to colonisation by such plants and considers in detail the biology and autecology of five such species: *Crassula helmsii* (swamp stonecrop), *Impatiens glandulifera* (Himalayan or Indian balsam), *Fallopia japonica* (Japanese knotweed), *Heracleum mantegazzianum* (giant hogweed) and *Tamarix* (salt cedar). These plants first came to the attention of botanists because of their attractive and impressive nature: *H. mantegazzianum* with its sheer size and its giant white umbels, *F. japonica* and *I. glandulifera* too because of their attractive foliage and flowers. They were brought from foreign climes to the botanical gardens of Europe and North America to be marvelled at. Perceptions have changed, and in the natural and semi-natural environment of the river bank these plants have become inappropriate and unwelcome. The management of such species is costing very large sums of money each year, expenditure which is not stopping their continuing and inexorable spread. Whilst our studies of them will continue to include extending our knowledge of their mechanisms of propagation, it has now become imperative to understand how they can be controlled effectively and permanently. A question arising from the studies of these species is "How long will it be before any given species becomes a problem in other parts of the world?". This volume is an important contribution to understanding where and under what conditions these and other species are likely to become of weed status.

Max Wade
February 1994

1 Spread of *Crassula helmsii* in Britain

F. HUGH DAWSON
NERC, Institute of Freshwater Ecology,
River Laboratory, East Stoke, Wareham, UK

THE PLANT

Crassula helmsii (T. Kirk) Cockayne (*Tillaea recurva* (Hook f.) to the water gardener or aquatic supplier) is identifiable in the field growing on damp soil near or in water by its short dense stands and mid- to yellowish-green, stiff, succulent-like appearance. Pairs of unstalked opposite leaves (4–24 mm) are borne on rigid stems which also bear single small white four-petalled aerial flowers on short stalks in their axils during summer. The joining of the leaf bases into a collar of approximately 1 mm is a distinctive character and allows the plant to be readily distinguished from other species, such as *Callitriche* spp., especially when growing at low density in its more flaccid underwater form. Leaf form varies from oblong-lanceolate to oblong-elliptical, acute to acuminate, rarely cuspidate and entire. The leaf tip is entire, which readily distinguishes this plant from species of *Callitriche* which have notched leaf tips.

INTRODUCTION TO BRITAIN

It appears that *Crassula helmsii* (Swamp stonecrop) was introduced into Britain before 1914, but was only commercially available from 1927, although the first site at which it became naturalized in Essex was only found in the mid-1950s (Dawson and Warman, 1987). It is possible that other introductions have occurred and anecdotal evidence suggests that it has been present on the Isle of Wight since the 1930s; this introduction is related to the import of sheep from Australia and is similar to a possible mechanism of transfer from eastern to western Australia (Dawson, 1989b).

However, it seems likely that there has been only one introduction, as plants examined from about 40 sites indicate that there is little morpholog-

Ecology and Management of Invasive Riverside Plants
Edited by L. C. de Waal, L. E. Child, P. M. Wade and J. H. Brock
© 1994 John Wiley & Sons Ltd

ical variation throughout Britain when compared with the range of form of plants (50) collected across Australia. Although geographically distinct areas were sampled, it is known that there has been some movement of stocks within Britain, for example from Norfolk to Lossiemouth in Scotland.

Field studies of the habitat in Australia or New Zealand would be expected to assist in highlighting critical points useful to the control of the plant, such as growth, habitat requirements and natural predators. The source, however, has not yet been definitively identified, although there are indications from studies of genetic variation as expressed in isoenzymes that only one introduction has been made into Britain. Preliminary determinations using starch–gel electrophoresis on shoot tips from a wide geographic range in Britain, showed no difference in expression of seven enzymes systems (FE, PGI, MDH, AAT, PGM, TPI and LAP; see glossary for full names at end of chapter, Richardson et al., 1986). Plant material in another more extensive series of British sites was invariate in its expression for four other enzyme systems (G6PDH, ICDH, MDH and ALD); such results indicate only one strain or little inherent polymorphism within the species. Australian material from 34 sites across its natural range, has been tested for 11 enzyme systems (AP, ADH, EST, GOT, G6PDH, ICDH, MDH, ME, PGI, SKDH, SOD) and whilst variation has been found it was only clear for two (ME and MDH), indicating that plants from the Northern Tablelands of northern New South Wales were different from other Australian and the British material. Preliminary but unclear results for another enzyme system (EST) could indicate that plants from Tasmania are also different and that plants from along the River Murray are the more likely source of the British introduction; this does not add much information as this river drains half the Australian continent.

EXPANSION RATE AND DISTRIBUTION

Crassula helmsii has rapidly expanded its range in natural and semi-natural sites across Britain and the plant has been found in approximately 390 sites to mid-1992 from approximately 270 sites in mid-1990 (Figure 1.1). Following the finding of the first naturalized site in Essex in the mid-1950s, there were several records for plantings in various types of pond mainly in the south of England during the 1960s and early 1970s, with two also in Scotland, but none in Wales. There were few records of the plant becoming naturalized until the late 1970s and early 1980s. Currently, however, the majority are still consolidating in the south-east quadrant of Britain and spreading across the remainder of England, with 15 sites in Wales including one in Anglesey and 10 sites in Scotland with one on the Isle of Skye, but none on the outer islands (Dawson, 1988). In addition, a few sites only have

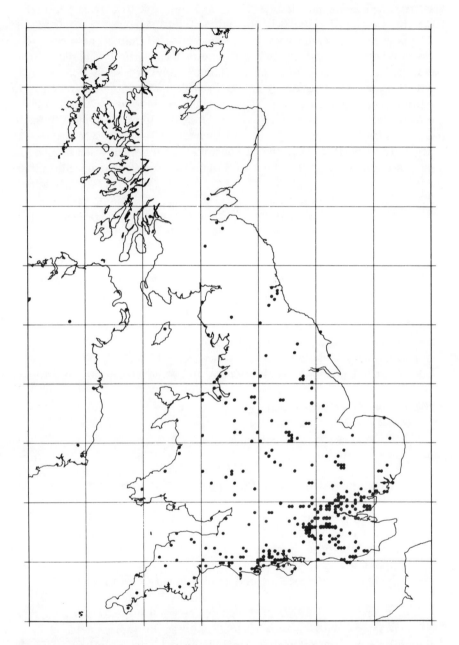

Figure 1.1 The distribution of *Crasssula helmsii* in Great Britain to mid-1992 as sites within 1 km squares (positions are indicated by a closed circle representing a 5 km size for visibility)

been recorded in Ireland despite the plant being said to be easily available; there are also records from Belgium and Germany.

There were two main types of invasion: firstly, that of new sites to a region or super county and, secondly, more local spread apparently from established sites. Significant local or secondary invasion seems to take 5–10 years to occur and preliminary analysis suggests that this rate is similar to the primary invasion rate. Sites at which such spread is clearly seen include the New Forest in Hampshire, in which 17 of the approximately 200 potential pool sites have been invaded with increasing rapidity over the last 25 years. Spread by drift along the Basingstoke Canal and transfer around the parks and commons around Greater London may be occurring at an even faster rate.

The annual rate of increase (Figure 1.2) relies to a major extent on the interest of botanists and recorders; there are several factors which must be taken into account in determining the actual rate. These factors include, on the positive side:

(i)   increased interest in *C. helmsii* as a new plant in the south of the country during the 1970s,
(ii) interest in producing new vice-county records,
(iii) the result of concern expressed by particular recorders and pond owners on the effects of the plant,
(iv) availability of description and drawings for identification,
(v)   continued publicity on the impact of this plant on various habitats and
(vi) the recent awareness-sheet jointly produced by the Institute of Freshwater Ecology and English Nature (Dawson and Warman, 1992);

and on the negative side:

(i)   reduced interest following the reporting of the first and second vice-county occurrences,
(ii) the perception that invasions were not as bad as forecasted, particularly for deep waters and for those with low nutrient concentrations and also the false optimism of loss of the plant from sites following supposed clearance and
(iii) difficulties of identification and confusion with *Callitriche* spp.

In addition, the recorded rate of spread of the plant lagged because of slow dissemination of records; it took up to 18 months for approximately 95% of the records to be completed, but occasional ones took several years. Many records were promptly disseminated by the end of the field season. The process was originally enhanced by direct mailings to vice-county recorders

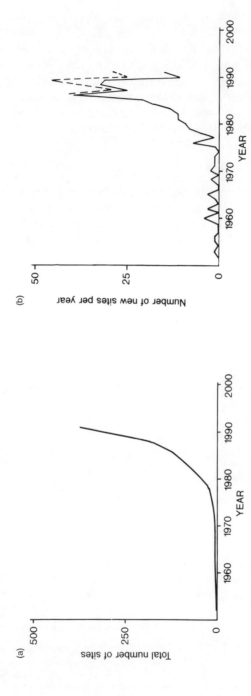

Figure 1.2 *Crassula helmsii* in Britain (a) the total number of new sites reported against year, and (b) the number of new sites reported annually to 1992 (———) with the additional reportings in 1992 for previous years (- - -) to indicate the lag-time in reporting new occurrences

in 1987/88, 1990 and 1992 and by regular exhibitions, pamphlets and publicity in the media.

Considerable variation was found in the precise definition of a "site", which has ranged from a single small patch to an area with six ponds, a lake and interconnecting channels. It was therefore necessary to define presence in a standard manner, thus 1 km squares were taken as single occurrences although actual National Grid Reference positions to 100 m are used in analysis of the distribution of secondary introductions.

TYPES OF SITE INVADED

Analysis of the types of site invaded indicates that small ponds are the most common, of which about one-third may dry-down. The majority of these are located in agricultural areas although there are also many in private land and nature reserves (Table 1.1) (Dawson, 1991b). Such an analysis does not

Table 1.1. Occurrence of *Crassula helmsii* in sites in Britain by (a) type of waterbody and (b) adjacent land use for sites, in the years to mid-1988 (190 sites), to mid-1990 (270 sites) and to the end of 1991 (370 sites)

Assessment date	Percentage occurrence			Public access
	Mid-1988	Mid-1990	End 1991	
Number of sites	190	270	370	
(a) Type of waterbody				
Small ponds (30% temporary or drying)	70	62		Variable
Tanks		4		Restricted
Shallow gravel sand or clay lakes	6	7		Variable
Large lakes or reservoirs	11	9		Open/closed
Linear watercourses near static	5	10		Open
Linear watercourses, flowing (or on banks)	5	4		Open
Damp ground, marsh	1	2		Variable
In cultivation	2	2		Closed
(b) Adjacent land use				
Nature reserves, SSSIs, etc.	15	16		Restricted
Natural or semi-natural areas	55			Open
Common land (and woodland)		12		Open
Parks, estates, country houses, moats	28	16		Restricted
Agricultural land		21		Restricted
Private gardens		12		Closed
Industrial, extraction of gravel, clay		11		Closed
Reservoirs, large tanks		6		Closed
Fish and ornamental ponds		4		Variable
in cultivation	2	2		Closed

fully indicate the area of plant stands. Some reservoirs in the south-east of England have extensive areas occupied by the plant, probably resulting from its tolerance to the large fluctuations in water level. These sites do not, however, have the high biomass which is found in seasonal ponds, particularly in the south, although the blockage of outlet pipes and screens is to be expected.

Preliminary analysis of the water chemistry of a selection of approximately 25 sites invaded indicates that biomass is highest in slightly alkaline and nutrient-rich waters; although the plant grows better than many native species in all but true acid waters, i.e. those of less than pH 5.5.

MECHANISMS OF SPREAD

Primary invasion seems to have been almost entirely by planting in the early 1950s and 1960s whereas secondary spread from these sites is now more common. Suppliers of aquatic plants have provided the plant both directly by name, and indirectly as an unnamed "oxygenator". Following initial publicity of the problem of invasion of natural sites, several suppliers withdrew such sales, but the plant is often readily available passively with a wide range of other named species of native and introduced marsh and aquatic plants.

Causes of expansion and invasion by this plant include (i) human activities, e.g. transfer on fishing nets, during transfer of fish, emptying aquaria, botanists and zoologists during surveys and pond clearance; and (ii) movement of wildlife, e.g. ponies in the New Forest and southern England. Passive drift has occurred along canals and drains, but not yet along rivers.

PLANT GROWTH FORMS AND GROWTH STRATEGY

The growth form and morphology of this plant vary with habitat (Figure 1.3). The variety of its forms and their environmental tolerances contribute to its success in both aquatic and moist terrestrial habitats.

DRY TO DAMP SOILS

The plant grows by runners of up to 0.3 m in length, which bear short side branches and which may be on the surface or buried. Thus, growth of these results in a low flat mat in dry areas, or a short turf, in moister or sheltered conditions. The leaves are typically succulent-like, being small, slightly fleshy and rigid, and ranging in colour from bright green to yellow or even red, depending upon water and nutrient status. They are often reflexed downwards.

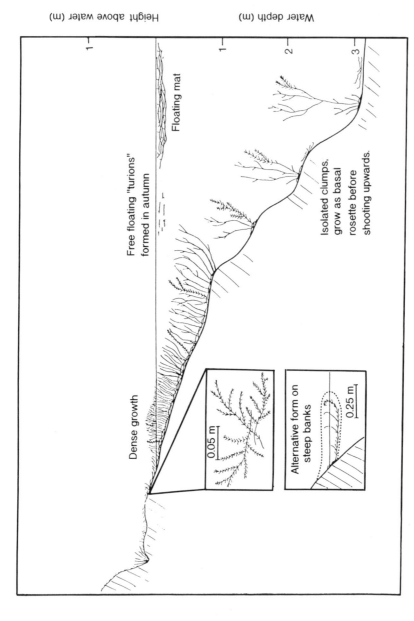

Figure 1.3 The growth form of *Crassula helmsii* at various depths below and heights above water level (leaves are shown on selected stems only. Figure extended from Dawson and Warman (1987). Reproduced by permission of Elsevier Applied Science Publishers Ltd).

WETTED PERIMETERS

On wet soils and around the margins of waterbodies, creeping and branching shoots rapidly colonize bare areas to form a loose rosette of creeping stems. After spreading 0.2–0.4 m, or less when shoot density is greater, the tips turn upwards and vertical shoots develop into a loose turf of 0.1–0.2 m in height which soon thickens as more shoots develop from the horizontal stems. Small local differences in substrata may cause the formation of small tussocks. Although branching is infrequent and many parallel shoots develop, much mutual support is achieved by the interlinking of the slightly recurved stiff leaves. In positions where the shoots can gain support, e.g. from other vegetation, the stand height may grade higher to approximately 0.25 m above the general stand height. This process smothers out other species, as *C. helmsii* remains throughout the year and shoots or germinating seeds of other species have difficulty in penetrating the stand. After as little as two years, many species can no longer penetrate these mats and are outcompeted. This even applies, surprisingly, to large species with strong rhizomes and acute shoot tips, such as *Typha* spp.

SHALLOW WATER

In shallow water down to depths of approximately 1 m, the shoots develop in the same manner as in wetted perimeters, but shoots develop with more flaccid underwater leaves; aerial leaves develop once the shoots pass to the air. Although underwater shoots may reach 0.5 m, the emergent part of the stand does not exceed 0.1–0.2 m. Emergent stands are shade tolerant and taller stands with relatively high biomasses have been found in sheltered wet areas shaded by deciduous trees.

DEEPER WATER

In deeper water down to depths of 3 m in Britain, shoots may grow to approximately 1.2 m in length. They branch sparsely when they are not emergent and their internodes are two to three times longer than emergent shoots. Colonization of deeper water is typically by the settlement of fragments which develop into rosettes. Stems may break away and float around the waterbody before settling and growing, but, in autumn, short shoots with very short internodes ("turions") are produced apically, which float or are blown around the waterbody, but have not been observed to sink. These turions seem to be very efficient at colonizing new areas. Water levels change seasonally in some waterbodies and this plant is well able to optimize its use of such areas, being well adapted to both aerial and submerged growth.

FLOWING WATER

In flowing water, the growth form is similar to the underwater form although stems appear tougher and are orientated in the direction of flow. Although experiments showed that the plant can grow at water velocities of greater than 0.3 m/s, the plant has not been found naturalized in flowing water in Britain, but may be present in sites adjacent to moving water, such as backwaters or on seasonally drying banks (Dawson and Warman, 1987).

ENVIRONMENTAL TOLERANCE BY PROPAGULES AND SHOOTS

Small pieces of shoot (5–10 mm) containing a node are frequently viable and most pieces will grow at least one new shoot, and sometimes two, under a wide variety of environmental conditions. Such pieces are also quite tolerant to drying conditions. Indeed shoots have been known to remain viable for several weeks in laboratory conditions and, in one extreme case, a shoot remained viable on correctly prepared (but not microwaved) herbarium sheets for approximately 4 months. Under adverse conditions, the die-back of stems occurs progressively from the base towards the tip, which remains viable for the longest period.

Shoots were observed to survive for several hours in ice and air temperatures of $-7°C$ after which only crushed leaves were lost from the plant; stems were blackened, but apical growth continued.

Preliminary trials show that the growth of shoots progressively declines with increasing salinity to approximately 15 000 ppm or approximately half that of sea water; further trials are necessary to clarify the growth form strategy.

Germination trials on seeds taken from flowering British plants have not yet found the conditions or pretreatments necessary for germination to occur. Results of material collected from colonized field sites are confused by the potential for development of nodal fragments as small as 1 mm.

ECOPHYSIOLOGY

The plants probably process carbon through the crassulacean acid metabolism (CAM) pathway as they show diel changes in titrateable acidity of the order of 30–60 mmol/g. However, whilst this indicates CAM, the presence of PEP carboxylase has not yet been confirmed as would be required by definition to confirm true CAM (e.g. Kluge, 1982). Diel acidity varies more in the short forms colonizing drying mud than in luxuriantly growing and partially submerged forms. This diel range is also more apparent in fully submerged stems and would be explained by the reduced availability of dissolved carbon dioxide in water by comparison with air.

FUTURE DISTRIBUTION

Most British freshwaters are susceptible to invasion by this plant. Preliminary analysis of data from Australia indicates that Britain lies within the range of requirements for this plant when considered in terms of water chemistry, rainfall, dryness, altitude, frost and snow conditions (Dawson, 1991a). In addition to this, the plant was found in one protected estuary in Tasmania within 0.05–0.1 m above the sea water surface. The consequence of this to its potential distribution in Britain is difficult to interpret because of the reduced tidal range of Australian waters.

CONTROL

One herbicide, diquat, has been found to be effective in control of the plant in underwater conditions. This is available either as a liquid (Reglone) or as the viscous gel diquat alginate (Midstream), which may be required to limit or optimize control in specific areas. Incomplete initial control rapidly leads to recolonization and invasion of new sites by actively growing fragments released from dying stems if economies of dose or area treated are made; mesh barriers have been recommended to reduce the movement of such fragments. Another herbicide, glyphosate, has been tested on emergent stands, but although more successful than any of the other herbicides approved for emergent weed control, it requires doses in excess of those generally accepted for normal use. Compounds such as hydrogen peroxide, which should directly kill this plant, have also been tested on emergent material, but without greater success (Dawson, 1989a, Dawson and Henville, 1991). New herbicides or even metabolites such as malic acid, might need to be tested to find more effective methods of control. Follow up monitoring after treatment is advised for several years to ensure that adequate control is achieved. Currently, it is felt that the continued expansion within sites and invasion of new sites justifies the use of extreme and thorough initial control. Partial control only creates additional space, which enhances growth of this plant while killing native plants. It is expected that native plants will recolonize waterbodies from seed banks after eradication of *C. helmsii* although some planting may be necessary from uncontaminated sites.

The alternative approach would be to accept the invasion of this species and find uses such as stripping nutrients from waste waters; the plant is well suited because it grows rapidly, it will tolerate a wide range of chemical conditions and it is amenable to handling and disposal. But, whilst feasibility trials have been attempted, this use is unlikely to be acceptable to the conservation lobby.

SUMMARY

(1) *Crassula helmsii*, an amphibious aquatic plant, has invaded approximately 390 natural sites (mid-1992) since the mid-1950s and invasion of approximately 1000 sites is predicted by AD 2000.

(2) Preliminary morphological and isoenzyme examination indicates that only a single introduction of this plant is likely to have occurred in Britain, probably originating from along the River Murray in southern Australia.

(3) The present distribution based mainly upon information from vice-county recorders indicates that the spread of the plant has been less from natural factors, e.g. animals, than from human activities. There have been deliberate introductions although passive distribution with other water plants, recreational and associated activities, particularly fishing and fish transfer, and the reintroduction of amphibians and reptiles, seem to be common, albeit nearly unconfirmable, modes of spread.

(4) Predicting the rate of invasion is made difficult by several factors, including the initial lack of information for identification, confusion with another common water plant. An increase in initial interest for new vice-county records was followed by a decline; subsequently, awareness of the problem has stimulated further interest.

(5) The growth form and morphology of the plant in its various habitats and its competitive mechanisms, together with an analysis of the type of waterbodies invaded, are discussed, with a prediction that the majority of temporary and permanent ponds and probably some drainage channels and streams in Britain and northern Europe will be rapidly invaded.

ACKNOWLEDGEMENTS

Thanks are due to Dr M. Earnshaw and Dr E. Sheffield of Manchester University for help, advice on CAM titrations and for undertaking the preliminary isoenzyme determination; to Dr A. Gray of the Institute of Terrestrial Ecology, Furzebrook, for advice; and Richard Saunders and Paul Henville of the Institute of Freshwater Ecology and Peter Sage on placement from Bath University for help with the electrophoretic apparatus and methodology; to Miss L Howton of MAFF Plant Health Division for help in issuing import licences; to the herbaria of western Australia, south Australia, New South Wales, Queensland and Tasmania for help and for licences to collect material in Australia. This study was funded by the Nature Conservancy Council (now English Nature and Scottish Natural Heritage), the Environmental Research Fund and the Natural Environment Research Council. F. H. Dawson was awarded a Winston Churchill Travelling Fellowship to study swamp stonecrop in Australia.

REFERENCES

Dawson, F.H. (1988). The alien aquatic *Crassula helmsii* continues to expand its distribution in Britain. *BSBI News*, **49**, 43.
Dawson, F.H. (1989a). Some attempts at the control of the alien aquatic *Crassula helmsii* (T. Kirk) Cockayne. *BSBI News*, **51**, 46.
Dawson, F.H. (1989b). *Natural Habitat and Population Control Mechanism of Crassula helmsii (Australian Swamp Stonecrop) in Australia.* Report to the Winston Churchill Memorial Trust, 33 pp.
Dawson, F.H. (1991a). *Crassula helmsii*: comparisons of the habitat in Australia with those in Britain. *BSBI News*, **57**, 48.
Dawson, F.H. (1991b). Distribution, dispersal and biology of the aquatic weed *Crassula helmsii* and its importance in agriculture. *Fifth Report of The Environmental Research Fund (TERF), a review of activities 1989–90*, pp. 5–6.
Dawson, F.H. & Henville, P. (1991). *An Investigation of the Control of Crassula helmsii by Herbicidal Chemicals (with interim guidelines on control). Final Report.* Report to the Nature Conservancy Council, 107 pp.
Dawson, F.H. and Warman, E.A. (1987). *Crassula helmsii* (T. Kirk) Cockayne: is it an aggressive alien aquatic plant in Britain? *Biological Conservation*, **42**, 247–272. (Abstract in *BSBI News* **45**, 38–39, April 1987 and updates: *Crassula Watch* 1, Nov 1987 4 pp., *Crassula Watch* 2, Nov 1988 4 pp., *Crassula Watch* 3, Nov 1990, 4 pp.
Dawson, F.H. and Warman, E.A. (1992) *Crassula helmsii Focus on Control.* Institute of Freshwater Ecology, Natural Environment Research Council & English Nature. Pamphlet 8 pp.
Kluge, M. (1982). Crassulacean acid metabolism (CAM). In Govindjee (Ed.) *Photosynthesis Vol. II. Development, Carbon Metabolism and Plant Productivity.* New York: Academic Press.
Richardson, B.J., Baverstock, P.R. and Adams, M. (1986). *Allozyme Electrophoresis. A Handbook for Animal Systematics and Population Studies.* Academic Press, 410 pp.

GLOSSARY OF ISOENZYME ACRONYMS

ADH　　　Alcohol dehydrogenase
ALD　　　Aldolase
AP　　　Alkaline phosphatase
EST　　　Esterase (colorimetric)
FE　　　Esterase (fluorescent)

GOT/AAT	Glutamate oxaloacetate transaminase/aspartate aminotransferase
G6PDH	Glucose-6-phosphate dehydrogenase
ICDH	Isocitrate dehydrogenase
LAP	Leucine aminopeptidase
MDH	Malate dehydrogenase
ME	Malic enzyme
PGI	Phosphoglucoisomerase
PGM	Phosphoglucomutase
SKDH	Shikimate dehydrogenase
SOD	Super oxide dismutase
TPI	Triosephosphate isomerase

2 Some Observations on the Use of Herbicides for Control of *Crassula helmsii*

DAVID SPENCER-JONES
Water Wise Consultancy, Forest Row, Sussex, UK

INTRODUCTION

Crassula helmsii (Swamp stonecrop) has spread rapidly throughout the United Kingdom since its introduction to the country before 1914 (Swale and Belcher, 1982) and commonly reaches pest proportions displacing native species and presenting management problems (Dawson and Warman, 1987). *C. helmsii* has also been recorded from Westfalen in Germany (Bücher *et al.*, 1990).

The trials described in this paper were conducted on a small privately owned lake of approximately 1800 m² which had become heavily infested with *C. helmsii*. The lake comprises a circular area approximately 1.5 m deep opening onto a larger and shallower area only 0.5 m deep. Water from an upstream gravel works ensures that the lake water is sufficiently warm never to freeze, thus encouraging growth all year round.

Although laboratory trials have provided some indication of herbicidal activity of dichlobenil, diquat and terbutryn, information from field trials is lacking. These three herbicides, each with its own specific but different mode of action, were considered as suitable candidates.

To control the infestation, the owner of the lake applied diquat alginate in 1989 but results were unsatisfactory. Subsequently, the lake was drained in the autumn in the hope that winter frosts might kill or seriously check the plant. These frosts never materialized. An excavator was then hired and as much as possible of the lake dredged, but, by May 1990, growth had once more become prolific throughout. The whole of the shallow area had become almost completely overgrown with numerous small but vigorous clumps of *C. helmsii* whilst, in the deeper part, the plant had developed into large submerged clumps which had reached the surface over much of the water. It was at this stage that the control programme described below was undertaken. In

Ecology and Management of Invasive Riverside Plants
Edited by L. C. de Waal, L. E. Child, P. M. Wade and J. H. Brock
© 1994 John Wiley & Sons Ltd

view of the owner's previous experience with diquat alginate, this was not used in the first instance

METHODS AND MATERIALS

The recommended timing for both dichlobenil and terbutryne is at the onset of vigorous growth in the spring, whilst diquat alginate should be applied in the late spring or early summer when growth is active. All three materials are surface applied, dichlobenil and terbutryn being in granular formulation, whilst diquat alginate is formulated as a viscous gel. Application rates used in this trial are shown in Table 2.1.

RESULTS

The 6.75% formulation of dichlobenil was applied on 1 June 1990 (Table 2.2). One month after application, all growth had been severely checked, with the plants pale and stripped of their leaves. After nine weeks, many of the small clumps in the shallow section had been killed whilst those in the deeper water had become blackened and brittle. Four weeks later, however, re-growth of the large deep-water clumps had become advanced and vigorous, whilst, in the shallow section, some re-growth could be seen in isolated areas.

Table 2.1. Herbicide application rates for treatment of *Crassula helmsii*

Chemical	Percentage	Rate (active ingredient)
Dichlobenil	6.75	10 kg/ha
Dichlobenil	20	10 kg/ha
Terbutryn	1	0.05 kg/ha
Diquat alginate	10	10 litres/ha

Table 2.2. Treatment programme for *Crassula helmsii*, June 1990 to October 1991

Year and date applied	Treatment	Period of control
1990 1 June	6.75% Dichlobenil	13 weeks
6 September	6.75% Dichlobenil	Throughout winter
1991 10 April	Terbutryn	12 weeks
30 July	20% Dichlobenil	11 weeks
14 October	Diquat alginate	24 weeks and continuing

Dichlobenil was reapplied on 6 September with the aim of preventing further growth throughout the winter. In this respect it proved successful, although by the following spring further treatment was again needed. It was decided to use terbutryn on this occasion because of its different mode of action from that of dichlobenil.

Accordingly, terbutryn was applied on 10 April 1991 at the lower of the manufacturer's two recommended rates. By then, large clumps were growing vigorously in the deep section, but with much smaller though more numerous clumps in the shallow section.

Six weeks later, although discoloured and pale, close examination showed active root and shoot growth which belied this apparent loss in vigour. There was no apparent change after a further two weeks, but, by mid-July, further treatment was again needed. This could not be effected until 30 July, when a further treatment of 20% dichlobenil was applied, the weed having by then reached the water surface over at least 25% of the surface area of the deep water. This mid-season treatment checked growth severely for a further 11 weeks when once again, to prevent further autumn and winter growth, re-treatment was deemed necessary.

The site was treated on 14 October with diquat alginate (Table 2.2), underwater growth being estimated at 90% of the water volume. Most large clumps in the deep water had almost reached the surface, some having become emergent whilst many of the small clumps in the shallow area had started to regenerate. The owner reported a dramatic effect after ten days and, when seen three weeks later, although many stems were still green and viable, they had been stripped of their leaves. Much vegetation by this time had broken away and was floating on the surface in various stages of vigour. Thereafter, with the exception of the floating debris, the plant gradually died out and when inspected some 24 weeks later, on 24 March 1992, the kill had become virtually complete.

DISCUSSION

For various reasons, the first application of dichlobenil in 1990 could not be made until 1 June. Considering the advanced stage of growth, this was far later than desirable. To be fully effective, dichlobenil granules need to reach the hydrosoil to enable chemical uptake by the plant roots. The propensity of growth at that time was such that a large proportion of the applied granules became lodged in the foliage, so greatly reducing efficacy. The extent to which results might have been improved had it been possible to treat much earlier is thus open to conjecture.

Terbutryn is approved for use at rates calculated to provide a concentration of 0.05 mg a.i./l water for listed susceptible plants and at 0.1 mg/l for those classified as moderately resistant (Ministry of Agriculture, Fisheries and Food, 1985). Of the treatments used, only terbutryn was applied at the recommended time. Further work is suggested to determine whether control could be improved by application at the higher rate.

Despite the somewhat indifferent results obtained from the owner's first use of diquat alginate, when inspected some 24 weeks after re-treating with this formulation in October 1991, all the *C. helmsii* had virtually disappeared apart from the occasional viable green stem and propagule which was present here and there in otherwise completely dead clumps. The floating vegetation which broke away after treatment was still green with viable propagules and would act as a source of re-infection unless cleared away.

Having conducted both tank and field treatments, Dawson and Henville (1991) recommend the use of diquat alginate. In view of their unsatisfactory results obtained with dichlobenil and terbutryn, they are of the opinion that these should not be used to treat *C. helmsii*. They also suggest that a repeat treatment of diquat alginate as late as November should be made if needed.

To date, the most effective treatment for this site has been diquat alginate applied in October 1991, although it is felt that the results from the other two herbicides were disadvantaged, either by late timing or possibly, in the case of terbutryn, by insufficient dose. Further more critical field trials are deemed necessary in order to predict with any accuracy the likely effects of the herbicides used in this study for control of the submerged growth of this pernicious alien species.

ACKNOWLEDGEMENT

The author wishes to thank ICI Professional Products for provision of the dichlobenil and diquat alginate used in this trial.

REFERENCES

Büscher, D., Raabe, U. and Wentz, E.M. (1990). *Crassula helmsii* (T. Kirk) Cockayne in Westfalen. *Floristische Rundbriefe*, **24** (1), 8–9.
Dawson, F.H. and Henville, P. (1991). *An Investigation of the Control of Crassula helmsii by Herbicidal Chemicals (with interim guidelines on control). Final report.* Report to the Nature Conservancy Council, 107 pp.
Dawson, F.H. and Warman, E.A. (1987). *Crassula helmsii* (T. Kirk) Cockayne: Is it an aggressive alien aquatic plant in Britain? *Biological Conservation*, **42**, 247–272.
Ministry of Agriculture, Fisheries and Food (1985). *Guidelines for the use of herbicides on weeds in or near watercourses and lakes.* Booklet B2078. London: HMSO.
Swale, E. and Belcher. H. (1982). *Crassula helmsii*, the swamp stonecrop, near Cambridge. *Nature in Cambridgeshire*, **25**, 59–62.

3 How Important are Rivers for Supporting Plant Invasions?

PETR PYŠEK[1] and KAREL PRACH[2]

[1]Institute of Applied Ecology, 281 63 Kostelec nad Černými lesy, the Czech Republic

[2]Department of Plant Ecology, Botanical Institute of the Czech Academy of Sciences, 379 82 Třeboň, the Czech Republic

INTRODUCTION

Invasion success of a plant species introduced to the region in which it did not previously occur depends on its dispersal. Habitats in central European landscapes differ in encouraging the movement of diaspores. Linear habitats usually contribute to easier spread of species through the landscape. With respect to the main dispersal agent, they may be divided into (a) terrestrial "transport habitats", including road verges and ditches as well as railway embankments and stations; and (b) water "transport habitats", including river and stream banks. Human activity is the main dispersal factor in the former group. In the latter, water acts as the main dispersal agent supporting downstream movement of diaspores (Skoglund, 1989; Thébaud and Debussche, 1991). In addition, seedling establishment and survival are made easier in these sites by periodic disturbances from flooding, which creates openings in vegetation cover (Ellenberg, 1988; Walker et al., 1986). The present paper analyses historical dynamics of four species alien to central Europe during their invasions in the Czech Republic. Special attention was paid to their performance in riparian habitats and to the role of this habitat type in supporting their invasion.

SPECIES SELECTION AND CHARACTERISTICS

The species selected for this study are those included in the *Control and Management of Invasive Riparian Weeds* project, launched by the International Centre of Landscape Ecology, Loughborough University, UK: *Impatiens glandulifera*, *Heracleum mantegazzianum* and *Reynoutria japonica*. In

Ecology and Management of Invasive Riverside Plants
Edited by L. C. de Waal, L. E. Child, P. M. Wade and J. H. Brock
© 1994 John Wiley & Sons Ltd

addition, another knotweed species, *Reynoutria sachalinensis*, showing similar biological attributes to *R. japonica*, but not so expansive so far in the study area, was added for comparison. All of them are troublesome weeds in riparian habitats. In central Europe, as well as in Great Britain, each species is the highest representative of its life form: *I. glandulifera* among annuals (maximum height 2.5 m), *H. mantegazzianum* among monocarpic perennials (4–5 m), and both *Reynoutria* species among polycarpic perennials (>2 m).

Impatiens glandulifera Royle is native to the Himalayas. It reproduces only by seeds and possesses an explosive seed capsule (Grime *et al.*, 1988; Perrins *et al.*, 1990).

Heracleum mantegazzianum, native to the western Caucasus, reproduces by seeds and regenerates from tuberous roots. Among the species studied, it is the one that may cause the most serious problems. Not only replacement of native vegetation but also injuries to human skin caused by phototoxic substances are the main reasons for efforts to eradicate the species from infested areas (Lundström, 1984; Pyšek, 1991).

Reynoutria japonica and *R. sachalinensis* have areas of origin in the Far East. The species are capable of effective vegetative regeneration, spreading by rhizomes, which is probably the only method of regeneration in the study region (however, see Bailey, 1994).

All species studied were introduced into the Czech Republic in the nineteenth century; the first reports are 1862 for *H. mantegazzianum* (but see Pyšek, 1991), 1869 for *R. sachalinensis*, 1892 for *R. japonica* and 1896 for *I. glandulifera*. They were originally planted as ornamentals in gardens and parks. They are capable of forming large monospecific stands spontaneously and hence, besides other serious problems, replace native vegetation and reduce species diversity.

METHODS

Historical reconstructions of the dynamics of spread were based on (i) published floristic records, (ii) unpublished floristic data obtained by personal communication and (iii) herbarium specimens (Charles University Prague, National Museum Prague). Information on the year of observation and habitat type, if available, was summarized for each record. If the year of observation was not provided by the original author, the year of publication was used instead, as both dates are closely related (Pyšek, 1991). The method of retrospective evaluation of plant species spread adopted in this paper has been discussed in detail by Pyšek (1991).

RESULTS AND DISCUSSION

TYPE OF INVASION AND THE ROLE OF RIPARIAN HABITATS

An increase in the cumulative number of localities (i.e. in the number of localities reported up to the respective year) follows an exponential curve in each species studied (Figure 3.1a). The increase was very fast in *I. glandulifera* and *H. mantegazzianum* and more gradual in *R. japonica*. In *R. sachalinensis* the number of localities increased only slightly during the twentieth century. Total numbers of localities currently known are given in Table 3.1.

If riparian habitats are considered separately (Figure 3.1b), the number of localities in 1991 was highest for *I. glandulifera* (340), followed by *R. japonica* (104), *H. mantegazzianum* (41) and *R. sachalinensis* (30). The contribution of riparian localities to the total number of localities was 51.1% in *I. glandulifera*, 27.5% in *R. sachalinensis* and 27.2% in *R. japonica*. *H. mantegazzianum* was the species with the lowest affinity to riparian habitats (only 10%). However, the detailed analysis of the invasion process revealed that even in this species there was a period when the species spread was considerably supported by rivers (Pyšek, 1994). Table 3.1 provides complete information on habitat preferences.

Invasion success of a species is determined by (i) its biological attributes related to the dispersal capabilities and ability to compete with the native flora; physiological attributes of successful invaders may be related to high biomass production, as this increases competitive ability as well as the number of offspring; and (ii) the characteristics of recipient habitats (Newsome and Noble, 1986).

In our data set, an increase in the number of localities (Figure 3.1a) may be considered as a measure of the former attributes, i.e. the ability to expand. Concentration of occurrence into one or more habitat types is, on the other hand, assumed to reflect ecological specialization of the species. Such a species may be expected to be restricted in its invasion by habitat types available. Correspondingly, a species occurring frequently in a wide range of habitat types is considered as less limited, if at all, in its invasion by the characteristics of the recipient habitat. The species included in this study may be classified with respect to the above mentioned criteria (Table 3.2).

Example 1: Strong invader restricted by the recipient habitat (*Impatiens glandulifera*)

This species rapidly invaded riparian habitats in the study region, which was made possible by the large number of seeds produced and easy dispersal by water, which is the main dispersal factor (Table 3.2; Lhotská and Kopecký, 1966). *I. glandulifera* is closely confined to wet and moist habitats. Its occur-

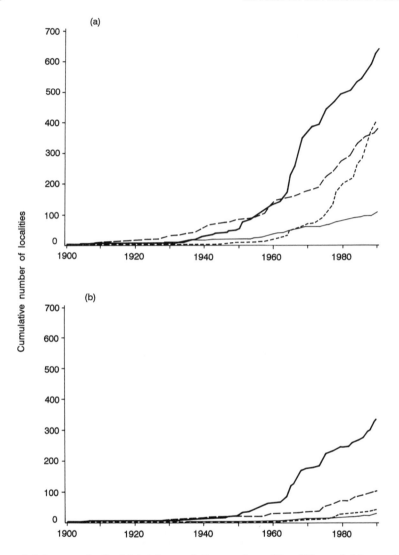

Figure 3.1 Increase in the (a) total cumulative number of localities and (b) cumulative number of localities reported from riparian habitats in the Czech Republic during the twentieth century, for *Impatiens glandulifera* (——), *Heracleum mantegazzianum* (- - -), *Reynoutria sachalinensis* (——) and *R. japonica* (– – –)

rence out of riverine habitats is rather rare in the Czech Republic. A high proportion of settlement localities, especially in the early years of invasion, is partly due to its escape from cultivation and occurrence as a garden weed. Moreover, in settlements and along roads it also prefers moist and wet sites.

Table 3.1. Contribution (%) of particular habitat types to the total number of localities known for the studied species in the Czech Republic in 1991

	Impatiens glandulifera	Heracleum mantegazzianum	Reynoutria japonica	R. sachalinensis
Rivers	51.1	10.0	27.2	27.5
Pond shores	5.5	4.2	3.2	2.8
Roads and railways	8.7	27.7	16.9	28.4
Settlements	27.3	36.5	40.8	28.4
Parks	0.7	5.0	5.9	11.0
Forests and meadows	5.8	15.6	5.9	11.0
Total no. of localities	665	411	382	109

Table 3.2. Species life-form and dispersal strategy of four plant species in relation to invasion status

Species	Life form	Spread	Dispersal agents* Human or animal	Water	Wind	Invasion status	Habitat limited
Impatiens glandulifera	Annual	Seeds	1	2	0	Strong	Yes
Heracleum mantegazzianum	Perennial	Seeds	2	1	1	Strong	No
Reynoutria japonica	Perennial	Vegetative	2	1	0	Weak	No
R. sachalinensis	Perennial	Vegetative	2	1	0	Weak	No

* Assessed according to 0 no importance, 1 important and 2 principal. The classification is based on authors' personal experience and holds for central Europe.

I. glandulifera is an invasive specis whose characteristics allow it to establish only under a narrow range of habitat conditions. It corresponds to type 2 of an invader according to Newsome and Noble (1986).

Examples of invaders limited only to a certain habitat have been reported from central Europe. The majority of permanently established aliens are limited to ruderal sites (Kornaś, 1990; Świeboda, 1963; van Soest, 1941). However, time plays an important role in our view of the species' habitat preferences: *Impatiens parviflora*, an early nineteenth century newcomer from the East, was limited to ruderal sites for many years and after several decades it massively invaded forests (Trepl, 1984).

Example 2: Strong invader less limited by recipient habitat (*Heracleum mantegazzianum, Reynoutria japonica*)

H. mantegazzianum invaded various habitat types at a similar rate (Pyšek, 1994). Some preference for settlements was found and, moreover, of all species studied this was the most successful in semi-natural vegetation, i.e. forests and meadows (Table 3.1). Water as a dispersal agent seems to be less important for its spread than wind and, especially, the direct transport of diaspores by man (Table 3.2); the plant is still popular as a garden ornamental and for dried flower arrangements (Lundström, 1984). *H. mantegazzianum* is an example of a species that invaded semi-natural habitats soon after its introduction without being preceded by the stage of establishment in disturbed sites, usually considered as a necessary stage in the naturalization process (Kornas, 1990).

In case of *R. japonica*, water is an important means of dispersal of the vegetative fragments, but the spread by man still prevails in the study region. Both dispersal agents often act simultaneously.

Both *H. mantegazzianum* and *R. japonica* are invading species having distinct competetive superiority over ecologically similar native species, which has allowed them to become a permanent part of the local flora (type 1 of an invader according to Newsome and Noble, 1986).

Example 3: Weak invader (*Reynoutria sachalinensis*)

Despite life history characteristics and time of introduction being similar to *R. japonica*, this species remains less successful as an invader. Vegetative fragments are spread by water and the affinity of the species to riparian habitats has increased in the last several decades. So far it has entered various habitats (including semi-natural ones, i.e. forests and meadows), and may, therefore, be considered as less habitat restricted. It might be that its invasion has just started. However, there are some indications that, in the past, *R. sachalinensis* was planted less frequently than *R. japonica*, which might have contributed to the differences in their present abundance in the Czech landscape.

EFFECT OF LANDSCAPE CHARACTER ON HABITAT
PREFERENCES

If our results are compared with reports on the same species from Great Britain (Gunn, 1986; Neiland *et al.*, 1987; Trewick and Wade, 1986), *R. japonica* and *H. mantegazzianum* are obviously more closely related to riparian habitats in Britain. Availability of recipient habitats is presumably partly responsible for this difference: in the Czech Republic, numerous disturbed and ill-managed sites provide openings in the spontaneous vegetation cover and these may be used by invaders for penetrating into communities of native species. Hence the proportion of localities situated in the open landscape is higher. In Great Britain, on the other hand, the landscape is more intensively managed and sites suitable for establishment of the species are rather rare. Suitable sites are therefore more confined to riparian areas.

ACKNOWLEDGEMENTS

Our thanks are due to the colleagues who provided their unpublished floristic data: J. Rydlo, Bohumil Slavík, V. Chán, K. Kubát, R. Hlaváček, S. Kučera, F. Krahulec, J. Kolbek and N. Gutserová. We thank J. Hadinec for help with herbarium collections, L. Klečková for technical assistance and E. Švejdová for drawing the figures. An anonymous reviewer kindly improved our English.

REFERENCES

Bailey, J. (1994). Reproductive biology and fertility of *Fallopia japonica* (Japanese Knotweed) and its hybrids in the British Isles. In L.C. de Waal, L.E. Child, P.M. Wade and J.H. Brock (Eds), *Ecology and Management of Invasive Riverside Plants*, pp. 141–158. Chichester: Wiley.

Ellenberg, H. (1988). *Vegetation Ecology of Central Europe*. Cambridge: Cambridge University Press.

Grime, J.P., Hodgson, J. and Hunt, R. (1988). *Comparative Plant Ecology. A Functional Approach to Common British Species*. London: Unwin Hyman.

Gunn, I.D.M. (1986). *Biology and control of Japanese knotweed* (Reynoutria japonica) *and Himalayan balsam* (Impatiens glandulifera) *on river banks*. MSc thesis, UWIST, Cardiff.

Kornaś, J. (1990). *Plant invasions in Central Europe: historical and ecological aspects*, In F. Di Castri, A.J. Hansen and M. Debussche (Eds), *Biological Invasions in Europe and the Mediterranean Basin*, pp. 19–36. Dordrecht: Kluwer.

Lhotská, M. and Kopecký, K. (1966). Zur Verbreitungsbiologie und Phytozönologie von *Impatiens glandulifera* Royle an den Flusssystemen der Svitava, Svratka und oberen Odra. *Preslia*, **38**, 376–385.

Lundström, H. (1984). Giant hogweed, *Heracleum mantegazzianum*, a threat to the Swedish countryside. *Weeds and Weed Control, 25th Swedish Weed Conference*, Uppsala, Vol. 1, pp. 191–200.

Neiland, R., Proctor, J. and Sexton, R. (1987). Giant hogweed (*Heracleum mantegazzianum* Somm. & Lev.) by the River Allan and part of the River Forth, *Forth Natural History*, **9**, 51–56.

Newsome, A.E. and Noble, I.R. (1986). Ecological and physiological characters of invading species. In R.H. Groves, and J.J. Burden (Eds), *Ecology of Biological Invasions: An Australian Perspective*, pp. 1–20. Canberra: Australian Academy of Sciences.

Perrins J., Fitter, A. and Williamson, M. (1990). What makes *Impatiens glandulifera* invasive? In J. Palmer (Ed.), *The Biology and Control of Invasive Plants*, pp. 8–33, British Ecological Society, University of Wales, Cardiff.

Pyšek, P. (1991). *Heracleum mantegazzianum* in the Czech Republic—the dynamics of spreading from the historical perspective. *Folia Geobotanica et Phytotaxonomica*, **26**, 439–454.

Pyšek, P. (1994). Ecological aspects of invasion by *Heracleum mantegazzianum* in the Czech Republic. In L.C. de Waal, L.E. Child, P.M. Wade and J.H. Brock (Eds), *Ecology and Management of Invasive Riverside Plants* pp. 45–54. Chichester: Wiley.

Skoglund, S.J. (1989). Seed dispersing agents in two regularly flooded river sites. *Canadian Journal of Botany*, **68**, 754–760.

Świeboda, M. (1963). Distribution of *Elsholtzia patrini* (Lep.) Garcke in Poland, *Fragmenta Floristica et Geobotanica*, **9**, 239–243.

Thébaud, C. and Debussche, M. (1991). Rapid invasion of *Fraxinus ornus* L. along the Hrault River system in southern France: the importance of seed dispersal by water. *Journal of Biogeography*, **18**, 7–12.

Trepl, L. (1984). Über *Impatiens parviflora* DC. als Agriophyt in Mitteleuropa. *Dissertationes Botanicae* **73**, 1–400.

Trewick, S. and Wade, P.M. (1986). The distribution and dispersal of two alien species of *Impatiens*, waterway weeds in the British Isles. *Proceedings 7th International European Weed Research Society/Association of Applied Biologists Symposium on Aquatic Weeds*, pp. 351–356 Loughborough.

van Soest, J.L. (1941). De verspreiding van Galinsoga in Nederland, *Nederlandsch Kruidkundig Archief*, **51**, 288–301.

Walker, L.R., Zasada, J.C. and Chapin, F.S. (1986). The role of life history processes in primary succession on an Alaskan floodplain. *Ecology*, **67**, 753–761.

4 *Tamarix* spp. (Salt Cedar), an Invasive Exotic Woody Plant in Arid and Semi-arid Riparian Habitats of Western USA

JOHN H. BROCK

School of Agribusiness and Environmental Resources, Arizona State University, USA

INTRODUCTION

In the early 1800s plants of the genus *Tamarix* were introduced to the United States of America as ornamentals. Towards the late 1800s, some of these plants began to invade rivers and streams in the arid and semi-arid areas of the south-western United States. Between 1900 and the 1960s the plants rapidly spread into areas impacted by human activities. Man's many impacts along the rivers include clearing land for agriculture; uncontrolled livestock grazing; trapping of beaver; cutting native trees for fodder, or to help control flood effects, and to reduce evapotranspiration losses on the watersheds; groundwater depletion; diversion of streams for irrigation; building of reservoirs; mining effects; urbanization with channeling of streams; and recreational impacts. The plant gets it common name, salt cedar, from its ability to tolerate salt and because its general appearance is like that of a juniper "cedar". Rapid *Tamarix* invasion in United States habitats, coincides with the time (1900–40) when most of the large dams were being built. *Tamarix* was apparently favoured by flood elimination and inundation (Everitt, 1980; Irvine and West, 1979; Petranka and Holland, 1980). In reviewing streamside vegetation from historic aerial photographs in Texas, Busby and Schuster (1973) found an increase of 52% in *Tamarix*, with a corresponding 47% decrease of visible sandbars and gravel in stream channels for the period. In the *Tamarix*-dominated habitats, plant diversity is low, with the plant growing in monospecific stands. Hildebrandt and Ohmart (1982), working along the Pecos River of New Mexico and Texas, found the community with the fewest associated plant species to be in those dominated

Ecology and Management of Invasive Riverside Plants
Edited by L. C. de Waal, L. E. Child, P. M. Wade and J. H. Brock
© 1994 John Wiley & Sons Ltd

by *Tamarix* while native communities had the greatest ground cover. *Tamarix* now occupies over 1 million acres (slightly less than 500, 000 ha) (US Soil Conserval Service and Texas Agricultural Extension Service, 1982; Hildebrandt and Ohmart, 1982; Hunter *et al.*, 1987; Robinson, 1965). *Tamarix* now exists as a naturalized exotic, difficult to manage effectively, and is located in the riparian habitat, one of the most ecologically important habitats in the western USA. Implications for the British Isles are that: (i) taxonomically similar species of *Tamarix* are present in Great Britain; (ii) with the potential of climatic change influenced by global warming, Britain's climate may become more semi-arid; and (iii) with low flow conditions currently being observed in several rivers in south-eastern England, *Tamarix* may be provided with establishment sites similar to conditions favouring its colonization of riparian habitats in the south-western USA.

This paper will address the taxonomy of *Tamarix* and its ecology and potential methods of management. Comprehensive literature reviews of *Tamarix* as an economic and ecological problem in the western United States are contained in reports to the US Bureau of Reclamation by DeLoach (1989) and Great Western Research (1989).

TAXONOMY

Tamarix is in the family Tamaricaceae. Kearney and Peebles (1960) state that *Tamarix* is a difficult genus which requires further study and that until this is done the identity of this widespread naturalized species is in doubt. Lawrence (1951) stated that one species, *T. gallica* had naturalized extensively in dry and saline habitats from South Carolina across the south to California. This is the common *Tamarix* of British horticultural landscapes. Baum (1967) recognized eight species of *Tamarix* in the United States and Canada. Most abundant were *T. ramossissima* and *T. chinensis* both with five stamens, deciduous and invasive to riverine systems, and *T. aphylla*, which is a large non-deciduous tree planted as an ornamental and in windbreaks, but is apparently not invasive. Four other species were not common, or of very recent introduction and include *T. gallica*, which seems to be the most common *Tamarix* in Great Britain. Horton (1977), after studying herbarium specimens and observing many live plants, was unable to distinguish between *T. chinensis* and *T. ramosissima*. Naturalized *Tamarix* plants in the south-western United States have been referred to as *T. chinensis, T. ramosissima* and *T. gallica*, all from the same region and habitat type.

To cloud the picture further, *Tamarix* is often seen with the scientific name of *Tamarix pentandra*. After consultation with taxonomists at the Royal Botanic Gardens, Kew, Herbarium and review of Baum's (1978) book *The Genus Tamarix*, the name *T. pentandra* does not seem to be acceptable. Subsequent authors have referred to this taxon as *T. chinensis* since this name has priority, including the plants resembling *T. ramosissima*. Taxonomic differentiation is apparently possible among the *Tamarix* species upon very careful examination. The following information was taken from Baum (1978), the world expert on *Tamarix*:

T. gallica has caducous petals which are elliptic to obovate, a glabrous rachis, entire sepals and a parabolic disk.

T. chinensis has persistent petals, sepals are entire and the lower bracts of the flower are more or less equal in length to the pedicel.

T. ramosissima has obovate persistent petals, not keeled, sepals are more or less eroded, denticulate, with bracts longer than the pedicels.

While these *Tamarix* species are distinguishable on a taxonomic level (Baum, 1978), S. Zmarzty of the Royal Botanic Gardens, Kew (personal communication, 1992) said that ecological variation could prevent trained botanists from being able to identify field plants correctly to any of the three above species. Not only do they appear to be morphologically similar, but are also ecologically similar.

DISTRIBUTION IN THE WESTERN UNITED STATES OF AMERICA

Tamarix distribution in the western USA is shown in Figure 4.1 (Robinson, 1965). While this distribution map shows *Tamarix* along major stream corridors, it is often a constituent of wetlands and shore lines of ponds and reservoirs. From research in Utah, Brotherson and Winkel (1986) reported that *Tamarix* distribution provided no relationship with various soil factors. *Tamarix* is believed by many observers, including Baum (1978), to be limited thermally in its distribution. Bowser (1957) working in the south-west USA reported that *Tamatix* did not spread rapidly above 1220 m, although it was present at 2740–3350 m. Similar observations hold for Arizona at present. A gradient of *Tamarix* abundance has also been reported by researchers in Kansas and the plains portion of eastern Colorado. Gesink *et al.* (1970) reported that *Tamarix* became the major constituent of plant cover along the Arkansas River in western Kansas, whereas, in central Kansas, plains cottonwood (*Populus sargentii*) and peachleaf willow trees (*Salix amyglyoides*) were dominant. Lindauer (1967) stated that *Tamarix* made up only 8% of plant cover along streams near the mountains, but was 67% of the cover on the Arkansas River in south-eastern Colorado. From central Kansas to the Rocky Mountains in Colorado there exists a precipitation gradient that decreases as one approaches the mountains from the east

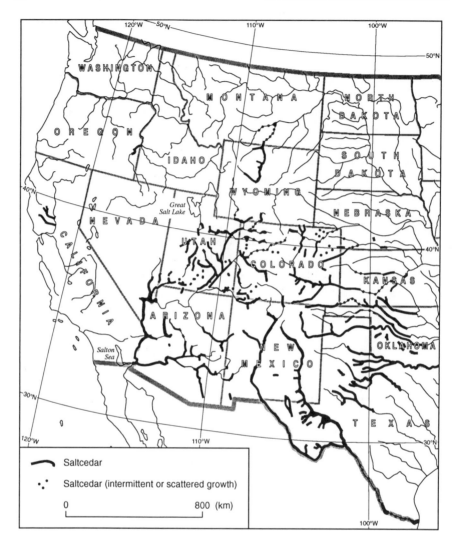

Figure 4.1 General distribution of *Tamarix* (saltcedar) along streams in the south-western USA (Robinson, 1965)

because of a rain shadow effect, and there is an increase in elevation. Given that average air temperature decreases with elevation, the observations of Bowser (1957), Gesink *et al.*, (1970) Lindauer (1967) and other scientists, the working hypothesis that *Tamarix* abundance, and perhaps distribution, is influenced most greatly by temperature seems to hold.

MORPHOLOGY

Tamarix plants are adaptable halophytic or xerophytic trees, or shrubs, with multiple stems and slender branches. Young branches are reddish brown and clearly marked in dormancy with light-coloured leaf scars. The leaves are of two sizes, whorled, overlapping and sessile. Scale-like leaves are about 3 mm in length and cauline leaves may be 8–9 mm (Wilkinson, 1966). Leaves comprise about 50% of the photosynthetic area, the rest of phothosynthesis being carried out in cladophyll stems. Stomate density averages $5045/cm^2$ (Davenport *et al.*, 1978). The plant bears small pink bisexual flowers in catkin-like racemes. The flower has five stamens rising from a nectiferous disk, and the sepals and petals are distinct. Seeds are densely tufted at the apex, aiding wind dispersal.

The root system of *Tamarix* is extensive and deep, with a strong tap root. Horton *et al.* (1960), found the root to exceed shoot length after 7 weeks of age. Gary (1963) reported that the root morphology was highly adaptable depending on water table and substrate. When growing in soils with dense clay layers, the root system tended to flatten rather than to penetrate the clay horizon vertically. Adventitious roots are produced endogensously, near the vascular cambium (Wilkinson, 1966).

PHYSIOLOGY

Tamarix reaches maximum photosynthesis at 44% full sunlight (Anderson, 1977). The optimum temperature for photosynthesis is between 23 and 28°C, tending to peak around 09:00 hour on summer days, and at 32–38°C photosynthesis is reduced by 20% below the maximum. Carbon dioxide uptake is tightly coupled with irradiation below light saturation. Stomatal resistance is least in the morning and transpiration reaches its maximum late in the morning, but is below potential transpiration rates during the afternoon (van Hylckama, 1969). Diurnal water potentials of *Tamarix* twigs closely follow incident sunlight (Anderson, 1982).

Tamarix leaves have the ability to exude salts, an adaptive strategy for tolerance of salt in a habitat. Davenport *et al.* (1978) report a mean of 1858, eight celled salt glands/cm^2 in epidermal leaf pits and cladophylls. Salt exudation enables the plant to tolerate saline soils in Death Valley, California, of up to 50 000 ppm of salt (Robinson, 1965). Ions excreted by *Tamarix* include chlorine, carbonate, sodium, potassium, bromine, calcium, nitrate, magnesium and sulfate (Berry, 1970; Hem, 1967; Waisel, 1961). Many *Tamarix* species, in addition to salt tolerance, are resistant to industrially generated gases, including sulfur dioxide (Smirnov, 1983, 1987).

Seedlings of *Tamarix* withstand total inundation by water for up to four weeks (Horton *et al.*, 1960). Warren and Turner (1975) reported survival of mature *Tamarix* root crowns submerged in still water for 98 days and total plant submergence for 70 days. This ability to survive inundation in low oxygen conditions contributes to the overall adaptability of this plant to aquatic sites.

Tamarix grows rapidly, stem heights of 3–4 m being attained in one season (Gary, 1960). One-year-old plants had lateral roots of up to 6 m, fibrous roots 0.3–0.5 m deep and a primary root 3.5 m long (Merkel and Hopkins, 1957).

ECOLOGY

PHENOLOGY

Tamarix breaks bud in the early spring (mid March) and foliage abscises in October, except in lower elevations of the Arizona Sonoran Desert, where the plant may stay evergreen (Brock, 1984; Wilkinson, 1966). There may be two periods of foliage growth and flowering common in the south-western United States, in spring and summer following rainfall, although flowering is common during the entire growing season (Brock, 1984). *Tamarix* blooms from early spring until late autumn and often in the first year after it becomes established. The seeds are small and weigh about 0.0001 g, one mature plant may produce 0.5 to one million seeds per season (Bowser, 1957; Tomanek and Zeigler, 1962). A seed rain of up to 15 seeds/cm^2 on the soil surface was produced in the summer (Warren and Turner, 1975), when seeds of other riparian trees are not present (Brock, in press). Seeds are readily wind dispersed and *Tamarix* has been estimated to have a rate of spread of 20 km/year in the Colorado River system (Christensen, 1962). *Tamarix* is said to be short-lived, observations indicate that they live longer than 20 years, but no longevity data are published. Replacement is not common in senescent stands of *Tamarix* (DeLoach, 1989).

GERMINATION AND ESTABLISHMENT

Seeds of *Tamarix* germinate within 24 hours of imbibition (Merkel and Hopkins, 1957; Horton, 1960;) Seeds germinate throughout the growing season, with a maximum of 51% in August. Exposed seeds in the wild loose their viability in about 4 weeks, but can be maintained in laboratory storage for over 40 weeks (Horton 1960; Merkel and Hopkins 1957). The most suitable germination substrate seems to be moist, fine silt deposits. Hopkins and Tomanek (1957), reported an average of 897 seedlings/m^2, of which 72% died during the first summer, and a year survival of less thant 10%. A seedling density of 170 000/m² on an Arizona mud flat has been reported (Warren and Turner, 1975).

VEGETATIVE REGENERATION

It is widely known that *Tamarix* has great capability to regrow from its crown area, stems and roots. A common form of vegetative propagation for this species is layering (Ginzburg, 1967; Wilkinson, 1966). In this case, a portion of a stem is covered with debris or sediment, adventitious roots form and the potential for a new individual plant is created. Despite this species' propensity for developing adventitious roots, Ando (1980) found only 17% survival of *Tamarix* stems planted in an irrigated field. Brock (1984) reported about 60% of stem tissues producing new shoots/roots under greenhouse conditions, while root cuttings were less successful, producing only about 10 % new shoot growth and those sections were removed from the parent plant near the crown. Prolific new shoot regeneration is reported by many sources from crown tissues following top removal by fire.

ALLELOPATHY

It is hypothesized that saline excretions serve as allelopathic agents in habitats occupied by *Tamarix*. As cited in DeLoach (1989), only potassium salts accumulated anomalously at the soil surface. The competitive nature of *Tamarix* and its physiological ability to tolerate and exude salts creates conditions believed, by many scientists, to be too saline for establishment and survival of most other riparian native species (Hoddenbach, 1987; Siegel and Brock, 1990). Other allelopathic materials of *Tamarix* are poorly known. Harbourne (1975) found some *Tamarix* species to have flavenol bisulfates and bisulfate-glucuronides. The constituents of resins and possible occurrence of phenols, tannins and other anti-herbivore chemical defences often associated with allelopathic plants have yet to be adduced for *Tamarix*.

HABITAT QUALITY

Plant species diversity in *Tamarix* stands is low, because of *Tamarix* density and exclusion of native plants (Brown, 1982). *Tamarix* communities along the Pecos River in New Mexico and Texas have the fewest associated plants (average of 5.2 for *Tamarix*-dominated sites compared with 12.0 for native plant stands) (Hildebrandt and Ohmart, 1982); additionally, native plant stands had the highest overall plant cover.

Monotypic stands of *Tamarix* are considered by many to be "biological deserts". Anderson and Ohmart (1977) found that *Tamarix* stands had 50% fewer small mammals than did native riparian stands. Jakle and Katz (1985), working with reptiles and amphibians, reported for desert riparian areas in Arizona a low species diversity for habitats dominated by *Tamarix*. They found a diversity value, using the Shannon and Weaver formula, of 1.81 for a desert wash, but a value for *Tamarix* stands of 0.63, attributed to a lack of light and shrub layer in the vegetation. Bird species richness and number was lower for *Tamarix* areas along the lower Colorado River in the south-west United States (Anderson *et al.*, 1983), but along the Pecos River of New Mexico birds were more common in *Tamarix*. Brown and Trossett (1989), in their work on habitats along the Colorado River in the Grand Canyon, Arizona, reported that *Tamarix* can be an ecological equivalent to other plants for some breeding bird species. The consensus seems to be that birds will use *Tamarix* differentially in various river habitats, depending on the bird species and its biological habits (resident or migratory). Conflicting work has been reported concerning insect populations and *Tamarix*. More research on plant-animal associations, and particularily the invertebrates, is needed for this invasive plant. Overall, *Tamarix* habitats are considered to be poor substitutes for native plant communities.

WATER USE BY TAMARIX

Tamarix is said to be a phreatophyte, a plant that obtains water directly from the water table or its capillary fringe (Meinzer, 1923). Data from various sources (Culler *et al.*, 1982; Gatewood *et al.*, 1950; Robinson and Bowser, 1959; US Bureau of Reclamation, 1973; van Hylckama, 1974) show that *Tamarix* water use is not linear to plant density (Figure 4.2a). At 100% plant density, water use on an area basis would be 6205 m^3/ha; and, at 50% plant density, water use would be 5274 m^3/ha. Water use varies by plant density and elevation, as shown in Figure 4.2b. Water use is much lower at higher elevations than at the warmer, and lower, elevations. This is an apparent response to lower evapotranspiration loses from *Tamarix* stands. Water use by *Tamarix* peaks when the water table is within 2 m of the soil surface, decreases rapidly and stablizes at water-table depths > 4 m, perhaps indicating a general depth of rooting (Figure 4.2b). Great Western Research (1989) reported that a total of 404 700 ha (1 million acres) of *Tamarix* would consume 3205 × 10^6 m^3 water/year, 80% of that coming from plants in Oklahoma, Texas, New Mexico and Arizona. In New Mexico, it was estimated by Blaney (1957, 1961), using the empirical Bowen Ratio method, that *Tamarix* would consume 180–1310 mm of precipitation, depending on geographical location. This is in excess of precipitation inputs to the water budget of most areas of New Mexico.

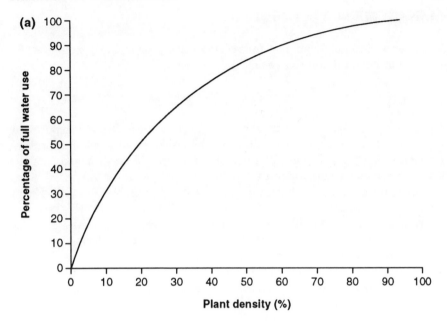

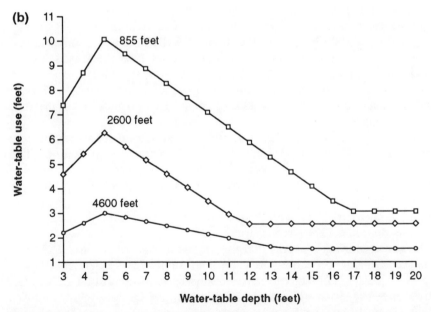

Figure 4.2 Water use by *Tamarix* (a) as influenced by plant density and (b) at three elevations (□ 855, ◇ 2600 and ○ 4600 feet) in the south-western United States (Great Western Research, 1989) (1 foot = 0.3 m)

MANAGEMENT TECHNIQUES

There are four main techniques for vegetation management: (i) biological, (ii) fire, (iii) mechanical and (iv) chemical.

BIOLOGICAL

No current biological control for *Tamarix* is known. Recent reports by Great Western Research (1989) on economic aspects and a literature review by DeLoach (1989), including potential for biological control, may set the stage for a major thrust for research.

Damaging insects have been reported on *Tamarix* in the USA by Hefley (1937) in Oklahoma, Liesner (1971) in New Mexico, and by Hopkins and Carruth (1954) and Glinski and Ohmart (1984) working in Arizona. The most host-specific and damaging seems to be an alien leafhopper (*Opsius stactogalus*), which suppressed *Tamarix* growth in trials in New Mexico, where protected plants showed 75% more growth than infected plants. But, in general, insect damage to *Tamarix* trees in the American south-west seems to be rare (Watts *et al.*, 1977).

In Sardinia, *T. gallica* was severely damaged by the insect *Apate monachus*, and following wind storms greatly reduced canopy cover of the trees (Luciano, 1982). In its native range, insects on *Tamarix* have been much studied, except in China (DeLoach, 1989). Research from Israel, Turkey, Iran, Pakistan and Georgia (in the former USSR) provides a consensus that about 13–15 insect species have good potential for further research as biological control agents. Within Azerbaijan (in the former USSR), Samedov and Mirzoneva (1985) report that plants in floodplains dominated by *Tamarix* had significant localized and mass areas damaged by attacks from insects of the Chrysomelidae family.

There are reports of potential *Tamarix* control from plant pathogens as well as insects. Brown (1953) isolated a bacterium from dying *Tamarix* plants in Arizona, which, when sprayed on healthy greenhouse plants, cause mortality. In Argentina, Frezzi, as cited in DeLoach (1989), reported that *Tamarix* plants 1.5–2 years old were killed by the plant pathogen *Botryosphaeria tamaricis*. DeLoach (1989) reports observing severely diseased trees in Argentina on a 1972 research trip.

Livestock grazing is a potential as a tool for *Tamarix* control and maintenance. Grazing by cattle can control invading *Tamarix* (Great Western Research, 1989), and intensive livestock grazing on a portion of the Gila River in New Mexico suppressed *Tamarix* size, but did not exclude establishment (J. H. Brock, field observations 1982, 1983). It is also hypothesized that grazing by goats maintains *Tamarix* and was reported to have been attempted as a maintenance treatment on the Pecos River in New Mexico, but no published reports of the efficacy of goats in controlling *Tamarix* were found.

FIRE

Fire is not an effective control technique for *Tamarix*. While a large fuel load is characteristic of *Tamarix* stands (large amounts of dried leaves and dead branches), *Tamarix* resprouts rapidly after fire (Horton, 1977) and regrows at 3–4 m/year (Hoddenbach, 1987). The effect of fire is illustrated in a report by Graf (1979), where a fire in the summer of 1975 in Utah burned about 20 acres. In the summer of 1976, fire effects could be plainly seen, with a surface cover of lush green *Tamarix* growth over the area. After 3 years, in 1978, it was difficult to find evidence of the fire. Research in Utah showed that repeat burning of *Tamarix*, in spring, summer and autumn fires over 2 years, was also ineffective because of vegetative regrowth (Howard *et al.*, 1982).

MECHANICAL

Mechanical treatments are designed to reduce top growth, or cause plant mortality. Activities such as shredding, rollerchopping, or chaining reduce canopy cover and under ideal conditions can reduce plant density. Grubbing or ploughing (root or disk) are designed to sever the plant from its roots. A major limitation of mechanical treatments for *Tamarix* control is its preferred habitat of moist stream channels, which can slow treatment and provide a ready medium for plant regeneration.

Shredding (brush mowing), rollerchopping (weighted drum fitted with blades) and chaining (anchor chains pulled between tractors) can all decrease the canopy coverage of *Tamarix*, but induce little mortality lessening plant density (J. H. Brock, field observations). Wiedemann and Cross (1979), in an experiment near Breckenridge, Texas with multiple cutting, found little plant mortality by shredding *Tamarix*.

Severing plant roots, usually increases woody-plant mortality. Grubbing (cutting individual trees to > 20 cm depth) can be very effective on trees with less sprouting ability than *Tamarix*. This technique results in low plant mortality on *Tamarix* (regrowth is readily evident within 6–12 months following treatment), but grubbing greatly reduces canopy coverage for several years and maintenance treatments are needed to retain initial gains. Root-ploughing (horizontal blade pulled at > 20 cm deep) alone gave about 40% control of *Tamarix* on sites in New Mexico (Hollingsworth *et al.*, 1979). While rootploughing is somewhat effective, the area needs to be treated more than once if high levels of control are desired. Ploughing and grubbing are effective treatments if combined with vegetation replacement to shade rapidly *Tamarix* regrowth (Graf, 1979). Ploughing with 1 m long ripper blades set about 1 m apart on tool bars of D-9 sized crawler tractors has kept a portion of the Salt River in central Arizona nearly free of *Tamarix* for the last 10 years (W.K. Knight revegetation ecologist, Maricopa County Flood Control District, personal communication, 1991). Maricopa County has an ongoing *Tamarix* control programme on a 51.5 km reach of the Salt River west of Phoenix, Arizona. The goal is to maintain a flood plain about 300 m wide, free of *Tamarix*, in a strategy to reduce flood damage, by increasing water conveyance. The average return period of this ploughing/ripping operation is approximately 10 months.

CHEMICAL

Herbicides commonly used in *Tamarix* control have included: 2,4-D, 2,4,5-TP (silvex), picloram, dicamba, tebuthiuron, triclopyr, hexazinone, glyphosate and imazapyr. Of these, only 2,4-D, triclopyr, glyphosate and imazapyr currently provide potential for uses near waterways, in the light of environmental concerns and use restrictions. 2,4-D can produce *Tamarix* mortality, but in most cases *Tamarix* has poor translocation of this herbicide to regrowth tissues and, as a result, does not provide confident treatment effects. A phenoxy herbicide with better results on woody plants, 2,4,5-TP (silvex), was used for *Tamarix* control and at 4 kg/ha as a foliage treatment provided about 60% mortality (Scifres, 1980). However, silvex was taken off the USA market about 10 years ago because of its close relationship with compounds in "agent orange". Picloram, dicamba and tebuthiuron were shown to have worked well in various tests on *Tamarix* in the mid 1970s (V.E. Jones, personal communication, 1978), but often caused environmental concerns about use near watercourses and persistence in the landscape.

In the early 1970s a new herbicide was introduced by Monsanto called glyphosate. J. H. Brock (unpublished data, 1972) treated plants of *Tamarix* on the Wichita River in north-west Texas, and found *Tamarix* to have a high mortality when treated with glyphosate at 1 kg/ha. Tests were discontinued as the manufacturer desired to have glyphosate marketed for agronomic and horticultural crops, rather than non-crop lands that have more marginal returns. In subsequent years glyphosate has been used very effectively as a *Tamarix* herbicide, although much of this work remains unpublished. Another 1970s herbicide is triclopyr, which can control *Tamarix* through foliage applications, but is more effective applied as a basal spray in a diesel solution to the tree trunk, or to freshly cut stumps. Howard *et al.* (1982), and J. E. Richardson (personal communication, 1990) reported that triclopyr provides a range of plant mortality to *Tamarix* from about 60 to 96%. In these cases, the high *Tamarix* mortality was from triclopyr applied in diesel to cut stumps. While this treatment is effective in killing

Tamarix, it is laborious, and as a result has an application limited to select areas.

The search for an effective *Tamarix* herbicide has been greatly aided in the past few years with the introduction of imazapyr; initial tests showed that it was effective when applied as a foliage or basal spray. The most comprehensive work with this compound has been carried out by K. Duncan, of New Mexico State University: in the spring of 1988, stands of *Tamarix* were treated with various rates of imazapyr (1–2%), hexazinone (2.0–6.0 ml/m plant height), and tebuthiuron (7.0 and 14.0 g/m plant height) in a herbicide rate test. The results are very encouraging, with *Tamarix* maximum mortality, 36 months after treatment, being 99, 80 and 10% for imazapyr, hexazinone and tebuthiuron, respectively (K. Duncan, unpublished data, 1991). Treatments applied by Duncan in 1989, explored more closely the effective herbicide rate of imazapyr, applied at 0.5, 0.75, 1.0, and 1.25% of solution on a volume/volume basis. These treatments resulted in *Tamarix* mortality of 87–95%, 23 months after treatment. Since imazapyr is an expensive compound, priced at $155 per gallon in 1989 with the recommended dose of 1.12 kg/ha (0.5 gallons/acre), treatments in 1990 by Duncan, consisted of imazapyr alone and imazapyr mixed with glyphosate, to reduce costs while maintaining high levels of *Tamarix* mortality. Imazapyr alone produced an average mortality (11 months after treatment) of 86.4%, while combinations of imazapyr and glyphosate provided average mortalities of 97.6% (K. Duncan, unpublished data, 1991), demonstrating that high *Tamarix* mortality can be achieved at more economic levels. Evaluations of these treatments at 24 and 36 months after treatment will be critical to determine whether the observed mortality of the *Tamarix* plants can be maintained by the herbicide combinations.

INUNDATION

Long-term flooding can cause mortality of *Tamarix* plants. Inundation of established *Tamarix* for a total of 28 or 36 months resulted in 99% mortality in the 1970s near Breckenridge, Texas (Wiedemann and Cross, 1978), when the flooding occurred during the growing season. Smith and Kadlec (1983), working with seed banks of *Tamarix*, found that flooding of even a few centimetres prevented seedling establishment, although established seedlings were reported by Horton *et al.* (1960) to withstand inundations for 4 weeks.

INTEGRATED METHODS FOR *TAMARIX* CONTROL

As with many noxious weeds, there is no one method of economical control for *Tamarix*. Combinations of treatments could hold potential for providing less expensive techniques for *Tamarix* management. One of the first considerations is what degree of management/control is desired for specific stands of *Tamarix*. If the aim of management is to keep the plants at a low height, a combination of fire and intensive livestock grazing, or mechanical treatments that reduce plant height, such as cutting and grazing, may be the selected treatments. Combining fire and herbicide controlled 99% of *Tamarix* in Utah, with a July fire and spraying resprouts with 2,4-D one month later (Howard *et al.*, 1982). If a site could be inundated, then a mechanical treatment, such as tree grubbing, or shredding and flooding, which gave 88% *Tamarix* mortality in Texas (Wiedemann and Cross 1978), might be selected. Mechanical techniques and herbicide treatments have been combined (root plough and soil herbicide injection with the plough) and provided 90–97% *Tamarix* control 48 mouth after treatment (Hollingsworth *et al.*, 1979). However, the persistence and high herbicide dose (picloram at 6 kg/ha) limits this treatment near water-bearing areas.

The greatest potential seems to be the use of cheap treatments, such as fire or grazing, or biological agents, such as insects or plant pathogens, to attack the weakened plants. Any treatment that would cause the *Tamarix* plants to expend energy to begin regrowth, and subsequent treatments to keep the plants stressed and then presented with another control agent, be it chemical or biological, could greatly increase mortality of *Tamarix* over the results of the individual treatments. Research with many other plants, which have been stressed, has shown that later treatments need not be at the same doses as non-stressed plants, this is especially true when using herbicides as the terminal treatment. The same logic may well prove true for *Tamarix*, with integrated methods of control planned to maximize mortality, and using knowledge of the plants' physiology and phenology, economic inputs could be minimized, and the programme spread over time to reduce high one-time budget expenditure.

REFERENCES

Anderson, B.W. and Ohmart, R.D. (1977). *Wildlife Use and Densities of Birds and Mammals in the Lower Colorado River Valley*. US Bureau of Reclammation, Lower Colorado River region.

Anderson, B.W., Ohmart, R.D. and Rice, J. (1983). Avian and vegetation community structure and their seasonal relationships in the Lower Colorado River Valley. *Condor*, **85**, 392–405.

Anderson, J.E. (1977). Transpiration and photosynthesis in salt cedar. *Hydrology and Water Resources in Arizona and the Southwest*, **7**, 125–131.

Anderson, J.E. (1982). Factors controlling transpiration and photosynthesis in *Tamarix chinensis*. *Ecology*, **63**, 48–56.

Ando, K. (1980). *Field Survival and Rooting Ability of* Elaegnus angustifolia *and* Tamarix pentandra. Reno: University of Nevada.

Baum, B.R. (1967). Introduced and naturalized tamarisks in the United States and Canada (Tamaricaceae). *Baileya*, **15**, 19–25.

Baum, B.R. (1978). *The Genus* Tamarix. Jerusalem: Israel Academy of Sciences and Humanities.

Berry, W.L. (1970). Characteristics of salts secreted by *Tamarix aphylla*. *American Journal of Botany*. **57**, 1226–1230.

Blaney, H.F. (1957). *Relationship of Pan Evaporation to Evapotranspiration by Phreatophytes and Hydrophytes*. Phreatophyte subcommittee of Pacific Southwest Inter-Agency Committee.

Blaney, H.F. (1961). Consumptive use and water waste by phreatophytes. *Journal of Irrigation and Drainage Division, Proceedings of American Society of Civil Engineers*, **87**, 37–46.

Bowser, C.W. (1957). Introduction and spread of the undesirable tamarisks in the Pacific Southwest section of the United States and comments concerning the plants' influence upon the indigenous vegetation. *American Geophysical Union Transactions*, **38**, 415–416.

Brock, J.H. (1984). *Some Autecological Studies on Regeneration and Maintenance of Selected Riparian Plant Species*. Final Report. US Bureau of Reclamation, p. 166.

Brock, J.H. (in press). Phenology of key riparian trees in the southwestern United States. *Desert Plants*.

Brotherson, J.D. and Winkel, V. (1986). Habitat relationship of salt cedar *Tamarix ramosissima* in central Utah. *Great Basin Naturalist*, **46**, 535–541.

Brown, B.T. and Trossett, M.W. (1989). Nesting-habitat relationships of riparian birds along the Colorado River in Grand Canyon, Arizona. *Southwestern Naturalist*, **34**, 260–270.

Brown, D.E. (1982). Biotic communities of the American Southwest-United States and Mexico. *Desert Plants*, **28**, 1–342.

Brown, J.G. (1953). Parasite for salt cedars. *Arizona Farmer*, **32**, 22–23.

Busby, F.E. and Schuster, J.L. (1973). *Woody Phreatophytes along the Brazos River and Selected Tributaries above Possum Kingdom Lake*. Texas, Water Development Board Report No. 168.

Christensen, E.M. (1962). The rate of naturalization of *Tamarix* in Utah. *American Midland Naturalist*, **68**, 51–57.

Culler, R.C., Hanson, R.L., Myrick, R.M., Turner, R.M. and Kiple F.P. (1982). *Evapotranspiration Before and After Clearing Phreatophytes, Gila River Floodplain, Graham County, Arizona*. USDI, Geological Survey Paper, 665-P.

Davenport, D.C., Hagan, R.M., Gay, L.W., Bonde, E.K., Kreith, F. and Anderson. J.E. (1978). *Factors Influencing Usefulness of Antitranspirants Applied to Phreatophytes to Increase Water Supplies*. US Office of Water Research and Technology Completion, California Water Resources Center, Davis, California, Report C-6030.

DeLoach, C.J. (1989). *Saltcedar, a Weed of western North America Riparian Areas: A Review of its Taxonomy, Biology, Harmful and Beneficial Values, and its Potential for Biological Control*. US Bureau of Reclamation, Yuma, Arizona, Final Report.

Everitt, B.L. (1980). Ecology of salt cedar—a plea for research. *Environmental Geology*, **3** 77–84.

Gary, H.L. (1960). *Utilization of Five-stamen Tamarisk by Cattle*. USDA, Forest Service, Rocky Mountain Forest and Range Experiment Station, Fort Collins, Colorado, Research Note 51.

Gary, H.L. (1963). Root distribution of five-stamen tamarisk, seepwillow, and arrow-weed. *Forestry Science*, **9**, 311–314.

Gatewood, J.S., Robinson, T.W., Colby, B.R., Hem, J.D. and Halfpenny, L.C.

(1950). *Use of Water by Bottomland Vegetation in Lower Safford Valley, Arizona*. US Geological Survey, Water-Supply Paper 1103.

Gesink, R.W., Tomanek, G.W. and Hulett, G.K. (1970). A descriptive survey of woody phreatophytes along the Arkansas River in Kansas. *Transactions of the Kansas Academy of Sciences*, **73**, 55–69.

Ginzburg, C. (1967). Organization of the adventitious root apex in *Tamarix aphylla*. *American Journal of Botany*, **54**, 4–8.

Glinski, R. and Ohmart, R.D. (1984). Factors of reproduction and population densities in the Apache cicada (*Diceroprocta* Apache.) *Southwest Naturalist*, **29**, 73–79.

Graf, W.L. (1979). *Potential Control Measures for Phreatophytes in the Channels of the Salt and Gila Rivers*. Department of Geography, Arizona State University, Tempe, Arizona, Report to US Army Corps of Engineers, Contract No. DACW09-79-C-0059.

Great Western Research (1989). *Economic Analysis of Harmful and Beneficial Aspects of Saltcedar*. Final Report, USDI, Bureau of Reclamation, Lower Colorado Region, Boulder City, Nevada.

Harbourne, J.B. (1975). Flavonoid bisulphates and their co-occurrences with ellagic acid in the Buxaceae, Frankeniaceae, and related families, *Phytochemistry*, **14**, 1331–1337.

Hefley, H.M. (1937). The relations of some native insects to introduced food plant. *Journal of Animal Ecology*, **6**, 138–144.

Hem, J.D. (1967). *Composition of Saline Residues on Leaves and Stems of Saltcedar* (Tamarix pentandra *Pallas*.) US GeologicalSurvey Professional Paper, 491-C, p. 9.

Hildebrandt, T.D. and Ohmart, R.D. (1982). *Biological Resource Inventory (vegetation and wildlife) Pecos River Basin, New Mexico and Texas*. Final Report, Bureau of Reclamation, Contract Number, 9–07–57-V0567.

Hoddenbach, G. (1987). Vegetation control of saltcedar (*Tamarix* spp). Paper presented at *National Park Service Conference*, Tucson, Arizona.

Hollingsworth, E.B., Quimby, P.C. and Jaramillo, D.C. (1979). Control of saltcedar by subsurface placement of herbicides. *Journal of Range Management*, **32**, 288–291.

Hopkins, H.H. and Carruth, L.A. (1954). Insects associated with saltcedar in southern Arizona. *Journal of Economic Entomology*, **47**, 1126–1129.

Hopkins, H.H. and Tomanek, G.W. (1957). A study of the woody vegetation at Cedar Bluff Reservoir. *Transactions of Kansas Academy of Science*, **60**, 351–359.

Horton, J.S. (1960). The ecology of saltcedar. *Proceedings: Arizona Watershed Symposium*, **4**, 19–21.

Horton, J.S. (1977). *The Development and Perpetuation of the Permanent Tamarisk Type in the Phreatophyte Zone of the Southwest*. USDA, Forest Service, General Technical Report, RM-43, pp. 124–127.

Horton, J.S., Mounts, F.C. and Kraft, J.M. (1960). *Seed Germination and Seedling Establishment of Phreatophyte Species*. USDA, Forest Service, Rocky Mountain Forest and Range Experiment Station,. Paper No. 48.

Howard, S.W., Dirar, A.E., Evans, J.O. and Provenza, F.D. (1982). *The Use of Herbicides and/or fire to Control Saltcedar* Tamarix. Photocopy of a report, Utah State University, Logan, Utah.

Hunter, W.C., Ohmart, R.D. and Anderson, B.W. (1987). Status of breeding riparian-obligate birds in southwestern riverine systems. *Western Birds*, **18**, 10–18.

Irvine, J.R. and West, N.E. (1979). Riparian tree species distribution and succession along the lower Esclante River, Utah. *Southwest Naturalist*, **24**, 331–346.

Jakle, M.D. and Katz, T.A. (1985). Herpetofaunal use of four habitats on the middle

Gila River drainage, Arizona. *Proceedings, First North American Riparian Conference*, Tucson, Arizona, pp. 355–358.

Kearney, T.H. and Peebles, R.H. (1960). *Arizona Flora*. Berkeley: University of California Press.

Lawrence, G.H.M. (1951). *Taxonomy of Vascular Plants*. New York: MacMillan.

Liesner, D.R. (1971). *Phytophagous insects of* Tamarix *spp. in New Mexico*, Unpublished thesis, New Mexico State University, Las Cruces.

Lindauer, I.E. (1967). Ecology of phreatophytes on the Arkansas River in southeastern Colorado. *Journal of the Colorado–Wyoming Academy of Sciences.*, **5**, 65.

Luciano, P. (1982). New damage caused in Sardinia by *Apate monachus* Fabr. Coleoptera, Bastrychidae. *Studi Sassaresi*, **29**, 67–71.

Meinzer, O.E. (1923). *Outline of the Ground Water Hydrology with Definitions*. US Geolological Survey, Water Supply Paper 494.

Merkel, D.L. and Hopkins, J.H. (1957). Life history of saltcedar (*Tamarix gallica* L.). *Transactions of Kansas Academy of Science*, **60**, 360–369.

Petranka, J.W. and Holland, R. (1980). A quantitative analysis of bottomland communities in south-central Oklahoma. *Southwest Naturalist*, **25**, 207–214.

Robinson, T.W. (1965). *Introduction, Spread, and Areal Extent of Saltcedar* Tamarix *in the Western States*. Geological Survey Professional Paper 491–A.

Robinson, T.W. and Bowser, C.W. (1959). *Buckeye Project—Water Use by Saltcedar*. Prepared for 59–3, Phreatophyte Subcommittee meeting, Pacific Southwest Inter-Agency Committee, p. 26.

Samedov, N.G. and Mirzoneva, N.B. (1985). A review of leaf-beetle (Coleoptera, Chrysomelidae) of the tugai forests of Azerbaijan. *Entomologicheskoe-Obozrenie*, **64**, 705–715.

Scifres, C.J. (1980). *Brush Management*. Texas A&M University Press, College Station.

Siegel, R.S. and Brock, J.H. (1990). Germination requirements of key southwestern woody riparian species. *Desert Plants*, **10**, 3–8, 34.

Smirnov, I.A. (1983). Resistance of woody species to gases in an arid climate. *Soviet Journal of Ecology*, **14**, 156–158.

Smirnov. I.A. (1987). Fume resistant trees and shrubs. *Lesnoe Khozyaistro*, **4**, 65–67.

Smith, A.M. and Kadlec, J.A. (1983). Seed banks and their role during draw down of a North American marsh. *Journal of Applied Ecology*, **20**, 673–684.

Tomanek, G.W. and Zeigler, R.L. (1962). *Ecological studies of* Tamarix. Fort Hays Kansas State College, Hays.

US Bureau of Reclamation (1973). *Phreatophyte Investigations, Bernardo Evapotranspirators*. USDI-USBR, Middle Rio Grande Project Office, Second Progress Report.

US Soil Conservation Service and Texas Agricultural Extension Service (1982). *Texas Brush Control Survey*. College Station, Texas A&M University

van Hylckama, T.E.A. (1969). Photosynthesis and water use by saltcedar. *Bulletin of the International Association of Scientific Hydrology*, **14**, 71–83.

van Hylckama, T.E.A. (1974). *Water Use by Saltcedar as Measured by the Water Budget Method*. US Geological Survey Professional Paper, 491-E.

Waisel, Y. (1961). Ecological studies on *Tamarix aphylla* (L.) Karst I-II. *Phyton*, **15**, 7–28.

Warren, D.K. and Turner, R.M. (1975). Saltcedar (*Tamarix chinensis*) seed production, seedling establishment, and response to inundation, *Journal of the Arizona Academy of Science*, **10**, 135–144.

Watts, J.G., Liesner, D.R. and Lindsey, D.L. (1977). *Saltcedar: a potential target for biological control*, Bulletin, New Mexico Agricultural Experiment Station, No. 650.

Wiedemann, H.T. and Cross, B.T. (1979). *Saltcedar Control Along Shorelines of Lakes*. Texas Agricultural Experiment Station, Texas A&M University, Consolidated Progress Report 3665.

Wilkinson, R.E. (1966). Adventitious shoots on saltcedar roots. *Botanical Gazette*, **127**, 103–104.

5 Ecological Aspects of Invasion by *Heracleum mantegazzianum* in the Czech Republic

PETR PYŠEK

Institute of Applied Ecology, 281 63 Kostelec nad Černými lesy, the Czech Republic

INTRODUCTION

HISTORY

Among aliens successfully naturalized in central European natural and semi-natural vegetation (Kornaś, 1990), so far only a few have caused practical problems. Giant hogweed (*Heracleum mantegazzianum* Somm. et Levier), introduced in the nineteenth century from western Caucasus, is at present becoming a serious threat to the landscape in some European countries, especially Sweden (Lundström, 1984), Scotland (Bingham, 1990; Neiland *et al.*, 1987) and the Czech Republic (Pyšek, 1991). Replacement of native vegetation (for a summary of possible consequences, see Pyšek, 1991) and injuries to human skin caused by phototoxic substances (Drever and Hunter, 1970) are the main reasons for efforts to eradicate the species from infested areas. However, once a large area is infested, eradication efforts have brought only limited success so far (Lundström, 1990; Williamson and Forbes, 1982).

Being the largest central European forb, part of the competitive superiority of *H. mantegazzianum* over other plants is ascribed to its size and its ability to shade the surrounding vegetation with huge ground leaves. High seed set (Brondegaard, 1990; Neiland, 1986) and dispersal encouraged by water, wind and human-related factors (Jehlík and Lhotská, 1971) also contribute to its rapid spread into various vegetation types.

In a previous paper (Pyšek, 1991), the historical dynamics of the spread of the species in the Czech Republic was reconstructed using floristic data. Having been introduced into the Czech Republic in the middle of the nineteeth century as a garden ornamental (Kratzmann, 1862), *H. mantegazzianum* was initially spread through cultivation in parks and gardens. Up to 1950, only nine localities had been reported, some of them serving as foci for sub-

Ecology and Management of Invasive Riverside Plants
Edited by L. C. de Waal, L. E. Child, P. M. Wade and J. H. Brock
© 1994 John Wiley & Sons Ltd

sequent spread. The beginning of rapid invasion occurred in the late 1960s and early 1970s. Since then, the number of reported localities has increased exponentially from 67 in 1970 to 472 in 1990 (Pyšek and Pyšek, 1994). The current distribution of *H. mantegazzianum* in the Czech Republic is presented in Figure 5.1. The species abundance in the landscape decreases with the distance from the region of the earliest introduction, which was in the westernmost part of the country (Pyšek, 1991).

The present paper, which is based on the same data set as the previous one (Pyšek, 1991), focuses upon ecological aspects of invasion by *H. mantegazzianum*. The following questions are addressed: (1) whether the dynamics of spread differ with respect to the type of invaded vegetation and (2) what was the role of climatic conditions in the process of the species' invasion?

DATA SOURCES

Analysis included both published and unpublished floristic data. The total number of localities registered in the Czech Republic in 1990 was 472. An updated reference list was provided by Pyšek and Pyšek (1994) for those localities described with sufficient accuracy in the original source. However, only those localities for which the information on habitat type was provided by the original author were analysed in this paper. This number ($n = 378$) is therefore lower than the total number of localities reported in the list mentioned above ($n = 410$).

Distribution of *H. mantegazzianum* was expressed as the presence or absence in squares 11×12 km (Schönfelder and Bresinsky, 1990).

RESULTS AND DISCUSSION

SPREAD IN VARIOUS VEGETATION TYPES: THE ROLE OF RECIPIENT HABITAT

The main habitat types were arbitrarily classified according to the intensity of disturbance. Habitats that encourage the greatest movement of diaspores (referred to as transport habitats) were included in group A, consisting of (i) pond margins and wetlands; (ii) valleys and banks of rivers and brooks; (iii) road verges, ditches and adjacent habitats; and (iv) railway areas including railway tracks and open spaces of railway stations. The following habitats were included among man-made, usually heavily disturbed, habitats in group B: (i) dumps, rubbish tips and various deposits, in settlements or in the open landscape; (ii) gardens and parks; and (iii) urban areas, i.e. habitats in towns and villages other than those belonging to (i) or (ii). The group of semi-natural habitats (C) was represented by (i) scrub communities, (ii) meadows and grasslands and (iii) forests and their margins.

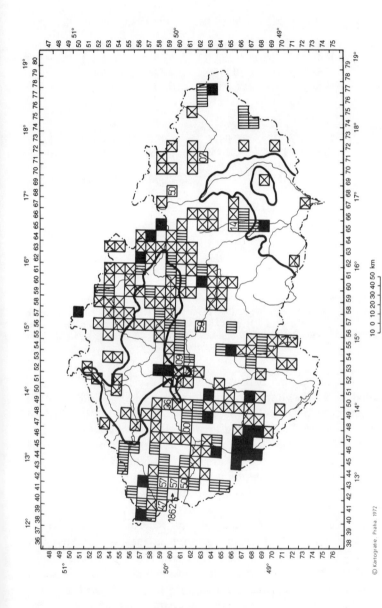

© Kartografie Praha 1972

10 0 10 20 30 40 50 km

Figure 5.1 Historical outline of distribution of *Heracleum mantegazzianum* in the Czech Republic. Earliest records (up to 1960) are indicated by the year of the first report. Different symbols are used to show subsequent spread: localities discovered in the 1960s ■, 1970s ▦ and 1980s ⊠; bold lines show the location of warm districts, which differ in having >50 summer days, <110 days with frost, mean April temperature >8°C, mean July temperature >18°C, and >160 days with mean temperature 10°C or more (Quitt, 1975)

Table 5.1. Summary of rate of spread of *Heracleum mantegazzianum* in different habitats in the Czech Republic

	1st record	n	Slope b	SE (10^{-3})	inter-cept a	SE
Transport habitats						
Ponds, wetlands	1963	16	0.0803	3.323	−4.412	0.234
River banks	1901	41	0.0851	2.037	−2.914	0.143
Roads	1963	76	0.1188	4.424	−6.452	0.312
Railway areas	1953	29	0.0834	4.534	−4.492	0.320
Total		162	0.1037	2.401	−4.255	0.169
Man-made habitats						
Dumps, deposits	1966	20	0.0894	4.212	−4.940	0.297
Urban areas	1947	118	0.1003	2.679	−4.387	0.189
Parks, gardens	1862	19	0.0524	1.791	−1.797	0.126
Total		157	0.0972	2.373	−3.704	0.167
Semi-natural habitats						
Scrub	1950	7	0.0395	2.181	−1.531	0.154
Meadow	1960	22	0.0848	3.708	−4.639	0.261
Forest	1947	30	0.0619	1.449	−2.289	0.102
Total		59	0.0822	1.908	−3.351	0.134
Grand Total		378	0.1031	1.932	−3.313	0.136

Slopes and intercepts of the regression equation LOG (CUMULATIVE NUMBER OF LOCALITIES + 1) = a + b × YEAR are given. Only records after 1945 were included in the calculation. Total number of localities known for a given habitat type in 1990 is given (*n*).

A study of the habitat groups indicates that the species occurs most frequently in man-made (41.5%) and transport habitats (42.8%); 15.8% of the localities were recorded in semi-natural habitats. At present, the highest number of records is reported from urban areas and road verges (Table 5.1).

The total number of localities has increased exponentially between 1947 and 1990 in each habitat type considered (Table 5.1, Figure 5.2). The rate of expansion was compared among habitats using a semi-log scale of the cumulative number of localities over time. The year 1947 was used as the starting point for regression equations, since, prior to this year only five records had been reported (see Figure 5.1) and thereafter the records started to occur more frequently. The slopes of regression lines reflect the rate of expansion (Table 5.1). The highest values of *b* were found in roads and settlements, whereas the lowest values were in scrub, parks and gardens. This indicates a tendency for a lower expansion rate of populations in semi-natural, less disturbed vegetation types. However, the pairwise comparisons did not reveal any significant differences between the slopes of regression lines (*F*-test, according to Snedecor and Cochran, 1965). Similarly, if pooled data for each

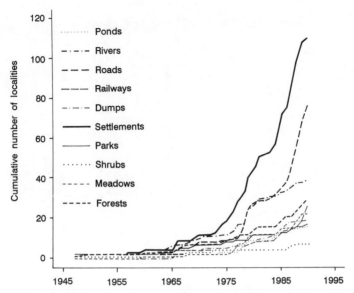

Figure 5.2 Spread of *Heracleum mantegazzianum* into different habitats in the Czech Republic

group of habitats (A–C) were analysed, no significant differences between slopes were found.

A conclusion may thus be drawn that the expansion rate in the last four decades was similar in each of the habitat types invaded. This suggests that the recipient habitat plays a less important role (Pyšek and Prach, 1994) than may be expected for a strongly competitive species (Newsome and Noble, 1986; Roy, 1990). Once *H. mantegazzianum* had entered a certain habitat type, it spread exponentially, regardless of the characteristics of the invaded vegetation.

Data on the first year of appearance (Table 5.1) show that, with the exception of (i) parks and gardens in which it had been originally cultivated and (ii) river habitats, the species was introduced in most of the habitat types during the 1950s or early 1960s. There was no difference between the man-made and semi-natural habitats.

The expansion was initially encouraged by the courses of main rivers. Mapping squares that contain main rivers (i.e. those indicated on the map in Figure 5.1) accounted for 66.7% of the total number of squares occupied by *H. mantegazzianum* in 1950. This proportion gradually decreased to 36.4% in 1990 (Figure 5.3a). Similarly, the percentage of occupied squares was higher among "river squares" than among squares without rivers (Figure 5.3b). The magnitude of this difference was greatest between 1965 and 1975, i.e. at the beginning of rapid exponential spread. If the data on

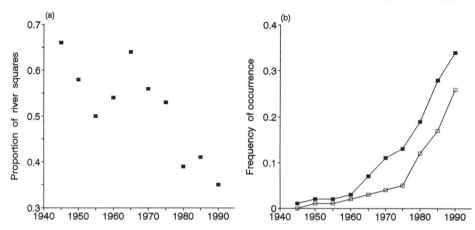

Figure 5.3 Spread of *Heracleum mantegazzianum* along the courses of main rivers in the Czech Republic: (a) river squares (i.e. those through which a main river flows, see Figure 5.1) occupied by the species as a proportion of the total number of squares occupied in the respective year; the value of Kendall non-parametric correlation coefficient was 0.64, significance level $\alpha < 0.01$, $n = 10$; and (b) probability of occurence of *H. mantegazzianum* in river squares ■ and terrestrial squares □

"river" and "terrestrial" squares are compared in the last decade, i.e. 1980s, the percentages of squares in which *H. mantegazzianum* was present were becoming similar, which indicates the species' spread from river squares to terrestrial ones.

Neiland (1986) has suggested that the increased occurrence on river banks in Scotland was not only because of the efficiency of seed dispersal by water but also because the river bank habitats are suitable for seedling establishment, being relatively free from competition by other species (see also Thébaud and Debussche, 1991).

TO WHAT EXTENT WAS THE SPECIES INVASION AFFECTED BY THE CLIMATE?

Comparison of altitude of localities with *H. mantegazzianum* over two decades showed an obvious shift towards lower elevation (Figure 5.4). At the beginning of the exponential phase of spread (approximately 1970, Pyšek, 1991), 28.5% of localities were >600 m above sea level; at present (1990), the respective value is only 14.7%. The mean altitude in 1970 was significantly higher than in 1990 ($t = 2.32$, $P = 0.02$). These results indicate that, at the beginning of spread, *H. mantegazzianum* occurred mainly at higher altitudes, which is no longer true. The frequency distribution of *H. mantegazzianum* according to altitude in 1990 corresponds closely to the overall

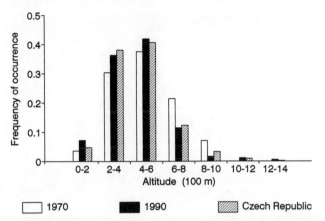

Figure 5.4 Frequency distribution of altitudes at which *Heracleum mantegazzianum* was found in the Czech Republic. Percentage of localities is shown for each altitudinal range. Data from the beginning of exponential phase of spread (1970, *n* = 56) are compared with the current state (1990, *n* = 375). Frequency distribution of altitudes in the Czech Republic (according to Novotný, 1971) is given in the third column. Number of localities in 1990 is lower than the total number known up to this year because in some cases it was not possible to obtain data on altitude owing to a vague location given in the original source

distribution of altitude in the Czech Republic (Novotný, 1971) (Figure 5.4).

Assessment of the effect of climate produced similar results. There are two large continuous warm climate districts in the Czech Republic: (i) the Elbe, Vltava and Ohře Lowlands, in the North of the country and (ii) the lowlands in south Moravia (Quitt, 1975; Figure 5.1). Up to 1970, only two localities were reported from the former district and one was known from south Moravia (i.e. only three out of 67 known at that time). During the next decade, the spread into both warm districts was represented only by four localities that appeared in the Elbe lowland. In the 1980s, *H. mantegazzianum* invaded partly into the Elbe lowland (remaining relatively unsuccessful along the Ohře river), but it is still almost absent in south Moravia. However, this evidence must be treated with caution since there is a large region adjacent to the south Moravian lowlands, which has a moderate climate, and *H. manteggazianum* is absent in this region as well. Nevertheless, from the beginning of massive spread up to recent time, the probability of a square being occupied was notably lower in those located in warm regions (Figure 5.5). Thus, it may be concluded that there was a strong tendency for *H. mantegazzianum* to avoid the warmest climatic regions. This trend is, to a certain extent, still obvious.

The preference for cooler, more humid areas corresponds to the fact that

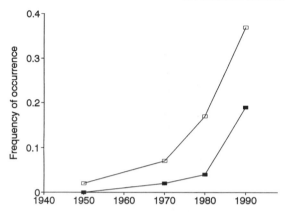

Figure 5.5 Probability of occurrence *Heracleum mantegazzianum* (expressed as a percentage of occupied squares, see Figure 5.5) in squares lying in warm climatic regions ■ and those in moderate or cold regions □

H. mantegazzianum is native to the upper forest belts of western Caucasus (Mladenova, 1950), i.e. it is originally a montane species. Similarly, on a continental scale, its more frequent occurence in northern Europe may reflect a more favourable climate for the species (Pyšek, 1991).

CONCLUSIONS

From the historical point of view, the performance of *Heracleum mantegazzianum* in the Czech Republic may be divided into three periods:

Period 1 (approximately 80 years): It appears that from the first introduction (1862) up to the 1940s the spread of *H. mantegazzianum* had been exclusively due to its cultivation as a garden ornamental. The localities where it occured in this period served as independent foci for the subsequent spread.

Period 2 (approximately 30 years): From the 1940s, the spread of *H. mantegazzianum* started along main rivers. In this period, the species invaded more successfully in the regions of higher altitudes and avoided the warmest districts.

Period 3 (Approximately 20 years): The 1960s and 1970s may be considered as the starting point of an exponential phase of the species' spread (Pyšek, 1991). Since then, *H. mantegazzianum* has invaded the landscape regardless of altitude, and the effect of warm climate was less restrictive. The rate of expansion was similar in the heavily disturbed, man-made habitats and in the semi-natural vegetation (meadow, scrub, forest). At the end of this period, the preference for river valleys was no longer evident, since *H. mantegazzianum* was spreading into the wider landscape.

The lack of quantitative data on spread dynamics from other European countries prevents direct comparisons. Although the duration of particular periods, as described in the previous paragraphs, may be expected to differ in different parts of Europe, the pattern of spread, at least in some of them, was similar (Pyšek, 1991) and the scheme presented appears to be generally valid.

ACKNOWLEDGEMENTS

Thanks are due to the following colleagues who provided their unpublished floristic records and other information: M. Marek, A. Pyšek, V. Skalický, P. Bureš, L. Faltys, V. Grulich, R. Hlaváček, V. Chán, J. Kaisler, J. Kurka, V. Pluhař, J. Rydlo, B. Trávínček, J. Vaněček, L. Vanečková and J. Sádlo. I am grateful to K. Prach for his comments on the early draft of the manuscript, S. Navratil and an anonymous reviewer for improving my English, and E. Švejdová for drawing the figures.

REFERENCES

Bingham, I.J. (1990). *Giant Hogweed: the Problem and its Control.* Leaflet, Scottish Agricultural College, Aberdeen.
Brondegaard, V.J. (1990). Massenausbreitung des Brenklaus. *Naturwissenschaftliche Rundschau*, **43**, 438–439.
Drever, J.C. and Hunter, J.A. (1970). Giant hogweed dermatitis. *Scotish Medical Journal*, **15**, 315–319.
Jehlík, V. and Lhotská, M. (1970). Contribution to the knowledge on the distribution and fruit dispersal of some synathropic plant sepecies from the Průhonice village, Průhonice park and the Botič brook valley. *Studies of the Czechoslovak Academy of Sciences, 1970/7*, pp. 45–95. [In Czech].
Kornaś, J. (1990). Plant invasions in Central Europe: historical and ecological aspects. In F. Di Castri, A.J. Hansen and M. Debussche (Eds), *Biological invasions in Europe and the Mediterranean Basin*, pp. 19–36. Dordrecht: Kluwer.
Kratzmann, E. (1862). Flora von Marienbad. In *Der Curort Marienbad und seine Umgebung*, 5th edn, pp. 339–359. Prague.
Lundström, H. (1984). Giant hogweed, *Heracleum mantegazzianum*, a threat to the Swedish countryside. *Weeds and Weed Control, 25th Swedish Weed Conference*, Uppsala, Vol. 1, pp. 191–200.
Lundström, H. (1990). New experiences of the fight against the giant hogweed, *Heracleum mantegazzianum. Weeds and Weed Control, 30th Swedish Crop Protection Conference*, Uppsala Vol. 2, pp. 51–58.

Mladenova, I.P. (1950). Caucasian species of the genus *Heracleum*, Tbilisi. [In Russian].

Neiland, M.R.M. (1986). *The distribution and ecology of giant hogweed* (Heracleum mantegazzianum) *on the River Allan, and its control in Scotland*. BSc dissertation, University of Stirling.

Neiland, R., Proctor, J. and Sexton, R. (1987). Giant hogweed (*Heracleum mantegazzianum* Somm. & Lev.) by the River Allan and part of the River Forth. *Forth Natural History*, **9**, 51–56.

Newsome, A.E. and Noble, I.R. (1986). Ecological and physiological characters of invading species. In R.H. Groves and J.J. Burden (Eds), *Ecology of Biological Invasions: An Australian Perspective*, p. 1–20. Canberra: Australian Academy of Sciences.

Novotny, J. (Ed.) (1971). *Czechoslovakia—a collection of maps*, 5th edn. Kartografia, Praha. [in Czech].

Pyšek, P. (1991). *Heracleum mantegazzianum* in the Czech Republic—the dynamics of spreading from the historical perspective. *Folia Geobotanica et Phytotaxonomica*, **26**, 439–454.

Pyšek, P. and Pyšek, A. (1994). Current occurrence of *Heracleum mantegazzianum* and survey of its localities in the Czech Republic. Prague: Zprávy Československé Botanické Společnosti, **27**.

Pyšek, P. and Prach, K. (1994). How important are rivers for supporting plant invasions? In L.C. de Waal, L.E. Child, P.M. Wade and J.H. Brock (Eds), *Ecology and Management of Invasive Riverside Plants*, pp. 19–26. Chichester: Wiley.

Quitt, E. (1975). *Climatic Regions of the Czech Socialist Republic*. Brno: Institute of Geography, Czechoslovak Academy of Sciences [In Czech].

Roy, J. (1990). In search of the characteristics of plant invaders, In F. Di Castri, A.J. Hansen, and M. Debussche (Eds), *Biological Invasions in Europe and the Mediterranean Basin*, 335–352 Dordrecht: Kluwer.

Schönfelder, P. and Bresinsky, A. (1990). *Verbreitungsatlas der Farn und Bltenpflanzen Bayerns*. Stuttgart: Eugen Ulmer.

Snedecor, G.W. and Cochran, W.G. (1967). *Statistical methods*. Ames: Iowa University Press.

Thébaud, C. and Debussche, M. (1991). Rapid invasion of *Fraxinus ornus* L. along the Hrault River system in southern France: the importance of seed dispersal by water. *Journal of Biogeography*, **18**, 7–12.

Williamson, J.A. and Forbes, J.C. (1982), Giant hogweed (*Heracleum mantegazzianum*): its spread and control with glyphosate in amenity areas. *Weeds, Proceedings of the 1982 British Crop Protection Conference*, pp. 967–972.

6 Cost and Impact of Current Control Methods Used Against *Heracleum mantegazzianum* (Giant Hogweed) and the Case for Instigating a Biological Control Programme

CLARE SAMPSON

Bunting Biological Control Ltd, Great Horkesley, Colchester, UK

INTRODUCTION

H. mantegazzianum Sommier et Levier (giant hogweed, family: Umbelliferae), native to the Caucasus, was introduced into Britain in 1893 as an ornamental plant. Since then, it has spread along river courses, roads, railways and wasteland and can now be found from the south coast of England to the Scottish highlands (Clegg and Grace, 1974). It has also spread through central and northern Europe up to Scandinavia (Tutin *et al.*, 1968) and into Canada (Morton, 1978).

H. mantegazzianum achieves an impressive size and, to some, is an attractive plant. However, it is invasive, replacing native flora and leaving bare ground exposed to erosion in winter (Williamson and Forbes, 1982). In amenity areas *H. mantegazzianum* prevents access both because of its large size and its phytotoxic sap (Berenbaum, 1981a; Drever and Hunter, 1970). Local authorities and private landowners need to take control measures to protect both the public and the environment.

Control of *H. mantegazzianum* has become a dilemma. Selective herbicides which may be safely used along watercourses have proven to be ineffective (Williamson and Forbes, 1982). The non-selective herbicide glyphosate can be applied as a spot treatment, achieving useful control (Kees and Krumrey, 1983; Lundström, 1984; Williamson and Forbes, 1982). For control to be

Ecology and Management of Invasive Riverside Plants
Edited by L. C. de Waal, L. E. Child, P. M. Wade and J. H. Brock
© 1994 John Wiley & Sons Ltd

successful, all the plants in the surrounding area must be treated to prevent re-seeding. Re-treatment may be neccessary, which can be impractical and prohibitively expensive. Cutting the stem is rarely effective, since the substantial root reserves allow regeneration. Cutting during seed set helps to spread the seeds even further. Both spraying and cutting can be hazardous to the operator owing to the noxious sap.

Because of the difficulties in achieving lasting control using chemical means, biological control could be considered as an alternative. The success of biological programmes often relies on the specificity of the control agent, ensuring that native flora, beneficial and crop plants remain unaffected. *H. mantegazzianum* sap contains a range of secondary chemicals such as furanocoumarins, which are specific either to the Umbelliferae family or to the species. Furanocoumarins are both repellent and toxic to generalist insect feeders (Yajima *et al.*, 1977), but lack toxicity to specialists which feed exclusively on Umbelliferae (Camm *et al.*, 1976). Furano-coumarins stimulate feeding and enhance growth in some specialists such as *Papilio polyxenes* (Lepidoptera: Papilionidae) (Berenbaum, 1981b). The complicated secondary chemistry of *H. mantegazzianum* may therefore aid the search for a specialist control agent.

Few studies have been made on the fauna of *H. mantegazzianun*. Only three species are recorded in the *Phytophagous Insect Data Base* (Institute of Terrestrial Ecology, Furzebrook Research Station). A full survey of species which have colonized *H. mantegazzianum* naturally since its introduction is needed as baseline information so as to avoid introducing ecologically and taxonomically similar species from the plant's native range.

The purpose of this study was twofold: firstly to establish the areas and habitats worst affected by *H. mantegazzianum* in Britain and to estimate the cost and efficacy of current control methods through a postal survey; and secondly, to assess the level of recruitment and the impact of native fauna on *H. mantegazzianum* as compared with *H. sphondylium*, the closest related British species to *H. mantegazzianum*, through a field survey. Part 1 of this paper deals with the postal survey and part 2 deals with the field survey.

PART 1. POSTAL SURVEY

A postal survey was carried out from May to August 1990. Brief information on *H. mantegazzianum* was given to 190 county councils, conservation groups and national park authorities. They were asked to complete a single-page questionnaire; 152 (80%) valid responses were returned, indicating a high level of interest.

RESULTS

Regions affected

Problem areas corresponded closely with the distribution of the plant. 10% of the respondents carried out control measures over large areas every year; these were centred along the Borders and up the east coast of Scotland as well as the Lee valley, Dartmoor National Park and the west Cumbrian coast in England. 43% found *H. mantegazzianum* an occasional problem and resorted to control measures of small areas, usually in response to public demand. 47% did not consider *H. mantegazzianum* to be a problem in their districts, these were mostly from a broad belt around the Midlands of England.

Control measures were taken largely to provide access to amenity areas, especially along river banks for recreation, salmon fishing and conservation areas. Other reasons mentioned were public safety, river bank protection, highway visibility and prevention of spread.

Habitats colonized

From the 150 sites recorded, *H. mantegazzianum* was most frequent along river banks, accounting for half of all habitats cited. With the exception of one cliff-top site and five woodland sites, all other habitats were split equally between roadsides and waste land.

Amongst conservation groups there is great concern over the spread of *H. mantegazzianum*. In Dartmoor National Park the spread was quoted as "rapid and in danger of destroying a vast number of habitats". Two conservation groups were concerned about the threat to ancient woodland Sites of Special Scientific Interest.

Methods of *H. mantegazzianum* control

Active control against *H. mantegazzianum* was undertaken by 81 local authorities and conservation groups, representing over half of the respondents. Three main control strategies were adopted. A third of the respondents were cutting the plant just above ground in the spring and treating the regrowth with glyphosate in spring or early summer. A third were using the chemical glyphosate alone, sometimes with necessary repeated applications to achieve success; this method was most popular in districts with large areas of *H. mantagazzianum* to control. The other third were using mechanical means of control by cutting the stem, although a poor success rate was reported. Two respondents (2%) had used glyphosate, followed by burning the surrounding area, using a flame gun in one case, and diesel oil in the other.

Cost of *H. mantegazzianum* control

Expenditure on control varied enormously between areas, according to the distribution and abundance of the plant. Local authorities are spending more than conservation groups, who generally treat smaller areas and make use of voluntary labour. The largest amount of money was spent in the central and border regions of Scotland.

Table 6.1 shows the cost of materials, hours of labour and area treated as quoted by respondents for the year 1989/90. The total expenditure is difficult

Table 6.1 Expenditure on control of *Heracleum mantegazzianum* for the year 1989/90

District Council	Area treated (ha)	Labour (hours)*	Costs (£'s)*
Scotland			
Banff and Buchan	9	4800	2500
Dumfries	–	1	1
Galashiels	–	10	50
Gordon	19	1600	500
Hawick	1	(200)	244
Inverness	–	280	600
Kilmarnock and Louden	–	16	(20)
Kincardine and Deeside	0.25	8	25
Lothian	4	200	1000
Moray	15	10800	14625
Nairn	–	80	50
Stirling	–	2280	3790
Stranraer	0.25	10	25
Tweed Valley (SWT)	–	16	10
England			
Aylesbury	0.05	1	10
Cheshire	–	100	300
Copeland	–	5	(20)
Darlington	–	5	100
Dartmoor National Park	1.1	(150)	458
Dover	0.25	5	100
Kendal	0.05	1	1
Lee Valley, Essex	1	18	(100)
Reading	0.04	(1)	(10)
Ribble valley	0.02	(1)	(10)
Rossendale	–	2	1
Scarborough	0.5	30	300
Suffolk	0.2	(10	(10)
31 councils cost unspecified	(6)	(155)	(1085)
Total	51.71	21085	25945

*Data in parentheses estimated.

to estimate as the form and quality of the information received were variable and 31 respondents were even unable to quantify their costs, but considered them to be minimal.

The minimum cost of *H. mantegazzianum* control from April 1989 to April 1990 was an estimated £89 200 assuming £3.00 per hour as a minimum wage. An increase in 1989/90 was caused by the initiation of an extensive eradication programme in the Moray district. Moray have initiated a 4-year eradication programme using 45 workers for 10 weeks/year. Some councils are returning to the same areas each year to carry out control measures, indicating the need for continuing treatment.

The postal survey indicated that there may be hidden costs caused by the injurious nature of the plant: twenty respondents reported such injuries. The majority of injuries occurred during control operations. The allergic reaction produced in some people merited medical attention.

Other comments

Eight Scottish councils called for the plant to be classified as an injurious weed requiring eradication. Several others are trying to control *H. mantegazzianum* in areas outside their jurisdiction by serving proprietors with notices under the Public Health (Scotland) Act 1897. Unfortunately, the legal process is time consuming and the plants have often seeded again by the time notices are served. Under the Wildlife and Countryside Act 1981, it is now an offence to "plant or otherwise cause to grow in the wild" certain plants, including *H. mantegazzianum*.

PART 2. FIELD SURVEY

A field survey was carried out during the growing season of 1990. Ten sites were chosen to represent a variety of habitats and geographical locations. A total of 93 *H. mantegazzianum* plants and 75 *H. sphondylium* plants were sampled. Where possible, ten plants of each species were sampled per site. A random-walk system was used to select plants for sampling. For each selected plant, full plant parameters and habitat details were recorded and subsequently searched systematically and destructively for phytophagous species, which were counted and identified from each unit of plant, i.e. leaves, buds, flowers, seeds and roots. Voucher specimens were collected and preserved in alcohol for verification. Larval stages were collected and bred through to the adult stage for identification. Specimens found on *H. sphondylium*, but not on *H. mantegazzianum*, were recorded, but not identified to species. A review of insect herbivores on *H. sphondylium* can be found in Sheppard (1987).

Damage was attributed to individual species where possible and scored as a percentage for each plant part. No quantitative damage assessments were made for sucking insects. Analysis of variance (ANOVAR) was conducted with the data using the GLIM (Generalized Linear Interactive Modelling) statistical package. ANOVARs were undertaken on each of the main herbivores found on *H. mantegazzianum* comparing the occurrence on both *Heracleum* species. Two ANOVARs used transformed data: the first used the records +1 to lessen the skew caused by many zero scores in the data: the second used these values divided by a measure of plant size (height × length of the largest leaf). This gave an estimate of the numbers of individuals per unit area of plant, corrected for the differing size of the two species.

RESULTS

Herbivores found on *H. mantegazzianum* and *H. sphondylium*

A total of 44 phytophagous species was recorded on *H. mantegazzianum* during this study. Of these, 19 were found frequently or in some abundance and 14 were single records, indicating that the species were visitors rather than feeders. The remaining 11 species were recorded occasionally (< five records). In addition, several generalist mollusc species (slugs and snails) were recorded, but not identified to species level. Thirteen species were recorded on *H. mantegazzianum*, but not on *H. sphondylium*. Table 6.2 shows a list of the main insect herbivores found on *H. mantegazzianum* during this study.

Plant diseases

Four diseases were observed during the survey. Aphid-transmitted virus diseases appeared to be the most damaging. Infected plants turned a distinctive mottled yellow. A total of 14 of the *H. mantegazzianum* plants sampled was infected (15%) and 7 of the *H. sphondylium* plants (9%). The damage levels on both *Heracleum* species were similar, averaging approximately 25%.

Powdery mildew (*Erysiphe heraclei*) was the second most frequent disease. It appeared towards the end of the season in response to humid weather conditions. Seven *H. mantegazzianum* plants were infected (7%) and eight *H. sphondylium* plants (11%). Infected plants were almost completely covered by the disease.

A leaf spot (*Alternaria alternata*) was observed on six *H. sphondylium* stems, but not on *H. mantegazzianum* stems. Miscellaneous leaf spots,

Table 6.2. Main insect species recorded on *Heracleum mantegazzianum* during the study in 1990

Order: genus: species	Plant part	Guild
Hemiptera: Heteroptera		
Orthops basalis Costa	Flower/leaf	Sap sucker
Hemiptera: Homoptera		
Philaenus spumaris L.	Leaf/stem	Sap sucker
Eupteryx aurata (L.)	Leaf	Sap sucker
Trioza apicalis (Forster)	Leaf	Sap sucker
Cavariella aegopodii (Scopoli)	Flower	Sap sucker
C. pastinacae (L.)	Flower	Sap sucker
C. theobaldi (Gillette & Bragg)	Flower	Sap sucker
Aphis spp.	Flower	Sap sucker
Paramyzxus heraclei	Leaf/root	Sap sucker
Thysanoptera		
Thrips atratus	Flower	Sap sucker
T. vulgatissimus	Flower	Sap sucker
Diptera: Acalyptera		
Phytomyza spondylii (Goureau)	Leaf	Leaf miner
Euleia heraclei (L.)	Leaf	Leaf miner
Lepidoptera		
Epermenia chaerophyllella (Goeze)	Leaf	Leaf chewer
Phaulernis dentella (Zeller)	Leaf	Leaf chewer
Depressaria pastinacella (Duponchel)	Flower/stem	Floral/stem feeders
Cydia aurana (Fabricus)	Flower/seed	Floral/seed feeders
Agonopterix heracleana (L.)	Leaf	Leaf roller
Coleoptera		
Phaedon tumidulus (Germar)	Leaf	Leaf chewer
Crepidodera ferruginea (Sp.)	Leaf	Leaf chewer
Meligethes sp.	Pollen	Pollen chewer
Byrrhus sp.	Pollen	Pollen chewer

possibly of the same species, were found on one *H. sphondylium* and three *H. mantegazzianum* plants.

An unidentified soft rot was observed in a few roots of both *Heracleum* species, sometimes moving up into the stem.

Recruitment of herbivores onto *H. mantegazzianum*

H. mantegazzianum had a greater total population and greater variety of herbivores per plant than *H. sphondylium*. A far greater proportion of the insects found on *H. mantegazzianum* was occasional or single records than those on *H. sphondylium*. Being an introduced species with unusual plant chemistry, fewer herbivores would be expected (Strong *et al.*, 1984). The apparent anomaly may be explained by the large size of *H. mantegazzianum*, which presents a greater target for insects and an increase in the variety and number of micro-habitats available for exploitation. Large plants are more likely to be colonized by insects than are small plants, both in ecological and evolutionary time (Lawton, 1983). Studies on British Umbelliferae have shown that larger species have more agromyzid miners than do smaller species (Lawton and Price, 1979).

The plant chemistry is of great importance in determining which species establish and the levels of damage caused by those species. Two differing schools of thought occur. One suggests that biochemically unusual plants reduce insect colonization and therefore predict a low insect diversity (Strong *et al.*, 1984). The other indicates that pre-adapted insects can shift hosts more easily because chemically diverse plants are more likely to share compounds with other plant species (Dethier, 1941). A study of British Umbelliferae (J.H. Lawton personal communication) found that unusual host-plant chemistry has no detectable effect on the number of insect species, whilst diversity of secondary compounds has an equivocal effect, but may enhance insect species richness.

The most frequent and damaging species found on *H. mantegazzianum* in this study were all specialist feeders recruited from the native *H. sphondylium*. These results show that *H. mantegazzianum* has already recruited the main damaging species found on *H. sphondylium* and that only three hemipteran species were found in some abundance on *H. sphondylium*, but not on *H. mantegazzianum*. It is likely, therefore, that further recruitment of the British fauna would have little impact on the distribution and abundance of the plant.

When comparing the fauna on *H. mantegazzianum* with that on *H. sphondylium*, the three species which were the most damaging to *H. sphondylium* plants were the most specialized feeders: *Cavariella pastinacae, Phaedon tumidulus* and *Depressaria pastinacella*. For these species, there were significantly more individuals ($P < 0.001$) per area of plant on *H. sphondylium* than on *H. mantegazzianum*. Two other specialists, *Phytomyza sphondylii* and *Eupteryx aurata*, were also more frequent per unit area of *H. sphondylium* ($P < 0.001$)

The three species which were significantly more abundant per area of *H. mantegazzianum* (but only to the 5% level) were *Orthops basalis, Agonopterix heracleana* and *Epermenia chaerophyllella*. *Orthops* and *Agonopterix* are specialized to family level (Umbelliferae) rather than to tribe level (Peucedanacae).

With the notable exception of *Euleia heraclei*, all the species showing no significant differences per unit area between the two *Heracleum* species were generalist feeders (including slugs, snails, thrips, *Aphis* sp. and *Meligethes*). As predicted, these were less damaging than specialist feeders.

The impact of herbivores on *H. mantegazzianum*

Generally, the levels of damage by folivores were low, except for sporadic high densities of *Epermenia chaerophyllella* and second-generation *Euleia heraclei*. It is not known what level of damage is required to influence the population dynamics of the plant. On *H. sphondylium*, folivores such as *Phaedon tumidulus* can reduce the reproductive performance of individual plants when present in high numbers (over 50% damage), or may even influence whether the plant produces flowers (Sheppard, 1987).

In the field, most leaf damage was caused by the four species shown in Table 6.3. Field observations indicated that this damage was not enough to kill the plant, prevent seeding or stop the spread of *H. mantegazzianum*.

The highest incidence of damage per plant was caused by *Epermenia chaerophyllella*, reaching 50% on one occasion. However, this species was too limited in distribution (on 18% of plants and at 6 out of 10 sites) to have an overall impact. The greatest damage was recorded on first-year seedlings.

Fewer species have been recruited to the flowers, stems and roots of *H. mantegazzianum*, and these are the areas which may have the most controlling impact on the plant. *Depressaria pastinacella* and *Cavariella pastinacae* generally have a significant and density-dependent effect on seed production on *H. sphondylium*, but the impact on *H. mantegazzianum* has not been quantified.

Damage by *D. pastinacella* was concentrated in the terminal umbels. Large populations of the moth would be needed to control *H. mantegazzianum*, as a few larvae only have a limited impact on the huge umbels. Although *D. pastinacella* has a high dispersal ability, it is limited to areas of high plant quality (Sheppard, 1987). Studies on *Heracleum lanatum* in North America (Hendrix, 1984) showed that 90% damage to the primary umbel by *D. pastinacella* reduced the number of seeds by 40% and seed weight by 53% compared with control plants. This suggests that the low incidence of damage observed on *H. mantegazzianum* in the field is having little overall impact.

Table 6.3. Summary of leaf damage by insects on *Heracleum mantegazzianum*

Damaging insect	No. of plants damaged	Range %	Average %
Phaedon sp.	20	< 1 to 25	2.85
Epermenia sp.	17	< 1 to 50	4.80
Agonopterix spp.	58	< 1 to 10	1.80
Euleia sp.	69	< 1 to 45	3.20

Cavariella spp. may have the greatest overall impact on *H. mantegazzia-num*. These aphids were found at all sites and on 89% of the plants sampled. Huge numbers built up on the umbels, and infected plants were stunted, with a reduced seed set. Further studies would be useful on the spread of virus diseases by these species and their impact on *H. mantegazzianum*.

DISCUSSION

Despite repeated control measures over large areas, *H. mantegazzianum* continues to spread, demonstrating the poor success of current efforts. Effective control can be achieved, but is beyond the resources of many private landowners and local authorities.

The cost of controlling *H. mantegazzianum* varied considerably depending on the methods used and the density of the treated plants. For example, it took Banff and Buchan district 4800 man hours to treat 60 miles of river bank, and Gordon district 1600 man hours to treat 80 miles of river bank using the same method. Although it is acknowledged that costs were considerably underestimated, a total of over £89 000 was spent by district councils on *H. mantegazzianum* control in 1989/90. Expenditure will increase as the plant continues to spread into new areas.

The plant has already spread into many areas outside the jurisdiction of local authorities where there are no laws enforcing control. Only four respondents were taking action to eradicate or prevent the spread of the plant, most were concentrating efforts into limited areas, to provide access to amenity areas.

Untreated areas serve as a seed source from which spread can take place. For successful control, a concerted effort must be taken by local authorities and private landowners. This would only be achieved with further legislation combined with government funding to publicize the campaign and inform landowners of control methods.

Although the field survey has its limitations, it has shown that recruited British species apparently have limited impact on *H. mantegazzianum* populations. Further studies are warranted on the impact of flower and seed feeders, but the search for suitable biological control agents should be widened to include the plant's native habitat.

ACKNOWLEDGEMENTS

Data are extracted from an MSc thesis supported by an SERC studentship and supervised by Prof. John Lawton with helpful comments from Simon Fowler.

REFERENCES

Berenbaum, M.R. (1981a). Patterns of furanocoumarin distribution and insect herbivory in the Umbelliferae. Plant chemistry and community structure. *Ecology*, **62**, 1254–1266.

Berenbaum, M.R. (1981b). Effect of linear furanocoumarins on an adapted specialist insect *(Papilio polyxenes)*. *Ecological Entomology*, **6**, 345–351.

Camm, E.L., C.K. Wat and Towers, G.H.N. (1976). An assessment of the roles of furanocoumarins in *Heracleum lanatum*. *Canadian Journal of Botany*. **54**, 2562–2566.

Clegg, L.M. and Grace, J. (1974). The distribution of *Heracleum mantegazzianum* (Somm. & Levier) near Edinburgh. *Transactions of the Botanical Society of Edinburgh*, **42**, 223–229.

Dethier, V.G. (1941). Chemical factors determining the choice of food plants by *Papilio* larvae. *American Naturalist*, **75**, 61–73.

Drever, J.C. and Hunter, J.A.A. (1970). Giant hogweed dermatitis. *Scottish Medical Journal*, **15**, 315–319.

Hendrix, S.D. (1984). Reactions of *Heracleum lanatum* to floral herbivory by *Depressaria pastinacella*. *Ecology*, **65** 191–197.

Kees, H. and Krumrey, G. (1983). *Heracleum mantegazzianum*—ornamental plant, weed and poisonous plant. *Gesunde Pflanzen*, **35**, 108–110.

Lawton, J.H. (1983). Plant architecture and the diversity of phytophagous insects. *Annual Review of Entomology*, **28**, 23–29.

Lawton, J.H. and Price, P.W. (1979). Species richness of parasites on hosts: agromyzid flies on the British Umbelliferae. *Journal of Animal Ecology*, **48**, 619–637.

Lundström, H. (1984). Giant hogweed, *Heracleum mantegazzianum*, a threat to the Swedish countryside. *Weeds and Weed Control, 25th Swedish Weed Conference*, Uppsala. **1**, pp. 191–200.

Morton, J.K. (1978). Distribution of giant cow parsnip *(Heracleum mantegazzianum)* in Canada. *Canadian Field-Naturalist*, **92**(2), 182–185.

Public Health (Scotland) Act 1897. London: HMSO.

Sheppard, A.W. (1987). *Insect herbivore competition and the population dynamics of Heracleum sphondylium L. (Umbelliferae)*. PhD thesis, University of London.

Strong, D.R., Lawton, J.H. and Southwood, T.R.E. (1984). *Insects on Plants. Community Patterns and Mechanisms*. Oxford: Blackwell Scientific Publications.

Tutin, T.G., Heywood, V.H., Burges, N.A., Moore, D.M., Valentine, D.H., Walters, S.M. and Webb, D.A. (Eds) (1968). *Flora Europaea*, **2**. Cambridge: Cambridge University Press.

Wildlife and Countryside Act 1981. London: HMSO.

Williamson, J.A. and Forbes, J.C. (1982). Giant hogweed *(Heracleum mantegazzianum)*: its spread and control with glyphosate in amenity areas. *Weeds, Proceedings of the 1982 British Crop Protection Conference*, pp. 967–972.

Yajima, T., Kato, N. and Munakata, K. (1977). Isolation of insect anti-feeding principles in *Orixa japonica* Thunb. *Agricultural and Biological Chemistry*, **41**, 1263–1268.

7 Spread and Management of *Heracleum mantegazzianum* (Giant Hogweed) along Irish River Corridors

JOE M. CAFFREY,
Central Fisheries Board, Glasnevin, Dublin, Ireland

INTRODUCTION

Heracleum mantegazzianum Sommier and Levier is a member of the Umbelliferae and is easily recognized by its large stature, mature plants often achieving a height of 4 m. The species was introduced as an ornamental plant to Victorian gardens in the British Isles towards the end of the nineteenth century. Based on a review of the limited literature available, Wyse Jackson (1989) suggests that *H. mantegazzianum* was growing in the National Botanic Gardens, Dublin, prior to 1889.

Since its introduction into Ireland, the invasive *H. mantegazzianum* has significantly expanded its range and is currently spreading rapidly through the country. By 1989 the plant had been recorded from 29 of the 40 Irish vice-counties (Wyse Jackson, 1989) and has probably since colonized a number of other vice-counties.

In Ireland, *H. mantegazzianum* is most prolific along the banks of rivers and streams. This probably reflects the dependence of the plant upon seed dispersal through the medium of flowing water (Williamson and Forbes, 1982). The plant is best suited to undisturbed or unmanaged sites and, as a consequence, is rarely found in tilled, landscaped or grazed habitats. Establishment is, however, most successful in sites that were disturbed prior to the arrival of seeds. The light requirements of the plant appear to be low, enabling it to grow in shaded habitats. It is capable of growing on all gradients, from low-lying mud-flats to steep banksides. In Ireland, it has been observed growing from cracks in old walls, at the edge of tarmacadam car parks, as well as in shallow streams. It is noteworthy that *H. mantegazzi-*

Ecology and Management of Invasive Riverside Plants
Edited by L. C. de Waal, L. E. Child, P. M. Wade and J. H. Brock
© 1994 John Wiley & Sons Ltd

anum is rarely recorded from lake shores or canal banks in Ireland, even where sources of possible seed recruitment are proximal.

Seed dispersal is passive and is normally effected by wind or water. In the absence of water dispersal, it is common for the heavy seeds to settle close to the parent plant in the same habitat. Personal observations in a number of *H. mantegazzianum* populations in Ireland suggest that few seeds travel more than 50 m from the parental stand. The seeds are generally large, with a large food reserve, and this facilitates vigorous seedling growth when suitable conditions permit. The period of seed dormancy in Ireland has not been determined, although it is clear that seeds of this plant can remain viable for several years (Beckwith, 1991).

Heracleum mantegazzianum might be regarded as a "competitive ruderal" species (Grime, 1979), with good competitor and invasive capabilities. The plant's competitive ability is reflected in the capacity to expand leaves early in the season, before associated species emerge, while its invader status is based on its large seed bank and its ability to disperse seeds by wind and water.

The uncontrolled spread of *H. mantegazzianum* in Ireland, and in many other European countries (Lundström, 1984; Pyšek, 1991) and Canada (Morton, 1975, 1978; Tutin *et al.*, 1968), is causing serious concern for a number of reasons, the most important of which relates to the direct hazard to human health. The plant produces sap which exudes from broken bristles on the stems, leaves or petioles. It is produced in copious quantities from broken stems. The sap contains active photosensitizing ingredients called furocoumarins, which induce phytophotodermatitis on contact with the skin of adults or children (Hipkin, 1991). This condition results in the formation of painful watery blisters and hyperpigmentation of the skin. In certain cases, the furocoumarins may permanently damage the skin's ability to filter ultraviolet A radiation, which is significant in bright sunlight. As a consequence, the blistering and hyperpigmentation may re-occur every time sunlight reaches the damaged tissue, often years after the initial contact with the plant (Powell, 1988).

The long, hollow stems of *Heracleum mantegazzianum* are particularly attractive to children who use them as "telescopes" and "blowpipes", often causing serious blistering around the eyes and mouth (Williamson and Forbes, 1982).

Dense populations of *H. mantegazzianum* present further problems by restricting public access to amenity areas. Along the Newport River in North Tipperary, Ireland, continuous stands of the plant have forced anglers to abandon this reputable trout fishery and divert their attention to rivers where this plant has not yet established. Dense populations of this plant may also alter the ecology of river banks by suppressing and ultimately replacing indigenous species, resulting in significantly reduced floral and faunal species diversity. The loss of plant species whose rooting parts consolidate river banks may lead to serious erosion when the *H. mantegazzianum* plants die back in winter, leaving bare soil (Williamson and Forbes, 1982). Furthermore, this plant is a host for the fungus *Sclerotinia sclerotiorum*, which attacks a wide range of arable and horticultural crops (Gray and Noble, 1965).

It is the object of the present study to investigate some aspects of the autecology of *Heracleum mantegazzianum* in Ireland and to formulate guidelines for the long-term control of this invasive and hazardous plant. This paper presents results from one year of study of *H. mantegazzianum* and forms the base for further research into this plant.

MATERIALS AND METHODS

In 1991, five trial sites, adjacent to river channels, were selected for study (Figure 7.1). All supported dense populations of *H. mantegazzianum*. At each site, two plots per treatment, averaging 60 m^2, were selected for study.

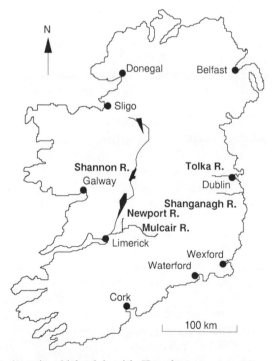

Figure 7.1 Irish rivers in which trials with *Heracleum mantegazzianum* were conducted in 1991

Table 7.1. Effect of treatments on *Heracleum mantegazzianum*, expressed as percentage plant kill, at five Irish trial sites in 1991

Site	Treatment	No. of plots	Date of application	May	July	September
R. Shannon	Triclopyr/Clopyralid	2	17 April	100	100	100
R. Mulcair	Triclopyr/Clopyralid	2	18 April	100	100	100
	Glyphosate	2	18 April	*	100	100
R. Newport	Glyphosate	2	18 April	*	100	100
R. Shanganagh	Triclopyr/Clopyralid	2	10 May	*	100	100
	Glyphosate	2	10 May	*	100	100
	Cut	2	10 May	*	5	5
R. Tolka	Glyphosate	2	4 July	–	*	80
	Cut	2	4 July	–	–	10

*No effect observed.
— No monitoring.

Treatments included the application of glyphosate (in the form of Roundup), triclopyr/clopyralid (in the form of Grazon 90) and cutting. Glyphosate was applied at 5, 10 and 20 litres/ha in April, May and July 1991, while triclopyr/clopyralid was applied at 4 and 6 litres/ha in April and May 1991 (Table 7.1). A knapsack sprayer fitted with a fan nozzle was used to apply the herbicides. Plants for the cutting trials were cut to just above ground level in May and July.

Both glyphosate and triclopyr/clopyralid are systemic herbicides with little or no residual activity. Glyphosate is active against a broad spectrum of plant species and, when used as an overall spray, can damage the flora in the vicinity of the target weed. It is approved for use in or near watercourses. Triclopyr/clopyralid is effective in controlling a range of broad-leaved herbaceous and scrub plants but has no effect on germinating grasses. It is not approved for use in or near watercourses, although triclopyr is currently registered under an experimental use permit in the USA for managing a range of submerged plant species (Netherland and Getsinger, 1992). Because triclopyr/clopyralid is not approved for use in or near water, spraying with this chemical was restricted to plots adjacent to, but not alongside, rivers. Both products show a very low order of toxicity to microbial communities and to mammals, birds, fish and insects (Dow Chemical Co., 1988; Monsanto, 1991; Netherland and Gestsinger, 1992; Sacher, 1978).

Control assessments were undertaken in May, July and September 1991 and in late March 1992. Observations were made of the effects of various treatments on the target vegetation and the associated flora.

RESULTS

At practically all of the sites where herbicides were applied, a 100% kill of
H. *mantegazzianum* plants was recorded (Table 7.1). No regrowth or recolonization with this species was recorded from these sites during the 1991
growing season. Triclopyr/clopyralid produced knockdown and twisting of
foliage after only six days. Thereafter, the vegetation remained green for a
further 4–5 weeks before completely dying off. The initial result with glyphosate was slower and knockdown was not achieved at any site for 4–5 weeks
after spraying. The plants decayed rapidly following knockdown.

Within 4 weeks of treating plots with triclopyr/clopyralid, healthy swards
of grass species were established around the twisted and limp H. *mantegazzianum* plants. The grasses continued to grow through the season and had
achieved an average height of 15 cm by September. By contrast, no grasses
were recorded from the glyphosate-treated plots in the weeks following
spraying, although localized dense stands of *Petasites hybridus* had established at some of the sites. The paucity of any vegetation at one of the sites,
that on the Shanganagh River treated with 20 litres glyphosate/ha, resulted
in considerable erosion of the bankside as winter floods stripped unconsoli-
dated soil from the bare bank.

The percentage plant kill recorded at sites where H. *mantegazzianum* was
cut was low (Table 7.1) and regrowth among the cut treatments was rapid.
Where a late cut (in July) was applied, the plant rapidly produced flower
stalks and set seed. In some instances the mature plant measured only 1.5 m
in height, compared with an average height of 3 m among adjacent, uncut
plants.

The winter of 1991/92 was mild and H. *mantegazzianum* plants were well
established by early February. An examination of the triclopyr/clopyralid-
treated plots in late March 1992 revealed very few seedling or regenerating
H. *mantegazzianum* plants. There was, however, complete cover with associated grassy and herbaceous vegetation at each site (Table 7.2). The
presence of a few regenerating plants at the River Mulcair site would suggest
that these had been missed when the herbicide was applied in April 1991.

Percentage ground cover was low with H. *mantegazzianum* at all glyphosate-treated sites, apart from the River Tolka (Table 7.2). At these sites,
practically complete cover with associated vegetation, including *Ranunculus
ficaria, Rumex* spp., *Urtica dioica, Anthriscus sylvestris, Heracleum sphondylium, Hedera helix* and various grasses, was present. At the glyphosate-
treated site on the River Tolka significant regrowth and seedling germination
among H. *mantegazzianum* plants was recorded in March 1992 (Table 7.2).
This was to be expected in view of the poor percentage plant kill achieved at
this site in 1991 (Table 7.1).

At the sites where H. *mantegazzianum* plants were cut in 1991, moderately

Table 7.2. Percentage ground cover with seedlings and regenerating plants of *Heracleum mantegazzianum* and associated vegetation in the year following treatment (March 1992) at five Irish trial sites

Site	Treatment	No. of plots	Percentage ground cover Seedlings	Regenerating plants	Associated vegetation
R. Shannon	Triclopyr/Clopyralid	2	0	0	100
R. Mulcair	Triclopyr/Clopyralid	2	2	5	100
	Glyphosate	2	8	0	95
R. Newport	Glyphosate	2	3	3	100
R. Shanganagh	Triclopyr/Clopyralid	2	0	0	100
	Glyphosate	2	3	5	100
	Cut	2	25	60	10
R. Tolka	Glyphosate	2	15	20	70
	Cut	2	5	30	65

dense stands were present in March 1992 (Table 7.2). The level of growth recorded at the River Shanganagh site was sufficient to preclude growth among the associated vegetation. At the River Tolka site, on the other hand, dense stands of *H. sphondylium* had established and were possibly curtailing the colonization of *H. mantegazzianum* seedlings and the regrowth of older plants.

It was clear from the results recorded at all sites treated with herbicide that increasing the dose above that recommended by the manufacturers, 5 litres/ha for glyphosate and 4 litres/ha for triclopyr/clopyralid, did not significantly affect the percentage plant kill achieved or significantly influence the rate of plant regrowth early in the season after treatment. For this reason, the results for dose trials at each site are combined in Tables 7.1 and 7.2.

DISCUSSION

EFFECTS OF SPRAYING

The results from the present trials clearly indicate that early-season spraying of *Heracleum mantegazzianum* colonies with glyphosate or triclopyr/clopyralid, at the dose recommended by the manufacturers, will effectively control this vegetation for the full growing season. Assessments made early in the season following spraying suggest that, while some re-colonization and regrowth among *H. mantegazzianum* was recorded, this was minimal when compared with that in untreated plots. This is broadly in agreement with the findings of Williamson and Forbes (1982) for glyphosate and Davies and Richards (1985) for triclopyr.

A late-season (July) treatment with glyphosate resulted in an unsatisfactory level of control, both in the season of treatment and in the following season. This probably reflects the protection afforded to small *H. mantegazzianum* plants by the large mature plants which, at this time of year, may reach 3 m in height and support leaves up to 1 m wide. The difficulty of attempting to provide an effective overall spray with vegetation this tall is compounded by the health hazard which the plant represents to operators. For these reasons the application of a first spray any later than early June is not to be recommended.

The low level of colonization of treated plots by *H. mantegazzianum* seedlings in late 1991 and early 1992 was unexpected, for two reasons. Firstly, as both herbicides have practically no residual effect, there was no chemical deterrent to seedling colonization and germination. Secondly, because all treated plots were contiguous with densely infested untreated areas, it was anticipated that seedling colonization in the former plots would be widespread. The low order of colonization recorded reflects the passive seed dispersal mechanism of the plant and the heaviness of the seeds. Observations at a number of areas infested with *H. mantegazzianum* revealed that most seeds and seedlings were located within 10 m of the parent colonies and that few were found more than 50 m distant. The principal exceptions occur where seed dispersal is operated by water or, unintentionally, by animals, birds or man. This probably explains why the plant rapidly expands its range along river corridors, but is less well represented with distance from water. Dispersal of seeds by wind, particularly where the parent plants are situated on high banks, or spoil heaps, may explain the occasional occurrence of *H. mantegazzianum* colonies up to 300 m from the nearest river or ditch.

Following spraying with triclopyr/clopyralid, recolonization of the treated plots with a wide range of grass and herbaceous species was rapid. This growth removed the bare appearance from the site and helped suppress young *H. mantegazzianum* seedlings. This probably accounts for the total lack of seedlings at two of the treated sites and the low level of colonization at the third in March 1992 (Table 7.2). Recolonization with grasses and herbaceous plants was slower at glyphosate-treated sites although, while the sites had a 'scorched' appearance for up to 12 weeks after spraying, levels of colonization with *H. mantegazzianum* were low. It was noticeable that, where the heaviest dose of glyphosate were applied, complete vegetation recovery among grasses and herbaceous plants was not achieved in the season of treatment. This resulted in some bankside erosion at the site on the Shanganagh River. In consideration of the damage caused, not only to non-target biota but also to the habitat, it is recommended that only the dose recommended by the manufacturer for treatment of *H. mantegazzianum* be used.

The damage to non-target organisms commonly associated with the use of glyphosate from a knapsack sprayer may be minimized by using a herbicide application system which allows accurate placement of product. Such an application system is currently available (Nomix Compact Lance) and allows glyphosate, as an oil emulsion, to be applied accurately in swaths ranging from 15 to 100 cm or to be used for spot treatment. As the emulsion is white it is possible to see the plants that have been treated, thus ensuring maximum application efficiency. This system also facilitates the accurate treatment of isolated seedlings growing amongst vegetation that is also sensitive to glyphosate. Clearance for the use of the oil emulsion formulation of glyphosate used in this application system has not yet been granted under the Control of Pesticide Regulations, 1986, and its use in or near water cannot yet be recommended. Trials with this system, under controlled conditions, will be conducted at a number of Irish sites in the coming seasons.

EFFECTS OF CUTTING

The effect of cutting *H. mantegazzianum* plants in the plots examined has been to induce vigorous vegetative regrowth or, when applied late in the growing season (early July), to induce flowering and seed production. This is broadly in agreement with work on this invasive plant conducted in northeast Scotland (Powell, 1988). Even the application of a severe cut, at ground level, has failed to kill significant numbers of the plant.

RECOMMENDATIONS

Before formulating clear guidelines for the long-term management of *H. mantegazzianum*, it will be necessary to compile more autecological information on the plant in a wide range of habitats. Furthermore, detailed data on the response of the plant to various forms of mechanical, chemical and environmental control must be obtained. Perhaps the most signifcant breakthrough in the control of this hazardous weed may be achieved through the agency of pathogenic organisms although, to-date, little work on this control strategy has been conducted.

It is possible, however, to suggest strategies that may temporarily confine the problem and arrest the hitherto uncontrolled spread of the plant along our watercourses. As seeds are dispersed along river corridors primarily by water, it is imperative that control commences at the most upstream site for the plant. At this juncture, herbicide application is the most effective control procedure available and results from present and other research (Davies and Richards, 1985; Williamson and Forbes, 1982) suggests that the use of glyphosate near watercourses and of triclopyr in adjacent infested areas will provide effective seasonal control.

It is strongly recommended that herbicides be applied early in the growing season, between March and early June, before the plants become too large to treat effectively and safely. A follow-up operation should be conducted in July or August and any *H. mantegazzianum* plants that survived the first spraying should be spot-treated. During this second operation any plants that have flowered should be de-headed and the flower or seed heads burned. If this control strategy is rigorously operated along a river course or within a river catchment, over a number of years, few problems with *H. mantegazzianum* will manifest themselves.

In Ireland the threat to the health of the population, and children in particular, and the probable loss of floral and faunal diversity which is associated with the spread of *H. mantegazzianum*, appears to be unrecognized. This is an issue of national importance which, if not tackled at a national level and in a co-ordinated and informed manner, will present very serious health, amenity and ecological problems in future years.

ACKNOWLEDGEMENTS

I wish to thank Kate Monahan for her assistance during field sampling. I am also grateful to Sydney Reid and Con Cashman (Monsanto Ireland) and Richard Barry (Duphar Ireland) for providing product for trials purposes and for their helpful comments. I would like to thank Mr Tom Harrington (Limerick City University) for providing information on *H. mantegazzianum* populations in the Limerick area. Dr P. Fitzmaurice is gratefully acknowledged for his constructive editorial comments.

REFERENCES

Beckwith, P. (1991). Giant hogweed. *Environmental Bulletin, British waterways* 5, 1–2pp.
Davies, D.H.K. and Richards, M.C. (1985). Evaluation of herbicides for control of giant hogweed (*Heracleum mantegazzianum* Somm. and Lev.), and vegetation regrowth in treated areas. *Annals of Applied Biology*, 106, 100–101.
Dow Chemical Co. (1988). *Triclopyr: Technical Information Guide*. Michigan: Midland.
Gray, E.G. and Noble, M. (1985). *Sclerotinia* diseases. *Scottish Agriculture*, 44, 265–267.
Grime, J.P. (1979). *Plant Strategies and Vegetation Processes*. Chichester: Wiley.
Hipkin, C. (1991). Phytophotodermatitis. *BSBI News*, 59, 7–8.
Lundström, H. (1984). Giant hogweed, *Heracleum mantegazzianum*, a threat to the Swedish countryside. *Weeds and Weed Control, 25th Swedish Weed Conference, Uppsala*, 1, pp. 191–200.
Monsanto (1991). *Aquatic Weed Control Research Review. Information guide*, Leicester: Monsanto. p. 15.

Morton, J.K. (1975). The giant cow parsnip, *Heracleum mantegazzianum* Umbelliferae, in Canada. *Canadian Field-Naturalist*, **89**, 183–184.

Morton, J.K. (1978). Distribution of giant cow parsnip (*Heracleum mantegazzianum*) in Canada. *Canadian Field-Naturalist*, **92**(2), 182–185.

Netherland, M.D. and Getsinger, K.D. (1992). Efficacy of triclopyr on Eurasian watermifoil: concentration and exposure time effects. *Journal of Aquatic Plant Management*, **30**, 1–5.

Powell, F. (1988). Giant hogweed control in north-east Scotland. *Plant Press*, **4**, 4.

Pyšek, P. (1991). *Heracleum mantegazzianum* in the Czech Republic: dynamics of spreading from the historical perspective. *Folia Geobotanica et Phytotaxonomica*, **26**, 439–454.

Sacher, R.M. (1978). Safety of Roundup in the aquatic environment. *Proceedings European Weed Research Society 5th International Symposium on Aquatic Weeds*, pp. 315–322, Amsterdam.

Tutin, T.G., Heywood, V.H., Burges, N.A., Moore, D.H., Walters, S.M. and Webb, D.A. (Eds) (1968). *Flora Europaea*. **2**. Cambridge: Cambridge University Press.

Williamson, J.A. and Forbes, J.C. (1982). Giant hogweed (*Heracleum mantegazzianum*): its spread and control with glyphosate in amenity areas. *Weeds, Proceedings of the 1982 British Crop Protection Conference*, pp. 967–972.

Wyse Jackson, M. (1989). Observations on the Irish distribution of a plant with serious public health implications: giant hogweed (*Heracleum mantegazzianum* Sommier and Levier). *Bulletin of the Irish Biogeographical Society*, **12**, 94–112.

8 Sheep Grazing as a Method of Controlling *Heracleum mantegazzianum*

ULLA VOGT ANDERSEN
Royal Veterinary and Agricultural University, Department of Botany, Dendrology and Forest Genetics, Copenhagen, Denmark

INTRODUCTION

The main conservation problem in Danish meadows is caused by cessation of grazing, leading to undesirable shifts in species composition and a decrease in diversity of the plant communities (Steen, 1981; Wells, 1969). Diversity may be exceptionally low in old-field ecosystems when there is strong dominance by species with allelopathic chemicals or other effective interference methods (Bazzaz, 1975). Many existing meadows, fens and freshwater marshes are commonly small areas in a predominantly agricultural landscape and are affected by drainage, eutrophication and dispersal of weeds from adjacent agricultural or urban areas (Grootjans *et al.*, 1985; Verhoeven *et al.*, 1983).

Among the species invading eutrophicated, abandoned and regenerating meadows in Denmark, *Heracleum mantegazzianum*, is causing the most serious problems (Jensen, 1976). The plant was introduced into Denmark in about 1830 as an ornamental and has spread all over the country, on moist roadsides, grasslands and meadows (Egholm, 1951).

DESCRIPTION OF THE SPECIES

Heracleum mantegazzianum is 2–3 m tall, vigorous and monocarpic. Each plant produces at least 5000 seeds/year, some of which are able to survive in the soil for 5–6 years before germinating (Rubow, 1990). The tremendous growth, the large leaf area and the enormous seed production makes the plant an extremely efficient competitor and it is able to overshadow and eliminate all other plants in occupied areas (Jensen, 1976). Only a few

Ecology and Management of Invasive Riverside Plants
Edited by L. C. de Waal, L. E. Child, P. M. Wade and J. H. Brock
© 1994 John Wiley & Sons Ltd

Danish indigenous plants can survive in association with *H. mantegazzianum*, and its presence leads to destruction of valuable plant communities.

Even though the plant is not considered a pest in agricultural fields, it is unwanted in the landscape by both public and local authorities. It is very annoying to human activities in recreational settings, because of the presence of furocoumarins, which are toxic and can cause photosensitization of livestock (Ivie, 1978) and dermatitis, when skin contaminated with plant sap is exposed to sunlight (Cooper and Johnson, 1984). It is suspected that furocoumarins possess allelopathic properties (Rice, 1974). None of the methods of controlling *H. mantegazzianum* has so far been efficient, without having a deleterious effect on surrounding vegetation (Rubow, 1990).

A decrease in biological diversity is often an undesirable effect of the expansion of introduced plant species (Huston, 1979). Both the decline of grazing on semi-natural grasslands and competition from introduced species will have severe consequences for both local biodiversity and a number of wild plant species in the near future. This problem is widely demonstrated all over northern Europe (Clegg and Grace, 1974; Lundström, 1984; Pyšek, 1991).

METHODS

STUDY AREA

Observations were carried out in an open mesotrophic meadow adjacent to Lake Furesoe in north-east Sealand, Denmark. The meadow (1.7 ha) is situated in a landscape with calcareous subsoil and local upwelling ground water. The area is surrounded by residential neighbourhoods, and eutrophicated waste water from households runs through the area in a small brook. Parts of the meadow are dominated by *Carex acutiformis, Phragmites australis* and *Calamagrostis canescens*. On the east and north sides, the study area is surrounded by stands of *Alnus glutinosa, Betula pubescens* and *Acer pseudoplatanus*. A swamp dominated by *Phragmites australis, Salix cinerea* and *Salix pentandra* is situated between the lake and the southern border of the area. When the observations started in 1987 the meadow had not been grazed for 25 years and no fertilizers had been applied.

VEGETATION ANALYSES

The research was carried out over 3 years. In May 1987, *H. mantegazzianum* stands were cut once and 10 sheep of the Swedish breed Goth (Adalsteinsson *et al.*, 1978) were introduced to graze the area. In the following years, six and nine sheep, respectively, were grazing in the meadow during the growing

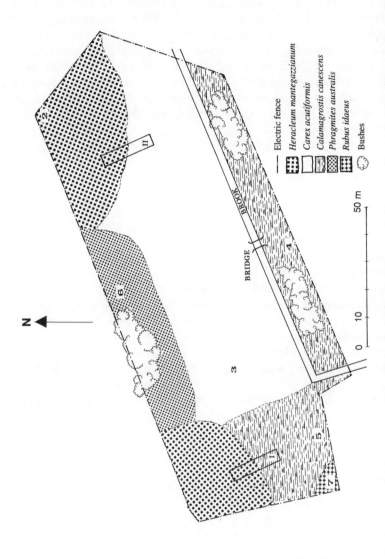

Figure 8.1 Map showing the study area in north-east Sealand, Denmark. Numbers 1–7 refer to the seven investigation zones (different plant communities); the "ungrazed" control plots I and II were established after two seasons of grazing, in 1989

N

BRIDGE

BROOK

0   10   50 m

Electric fence
Heracleum mantegazzianum
Carex acutiformis
Calamagrostis canescens
Phragmites australis
Rubus idaeus
Bushes

period from early May to late October. The sheep were constantly under veterinary control.

The meadow was divided into seven zones, i.e. seven plant communities. A detailed vegetation map was drawn and all large woody plants were recorded (Figure 8.1). In each of the seven vegetational zones, the floristic composition of the stands was analysed, using the Raunkiaer circle method (Malmer, 1974): 10 circles (0.1 m^2) were placed at random, and all plants rooted inside the circles were recorded. These results are expressed as percentage frequency. In 1989 the Hult-Sernander method (Malmer, 1974) was used to determine the percentage cover: three quadrats (1 × 1 m) were positioned at random in each of the seven plant communities. In each quadrat, plant species present were recorded, with estimated covering scored on a scale of 1 to 5, with species covering (1) <6, (2) 6–13, (3) 13–25, (4) 25–50 and (5) >50% of the quadrat. In dealing with results of the vegetation analysis, the cover index of Hult-Sernander was converted into the numerical means of the index intervals as follows: (1) 2%, (2) 9%, (3) 18%, (4) 36% and (5) 72% (Hansen and Jensen, 1972).

Vegetational analyses were carried out before grazing started in 1987 and three times during the growth period (early May, late July and early October) in 1988 and 1989.

The effects of discontinued grazing were analysed by comparing the results from grazed and ungrazed plots. In 1989 two control plots, I and II, were established and fenced to prevent grazing. The plots were 80 m^2 (4 × 20 m), and each plot included two plant communities, where similar vegetation was present on either side of the fence: a western stand of *Heracleum mantegazzianum* (further refered to as *H.m.* west) and *Calamagrostis canescens* community for control plot I, and an eastern stand of *H. mantegazzianum* (*H.m.* east) and *Carex acutiformis* community for control plot II. The position of the control plots is shown on the map (Figure 8.1). Ten Raunkiaer circles and three Hult-Sernander quadrats were laid out at random in each control plot as well as in the surrounding plant community. The results of the analysis from the ungrazed plots were compared with the results from the grazed surroundings.

Nomenclature follows Hansen (1981) except for *Heracleum mantegazzianum* Somm. & Lev.

RESULTS

STUDY AREA BEFORE TREATMENT

Before grazing started in 1987, the *H. mantegazzianum* communities were dominated by *H. mantegazzianum* nearly 2 m tall. Because of the massive competition from *H. mantegazzianum*, the soil underneath the dense population was bare and the number of other species as well as their frequencies were very low. The other species occurring in the two communities dominated by *H. mantegazzianum* in 1987 were mostly competitive, shade-tolerant species or early spring species able to complete their life cycle before *H. mantegazzianum* closed the community.

CHANGES IN PLANT COMMUNITIES DUE TO GRAZING

Changes in the composition of life forms in the meadow over time are shown in Figure 8.2., and the changes in the number of species in the seven zones, are shown in Figure 8.3.

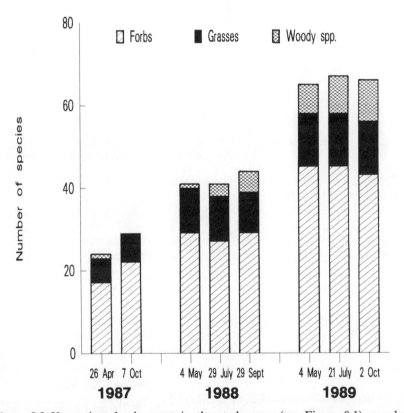

Figure 8.2 Vegetation development in the study area (see Figure 8.1): number of species, herbaceous (including Equisetaceae), grasses (including Cyperaceae and Juncaceae) and woody species

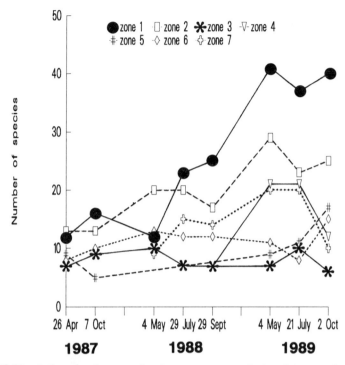

Figure 8.3 Vegetation development in the seven zones, during 3 years, showing the changes in the number of species in the different plant communities: (1) *Heracleum mantegazzianum* west, (2) *H. mantegazzianum* east, (3) *Carex acutiformis*, (4) *Calamagrostis canescens* south of brook, (5) *C. canescens* west, (6) *Phragmites australis* and (7) *Rubus idaeus* (see Figure 8.1)

Conspicuous changes in the floristic composition appeared in the *H. mantegazzianum* communities during the study period (Table 8.1). The vegetation changed from a deeply shaded community with a low species diversity, to an open grassland with a rich flora of low, dense grasses and herbs. The frequency of *H. mantegazzianum* showed a small decrease in both *H.m.* west and *H.m* east. The Raunkiaer circle method, however, does not distinguish between 2 m tall, mature plants and small seedlings, and no mature *H. mantegazzianum* plants were present in the area after cutting and grazing (Figures 8.4 and 8.5.). Species emerging in the meadow after clearing were common weeds in Denmark as well as typical meadow or wetland plants. Species tolerant of grazing showed the highest frequency and covering rates at the end of the study period.

The grazing had only a slight impact on the *Carex acutiformis* and *Calamagrostis canescens* populations, but, because of the trampling, the litter was

Table 8.1. Average frequency (%) of species in two *Heracleum mantegazzianum* plots (see Figure 8.1)

Species	I *H.m.* west			II *H.m.* east		
	1987	1988	1989	1987	1988	1989
Achillea millefolium†			3			
Aegopodium podagraria	5*	23	3			
Alliaria petiolata	5*		3	5*		
Angelica sylvestris	25		3			
Arabidopsis thaliana			3			
Barbarea vulgaris ssp. *vulgaris*			3			3
Bellis perennis†					3	3
Caltha palustris			3			
Cardamine amara						3
Cerastium fontanum spp. *triviale*		3	17	10	3	17
Chrysosplenium alternifolium					3	
Cirsium arvense			3	5*		3
Cirsium oleraceum		7	20		10	7
Cirsium vulgare	5	7	13		3	
Corydalis bulbosa				5*		
Epilobium obscurum	5	47	10		30	13
Epilobium parviflorum	30*		7	15*	7	10
Equisetum arvense			3			
Equisetum fluviatile		3	7			
Eupatorium cannabinum		3	7			3
Ficaria verna	5*	3	3	15*	20	10
Filipendula ulmaria		7				3
Galeopsis bifida						3
Galium aparine		13	7		7	
Geum rivale†		3	3			
Glechoma hederacea		3	10	5*	10	30
Gnaphalium uliginosum					7	3
Heracleum mantegazzianum	90*	67	73	100*	87	67
Hypericum tetrapterum	5	10	7	5	7	7
Impatiens noli-tangere		27	7			
Impatiens parviflora		17	13			
Lathyrus pratensis†	5	3			3	3
Lychnis flos-cuculi					3	
Lysimachia vulgaris			3		3	
Lythrum salicaria			10			
Mentha aquatica x *arvensis*		3	10			
Myosotis palustris					3	
Myosoton aquaticum	5	3	7		3	
Plantago lanceolata						3
Plantago major†			10		3	3
Polygonum amphibium					3	
Potentilla anserina†			3			
Primula elatior			3			
Ranunculus repens†	20	53	83	40*	90	97

Continues

* Indicates that the species was present before grazing was started
† Indicates that the species is adapted to grazing

Table 8.1. *Continued*

Species	I *H.m.* west 1987	1988	1989	II *H.m.* east 1987	1988	1989
Rumex obtusifolia				5		3
Sagina procumbens			3		3	7
Scrophularia nodosa	10*	3				
Senecio vulgaris				5		
Stachys palustris		7	7		7	
Stachys sylvatica		3	3			
Stellaria media†			10			
Taraxacum sp.†		3	20			7
Trifolium repens†			10			3
Tripleurospermum inodorum			3			
Tussilago farfara						7
Urtica dioica	25*	23	30	55*	37	30
Veronica beccabunga	20	53	63	30*	37	20
Veronica filiformis			7		20	17
Veronica serpyllifolia				5		7
Acer pseudoplatanus		3	7			
Betula pubescens			3			
Crataegus monogyna		3				
Fraxinus excelsior			3			
Rubus idaeus	5*	3	10			
Salix alba			3			
Salix caprea			13			3
Salix cinerea			3		3	
Salix daphnoides			7			
Salix pentandra			3			3
Salix rosmarinifolia		3	7		10	
Salix smithiana			3			
Sambucus nigra			3			
Agrostis stolonifera†		13	63		27	43
Calamagrostis canescens		30	7			
Carex acutiformis	35*	37	17	5*	20	23
Carex hirta			10			13
Dactylis glomerata†			3			
Deschampsia caespitosa†	5*		7		7	3
Glyceria maxima	5*	3	3			
Holcus lanatus†			3			
Juncus articulatus	10	10	20	10	13	10
Juncus compressus			3			
Juncus effusus†			7		20	30
Lolium perenne			3			
Phalaris arundinacea		3				
Phragmites australis	10*	30	23	16*	3	3
Poa annus	15	50	27			50
Poa pratensis†			80	55*	90	93
Total number of species	22	39	68	19	34	42

Figure 8.4 (a) View of the eastern corner of the meadow (see Figure 8.1), showing the growth of *Heracleum mantegazzianum* before grazing (and cutting), on 25 May 1987; (b) same view on 25 October 1989 after three seasons of grazing, showing control plot II. The changes in the plant community are obvious, with tall tufts of *Juncus effusus* in the foreground

Figure 8.5 (a) View of *Heracleum mantegazzianum* community east, looking SE, before cutting, 25 May 1987; (b) same view on 26 July 1987 showing sheep grazing on *H. mantegazzianum*

Table 8.2. Percentage cover of species in grazed area and *H.m.* west section of ungrazed control plot I in 1989

Species	Grazed	Control
Agrostis stolonifera	27	60
Carex acutiformis	1	4
Cerastium fontanum spp. *triviale*	4	1
Cirsium oleraceum	4	13
Glechoma hederacea	6	1
Heracleum mantegazzianum	8	36
Phragmites australis	1	7
Poa pratensis	48	13
Ranunculus repens	51	25
Salix caprea	2	8
Urtica dioica	24	8
Veronica beccabunga	15	1

mixed with the soil and partly decomposed. Visually estimated, the litter layer was reduced by 90% by the end of the study period.

RESPONSE TO CESSATION OF GRAZING IN CONTROL PLOTS

The vegetation in the ungrazed controls grew taller than that outside the fences, and both grasses and herbs were allowed to flower. The results show a higher frequency of tall, competitive herbs inside the ungrazed control plot (Table 8.2). The percentage cover of *H. mantegazzianum* increased in the control compared to the surroundings, while the grazing-adapted *Poa pratensis* showed the opposite tendencies. It is obvious that *P. pratensis* takes advantage of the grazed situation, and the results indicate that formation of a dense cover of this species can help to prevent re-establishment of *H. mantegazzianum*. Competitive species avoided by grazing animals have an advantage in the grazed situation, whereas species adapted to grazing and forming a short sward, such as *Ranunculus repens*, obviously are suppressed by competition when grazing ceases.

DISCUSSION

Diversity can be maintained by reducing the intense competition, which forces niche restriction, and effects which reduce the most abundant competitor will have a stronger effect in maintaining diversity (Grime, 1979; Huston, 1979). As an efficient competitor, *H. mantegazzianum* is able to monopolize resources and space, and light stress is probably the most important factor in this competition. Local species diversity is directly related to the efficiency with which grazing sheep prevent the dominance of one species (Huston, 1979). The results of this research indicate that the sheep selected the most abundant competitor and seemed to prefer it to other plants.

When given a free choice between the more succulent and apparently more nutrious plants and rougher fibrous vegetation, the sheep prefer the younger and more succulent herbage and select the leaf before the stem material, the leaf containing the most nitrogen in the form of protein at any given time (Hughes *et al.*, 1962; Martin, 1962). Plants with a high content of ethereal oils may be distasteful to the animals and the oils might possess certain toxic properties (Buttenschön and Buttenschön, 1982b). The sheep obviously seem to prefer *H. mantegazzianum*, instead of the rough, tough almost tasteless and indigestible grasses and *Carex* spp. They also seem to prefer bitter and acid species, such as *Taraxacum* sp., *Ranunculus repens* and *Mentha aquatica*. All tasty, aromatic, crisp and juicy herbs, including *H. mantegazzianum*, showed, of course, a higher average percentage cover in the ungrazed control.

Some species which are not favoured or avoided by the animals may be subject to disturbance as a result of treading and may take advantage of the more shallow vegetation in the grazed situation (Bakker *et al.*, 1983; Buttenschön and Buttenschön, 1982a). This was observed for *Urtica dioica, Cirsium vulgare, Deschampsia caespitosa* and *Juncus effusus*. Avoidance of these species resulted in an increase in abundance.

In the absence of grazing, tall competitive grasses and broadleaved herbs increase in size to such an extent that they supersede and eliminate the low-growing and more light-dependent perennials and annuals (Grime, 1979). The vegetation in the plots responded to the absence of grazing with increased yields and expansion of *H. mantegazzianum* and other nitrophilous herbs typical of overgrown wetlands, such as *Urtica dioica, Filipendula ulmaria, Anthriscus sylvestris, Lysimachia vulgaris, Lythrum salicaria, Angelica sylvestris* and *Stellaria media* and a drop in species richness. Similar results were obtained by Grootjans *et al.* (1985).

The total number of species may have increased more in the *H.m.* east plot because of the large amount of bare soil present in this area after clearing. Areas of bare ground created by sheep trampling and grazing provide suitable habitats for the establishment of seed from annuals (Regnell, 1980; Wells, 1969). This might be why the number of annuals such as *Poa annua, Impatiens noli-tangere* and *Impatiens parviflora* was at its highest in the second year of grazing when the soil was uncovered after the clearing of *H. mantegazzianum*. The majority of "new" species emerging in the area had been present in the soil as a seed bank (Oedum, 1978). Others were possibly introduced with the sheep or dispersed form adjacent areas.

A dense sward and/or a thick layer of litter prevents seeds from reaching the soil surface and hinders germination and seedling establishment (Regnell, 1980). The large quantities of litter formed by grasses such as *Poa pratensis* and *Calamagrostis canescens* play a significant role in this process (Grime, 1979; Wells, 1969). Furthermore, these species are both competitive and efficient absorbers of nitrogen. As *H. mantegazzianum* totally dies down in the winter, it is possible for rapid-growing species to establish from seeds if *H. mantegazzianum* is suppressed. A dense population of grasses, created and maintained by sheep grazing, could prevent *H. mantegazzianum* from reestablishing.

Species diversity will probably drop again after cessation of grazing. If the meadow is abandoned again, it will be subject to secondary succession (Horn, 1974). In some ways, the condition of the area will be worse than it was before the start of the grazing regime, because *H. mantegazzianum* will be able to establish itself from seedlings in the zones that previously were covered by a thick layer of litter, i.e. the *Carex acutiformis* and the *Calamagrostis canescens* zones. Establishment of woody species is advanced after enclosure of previously grazed wetlands, compared with ungrazed areas with a dense population of competitive species (Regnell, 1980). The establishment of *Salix* spp. in the control plots is of great importance to the future succession.

If the meadow is to be kept open and attractive for recreation and amenity purposes, grazing must continue. Under continued sheep grazing, *H. mantegazzianum* will be efficiently controlled and the grazed meadow will contain more species than an ungrazed one. However, there is an optimum grazing pressure at which species diversity will be at its highest. Species diversity is expected to remain rather low if the grazing is too heavy, because of the high frequency of disturbance (Grime, 1979; Huston, 1979). Heavy grazing pressure might prove fatal to sensitive species and diversity can also be reduced as a result of eutrophication from the animal dung (Bakker *et al.*, 1983; Steen, 1981). Vermeer and Berendse (1983) and Vermeer (1986) showed a negative relationship between increasing nutrient availability and species diversity in wetlands.

ACKNOWLEDGEMENTS

I would like to thank Joergen Jensen for constructive discussions and comments on the manuscript, Gitte Pedersen, who assisted in collecting the field data, Rolf Jess Joergensen who was in charge of the veterinary control, Ellen Brabaek Andersen and Birgitte List for correction of the English text, and Torben Bo Andersen for assistance with the computer graphics.

REFERENCES

Adalsteinsson, S. Lauvergne, J.J., Boyazoglu, J.G. and Ryde, M.L. (1978). A possible genetic interpretation of the colour variants in the fleece of the Gothland and sheep. *Annales de Genetique et de Selection Animale*, **10**, 329–342.

Bakker, J.P., de Leeuw, J. and Van Wieren, S.E. (1983). Micropatterns in grasslands vegetation, created and sustained by sheep-grazing. *Vegetatio*, **55**, 153–161.

Bazzaz, F.A. (1975). Plants species diversity in old-field successional ecosystems in southern Illinois. *Ecology*, **56**, 485–488.

Buttenschön, J. and Buttenschön, R.M. (1982a). Grazing experiments with cattle and sheep on nutrient poor, acidic grassland and heath. I Vegetation development. *Natura Jutlandica*, **21**, 1–18.

Buttenschön, J. and Buttenschön, R.M. (1982b). Grazing experiments with cattle and sheep on nutrient poor, acidic grassland and heath. II Grazing impact. *Natura Jutlandica*, **21**, 19–27

Clegg, L.M. and Grace, J. (1974). The distribution of *Heracleum mantegazzianum* (Somm. & Levier) near Edinburgh. *Transactions of the Botanical Society of Edinburgh*, **42**, 223–229.

Cooper, M.R. and Johnson, A.W. (1984) *Poisonous Plants in Britain, and their Effects on Animals and Man*. London: Ministry of Agriculture, Fisheries and Food.

Egholm, B. (1951). The distribution of the Umbelliferae in Denmark. [English summary] *Dansk Botanisk Tidsskrift*, **47**, 373–480.

Grime, J.P. (1979). *Plant Strategies and Vegetation Processes*. Chichester: Wiley.

Grootjans, A.P., Schipper, P.C. and Van der Windt, J.H. (1985). Influence of drainage on N-mineralization and vegetation response in wet meadows. *Acta Oecologia*, **6**, 403–417.

Hansen, K. (Ed.) (1981). *Dansk Feltflora*. Kbenhavn: Gyldendal.

Hansen, K. and Jensen, J. (1972). Vegetation on roadsides in Denmark. Qualitative and quantitative composition. *Dansk Botanisk Arkiv*, **28**, 1–143.

Horn, H.S. (1974). The ecology of the secondary succession. *Annual Review of Ecology and Systematics*, **5**, 25–37.

Hughes, R.E., Milner, C. and Dale, J. (1962). Selectivity in grazing. In D.J. Crisp (Ed.), *Grazing in Terrestrial and Marine Environments*. Oxford: Blackwell Scientific Publications.

Huston, M. (1979). A general hypothesis of species diversity. *American Naturalist*, **113**, 81–101.

Ivie, G.W. (1978). Toxicological significance of plant furocoumarins. In R.F. Keeler, K.R. van Kampen and L.F. James (Eds), *Effects of Poisonous Plants on Livestock*. pp. 475–485. New York: Academic Press.

Jensen, J. (1976). Conservation problems in eutrophic fens. [English summary] In A. Jensen and C.H. Ovesen (Eds) *Drift og Pleje af Våde Områder i de Nordiske Lande*. Reports from the Botanical Institute, University of Aarhus, No. 3.

Malmer, N. (1974). *Scandinavian Approach to Vegetation Science*. Meddelanden från Avdelningen för Ekologisk Botanik, *Lunds Universitet*, **2**.

Martin, J.D. (1962). Analysis of sheep diet utilizing plant epidermal fragments in faeces samples. In D.J. Crisp (Ed.) *Grazing in Terrestrial and Marine Environments*. Oxford: Blackwell Scientific Publications.

Lundström, H. (1984). Giant hogweed, *Heracleum mantegazzianum*, a threat to the Swedish countryside. *Weeds and Weed Control, 25th Swedish Weed Conference*, Uppsala. Vol. 1, pp. 191–200.

Oedum, S. (1978). *Dormant Seeds in Danish Ruderal Soils.* Hoersholm Arboretum, Denmark: Royal Veterinary & Agricultural University.

Pyšek, P. (1991). *Heracleum mantegazzianum* in the Czech Rebublic: dynamics of spreading from the historical perspective. *Folia Geobotanica* et *Phytotaxonomica*, **26**, 439–454.

Regnell, G. (1980). A numerical study of succession in an abandoned damp calcareous meadow in S Sweden. *Vegetatio*, **43**, 123–130.

Rice, E.L. (1974). *Allelopathy.* London: Academic Press.

Rubow, T. (1990). Giant hogweed. Importance and control. *7. Dansk Plantevaerns Konference, Ukrudt.*

Steen, E. (1981). Dynamics and production of seminatural grassland vegetation in Fennoscandia, in relation to grazing management. *Acta Phytogeographica Suecica*, **68**, 153–156.

Verhoeven, J.T.A., Van Beek, S., Dekker, M. and Storm, W. (1983). Nutrient dynamics in small mesotrophic fens surrounded by cultivated land. Productivity and nutrient uptake by the vegetation in relation to the flow of eutrophicated groundwater. *Oecologia*, **60**, 25–33.

Vermeer, H.J.G. (1986). The effect of nutrients on shoot biomass and species composition of wetland and hayfield. *Acta Oecologia*, **7**, 31–41.

Vermeer, H.J.G. and Berendse, F. (1983). The relationship between nutrient availability, shoot biomass and species diversity in grassland and wetland communities. *Vegetatio*, **53**, 121–126.

Wells, T.C.E. (1969). Botanical aspects of conservation management of chalk grasslands. *Biological Conservation*, **2**, 36–43.

9 The *Heracleum mantegazzianum* (Giant Hogweed) Problem in Sweden: Suggestions for its Management and Control

HARALD LUNDSTRÖM[1] **and ED DARBY**[2]

[1]*Borgmastaregata 3, Trelleborg, Sweden*
[2]*International Centre of Landscape Ecology, Loughborough University, UK*

INTRODUCTION

Heracleum mantegazzianum Sommier et Levier (giant hogweed or Jätteloka in Swedish) was first introduced into Sweden in the middle of the nineteenth century by plant nurseries (Lundström, 1984). Since then it has spread naturally by seed propagation throughout southern and central Sweden. In this way it has become increasingly widespread, not only where it is cultivated in parks and gardens, but also along roads and ditches and in other habitats. The spread of the plant has been greatly aided by anthropogenic activities. During the 1960s it was popular to hang dried full-size *H. mantegazzianum* plants on the walls of recreation rooms. The plants were often transported on car roof-racks and spilt seeds resulted in stands developing along road verges. Eventually when the dried plants were discarded and taken to rubbish tips the growth of immense stands on and around the tips followed. Seeds were also redistributed on the tyres of refuse lorries and tractors. Once *H. mantegazzianum* had spread to river banks, there was rapid colonization downstream. In some districts, wholesale changes have taken place in the landscape. Original vegetation has been totally replaced by the plant, leading to yet further infestation. Historically, the distribution of *H. mantegazzianum* along river banks in Sweden shows similarities to that reported from the British Isles (Dodd *et al.*, 1994) and the former Czechoslavakia (Pyšek, 1991). Initially, expansion of *H. mantegazzainum* followed river banks. Later, when much larger areas of the landscape had been invaded, this pattern of initial spread along the rivers could no longer be discerned (Pyšek, 1991).

Ecology and Management of Invasive Riverside Plants
Edited by L. C. de Waal, L. E. Child, P. M. Wade and J. H. Brock
© 1994 John Wiley & Sons Ltd

One of the difficulties of determining the exact status of *H. mantegazzianum* in Sweden is the lack of data. An inventory of its distribution along Swedish rivers is incomplete. Invasive stands have been studied since 1956 in Österlen in south-eastern Sweden, but there is little up-to-date information on this study. Data concerning the mapping of stands before control measures began have been received from some municipalities in southern Sweden. Attempts have been made to question river committees in southern Sweden, but with little success. One reason may be that many landowners are unaware of the likely consequences of failure to take action against *H. mantegazzianum*.

CONTROL METHODS

There is a need to control *H. mantegazzianum* for two reasons: firstly because of its invasive nature, out-competing and smothering native flora; and secondly, because of the injuries caused by skin contact with the phototoxic sap (Drever and Hunter, 1970). The plant is characterized by rapid growth and the production of large numbers of viable seeds, which remain capable of germinating over 7–8 years. Because of these factors, vigorous control measures are required over a number of years in order to control and eradicate the plant (Dodd *et al.*, 1994). Suggested methods of control include mechanical, chemical and grazing. In general, chemical control is necessary in large, dense stands. Single small specimens can easily be removed with a hoe.

CHEMICAL METHODS

It is usual, especially when attempting to control large stands of *H. mantegazzianum*, to spray using an appropriate herbicide, e.g. glyphosate (Williamson and Forbes, 1982). It is necessary to spray at least twice during every growing season. Spraying with herbicides should be done under suitable weather conditions (except when using the leaf-turner (see 'Selective control' below)). Clothing must be watertight and should include rubber gauntlets and face protection. Regular checks need to be made to prevent new stands developing. When such large-scale control has been practised for several years and only a few plants remain, it is cheaper to switch to selective measures until all visible specimens have been eradicated. Total control is usually only achieved after many years of spraying.

The main problem in controlling the plants is the large numbers of seeds produced and their long-term viability. The most efficient way of controlling the plant is to treat it before the production of seeds. In the past, control measures have been carried out too late in the season, requiring yet more expensive control later on. Any movement of plants off-site should be avoided, but if considered necessary every effort should be made to prevent loss of seeds *en route*.

Control measures should be commenced as soon as possible in the year after the last night frost. Surviving plants can be treated with the L-Stampler (Lundström, 1989).

MECHANICAL METHODS

Initial control using mechanical methods is only advisable for very small stands. The fast growth of the plant makes large and widespread stands very expensive to control by hand. There is the added disadvantage of the hazards associated with control of fully grown plants.

The stem can be cut close to the ground, but the root will sprout after little more than a week. Sometimes a single new umbel will develop close to the ground with flowers capable of producing viable seeds. Especially on steep river banks, it is advisable to avoid cutting full-grown plants with any other tool than a blade attached to a 2.5 m plastic tube (Lundström, 1989). Using a scythe is not a suitable method, since work-related accidents are common.

All methods that entail cutting the stem must be considered potentially dangerous. Caution needs to be exercised by workers and thought given to others, such as children, who may inadvertently come into contact with the cut plant material.

GRAZING

In Denmark and on the south coast of Skåne, stands have been grazed by sheep and cattle. This method's impact will require time to evaluate, but initial studies confirm that it can be successful (Vogt Andersen, 1994).

SELECTIVE CONTROL

The first tools to be used for selective control in Sweden are described in Lundström, (1984). At that time, the use of a hand sprayer proved to be most effective. The most significant observation during 1984 was the importance of treating plants early in the season. When the species is controlled at an early stage, there is also less risk of skin contact with the phototoxic sap from the stem and foliage.

Attention was focused on the problem of finding new methods and the use of cheap, light and simple tools adapted for early application.

This resulted in the following designs:

(1) A kit consisting of an L-stampler (Figure 9.1) and a plastic petrol can, (Figure 9.2). After cutting the top off the can, it can be anchored in the ground with a metal peg.
(2) The collapsible leaf turner (Figure 9.3) made of wood, a bolt and some galvanized nails with heads protruding, to be used to lift the underside of the leaf before spraying. The tool can be used with a hand sprayer and is effective even in wet weather.
(3) The tube sprayer (Figure 9.4), is used in conjunction with a hand-sprayer, controls weeds where conventional spraying poses a risk to

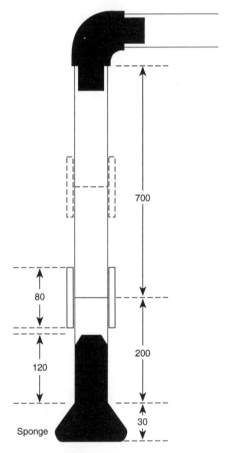

Figure 9.1 L-stampler made of plastic 40-mm tubes, coupling box, artificial sponge with fine pores: vertical application for selective use on rosettes of large dicotyledonous weeds or as a wiper for a leaf turner. Dimensions in mm (not drawn to scale)

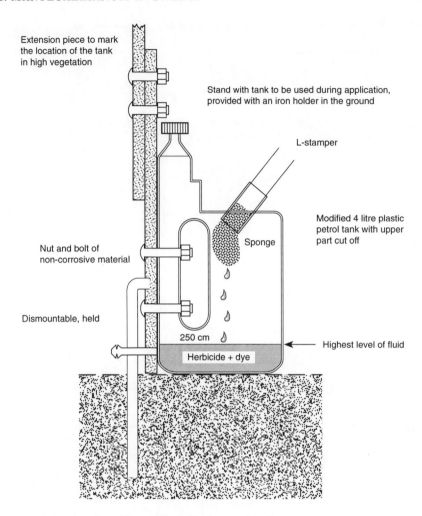

Figure 9.2 L-stampler with modified plastic petrol tank

valuable surrounding vegetation. The tube reduces spray drift. The tool consists of a plastic tube fastened to a wooden handle. Where spraying takes place directly into the tube, it has to be twisted a little before being moved to a new spot to prevent dripping close to the tube.

In all three of these selective application methods, a very small quantity of a marker must be added to the solution of herbicide. This dye is needed to mark the treated leaves, preventing duplication of work. The three tools

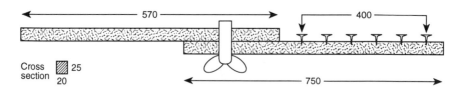

Figure 9.3 Collapsible leaf turner: made of wood (20 × 25 mm), nails (30 mm long) and bolt and wing nut (60 mm): total length 110 mm

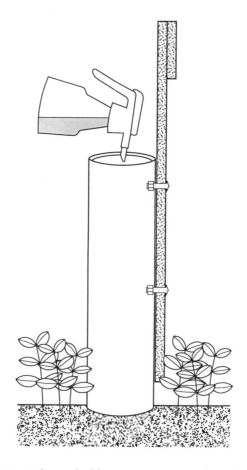

Figure 9.4 Tube sprayer: can be used with a sprayer to control weeds where there is a risk of spraying close to other plants: tube is twisted a little before being moved, to prevent dripping on surrounding foliage close to the tube sprayer: the spray is sheltered from the wind

described have been designed and tested in the field for use under different weather conditions, except extreme conditions.

DISCUSSION

There is a need for the development of a control policy for *Heracleum mantegazzianum* in Sweden. In 1973 the Swedish Environmental Protection Agency (SNV) decided to adopt a policy of limited control of *H. mantegazzianum*. A decade later, in the face of accelerated invasion by the plant, the agency changed that policy to one of control, as far as possible. One result of that policy change was a marked reduction in the number of stands along roads and railway embankments, although large stands still exist in woods and on rubbish tips. During 1984–91 there was a great deal of publicity about control of *H. mantegazzianum* and the use of herbicides. A significant outcome of that debate was public opposition to the use of herbicides. This opposition lead to many local authorities banning the use of herbicides within their areas. The threat of cost cutting by local authorities is also likely to reduce the programme of control. The inevitable outcome of a continuing reduction in effort to control *H. mantegazzianum* will be an increase in the size of existing stands and renewed expansion of stands of the plant in previously cleared areas.

A good example of how to deal with *H. mantegazzianum* is evident along the Vege river in Skåne in southern Sweden, where a successful struggle is being waged against the huge stands. Concerned farmers are now being paid by the river committees to eradicate the stands of *H. mantegazzianum* close to the river and its tributaries with a herbicide containing glyphosate. The results are promising and are a combination of teamwork, aided by contributions from surrounding local authorities. It is now possible to fish from certain beaches, which have previously been inaccessible, except during the winter, because of the presence of *H. mantegazzianum*. The efforts being undertaken along the Vege river include encouraging landowners to take swift action against the plant.

The SNV has recommended to the Swedish Riksdag placing restrictions on the spread of *H. mantegazzianum*, similar to the provisions of the Wildlife and Countryside Act 1981 (London: HMSO) in Britain. Such a law in Sweden would hopefully include measures to control *H. mantegazzianum* along watercourses. It is clear that something must be done to control the spread of this plant before it is too late. It is necessary to start such a project with accurate mapping of the distribution of the plant in order to assess the effectiveness of the treatment programme. Mapping should be carried out during the spring and summer, preferably followed by appropriate control measures. This will be a long-term project and will require adequate resources to achieve good results. An essential ingredient of successful control is the need to employ adequate manpower. Delay will only increase the cost of control in the future.

More is known about the autecology of the plant and the importance of control early in the season. What is required now is a publicity campaign to remind both public and private landowners of the threat that *H. mantegazzianum* poses to the natural flora and to the public at large. Successful control, however, will only come from the acknowledgement of the need for a planned campaign to be funded adequately and supported by local authorities, environmental agencies and private landowners. The tools described in this paper are a contribution to that campaign. They have been designed for ease of use in selective control of small specimens or following control of large stands, when only a few plants still remain.

REFERENCES

Dodd, F., de Waal, L., Wade P.M. and Tiley, G. (1994). Control and management of *Heracleum mantegazzianum* (giant hogweed). In L.C. de Waal, L.E. Child, P.M. Wade and J.H. Brock (Eds), *Ecology and Management of Invasive Riverside Plants*, pp. 111–126 Chichester: Wiley.

Drever, J.C. and Hunter, J.A.A. (1970) Giant hogweed dermatitis. *Scottish Medical Journal*, 15, 315–319.

Lundström, H. (1984). Giant hogweed, *Heracleum mantegazzianum*, a threat to the Swedish countryside. *Weeds and Weed Control, 25th Swedish Weed Conference*, Uppsala. Vol. 1, pp. 191–200.

Lundström, H. (1989). New experiences of the fight against the giant hogweed, *Heracleum mantegazzianum Weeds and Weed Control, Swedish Crop Protection Conference*, Uppsala, Vol. 2, 51–58.

Pyšek, P. (1991). *Heracleum mantegazzianum* in the Czech Republic: dynamics of spreading from the historical perspective. *Folia Geobotanica et Phytotaxonomica*, 26, 439–454.

Vogt Andersen, U. (1994). Sheep grazing as a method of controlling *Heracleum mantegazzianum* In L.C. de Waal, L.E. Child, P.M. Wade and J.H. Brock (Eds), *Ecology and Management of Invasive Riverside Plants*, pp. 77–91. Chichester: Wiley.

Wildlife and Countryside Act 1981. London: HMSO.

Williamson, J.A. and Forbes, J.C. (1982). Giant hogweed (*Heracleum mantegazzianum*): its spread and control with glyphosate in amenity areas. *Weeds, Proceedings of the 1982 British Crop Protection Conference*, pp. 967–972.

10 *Heracleum mantegazzianum* (Giant Hogweed) and its Control in Scotland

GORDON E. D. TILEY and BRUCE PHILP
Scottish Agricultural College, Auchincruive, UK

INTRODUCTION

Heracleum mantegazzianum Somm. and Lev. (Giant hogweed) was introduced into Scotland from the Caucasus mountains during the nineteenth century as a garden ornamental. It has since escaped and spread to become a locally serious weed, especially in river valleys. Its prolific seeding and invasive character has resulted in colonization away from rivers onto roadsides and waste places in both countryside and urban areas.

Methods of control were studied in Scotland by Williamson and Forbes (1982) and recommendations were subsequently revised (Bingham, 1989). However, the spread of *H. mantegazzianum* has continued unabated and a more co-ordinated control strategy is required to prevent the problem from becoming unmanageable.

This paper describes the distribution of *H. mantegazzianum* in Scotland, its disadvantages and means of control, as illustrated by a case study on the River Ayr in western Scotland (Tiley and Philp, 1992).

DISTRIBUTION

A recent distribution map from the Biological Records Centre (1993), reproduced in Figure 10.1, indicates that *H. mantegazzianum* occurs mainly in central and eastern lowland Scotland. The main concentrations of infestation are along river valleys, especially near Edinburgh, in the Borders and in the north east. The number of 10 km^2 records has approximately doubled since 1960. This map incorporates all records reported to the Biological Records Centre up to 1992, though it is not necessarily comprehensive. The recent rapid spread of *H. mantegazzianum* in many areas of Scotland is not

Ecology and Management of Invasive Riverside Plants
Edited by L. C. de Waal, L. E. Child, P. M. Wade and J. H. Brock
© 1994 John Wiley & Sons Ltd

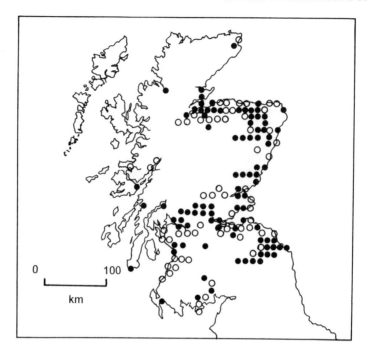

Figure 10.1 Distribution of *Heracleum mantegazzianum* in 10-km squares in Scotland: ○ recorded up to but not since 1959 (66 records), ● recorded since 1959 (91 records). Reproduced by permission of the Biological Records Centre, ITE Monk's Wood (1993)

adequately represented on the map and a survey is in progress to update records of the current distribution in Scotland. In many areas, the source of *H. mantegazzianum* can be traced to the sites of former country houses, some now derelict, from which spread has occurred. *H. mantegazzianum* on the River Leith in Edinburgh occurs downstream from the Royal Botanic Garden (Clegg and Grace, 1974).

In Scotland the principal riparian habitats bearing *H. mantegazzianum* are sandy banks and moist hollows which are open or partly shaded by trees. Densely wooded, steep rocky banks and grazed areas are largely free of the plant. Primary distribution of seeds appears to be by water with deposition concentrated along the edges of ebb-flows. Secondary spread locally is by wind. Occurrence on roadsides and in waste places has been attributed to the collection and discarding of dried flower heads (Lundström, 1984). Other possible agents of dispersal are birds and transport of soil. Until recently, several UK nurseries and seedhouses were marketing *H. mantegazzianum* as an ornamental. It is an offence under the Wildlife and Countryside Act 1981, "to plant or cause to grow (*H. mantegazzianum*) in the wild".

DISADVANTAGES OF *HERACLEUM MANTEGAZZIANUM*

The British flora contains many examples of introduced species which have become naturalized and have subsequently blended with the native flora. However, the presence and further spread of *H. mantegazzianum* in Scotland and the rest of Britain is considered undesirable for the following reasons.

RATE OF SPREAD

H. mantegazzianum is a very invasive species, being large (at flowering stage >4 m, at vegetative stage >2 m) and extremely prolific (50 000 or more seeds per plant). Data from the Czech Republic (Pyšek, 1991) and Britain (Williamson and Forbes, 1982) indicate an exponential increase in the occurrence of *H. mantegazzianum*, since 1950–60 into the general countryside after initial consolidation in river valleys. Unmanaged areas or land under extensification or set-aside management is at particular risk.

EFFECT ON NATIVE FLORA

The seedlings are vigorous and readily established in a number of habitats and vegetation types, including dense grass swards. The large leaf size makes the plant very competitive and in dense stands it rapidly shades out the indigenous flora.

HYBRIDIZATION

There is a possibility of hybridization with the native *Heracleum sphondylium* L. with potentially deleterious effects. Natural hybrids have been recorded by Wyse Jackson (1989) and McClintock (1975). These are intermediate in size and botanical characters between the parents and are sterile or of low fertility. The majority of occurrences of natural hybrids between *H. mantegazzianum* and *H. sphondylium* are from Scotland (McClintock, 1975).

RIVER BANK EROSION

The loss of smaller, more densely growing species can predispose river banks to erosion in winter. Dominant *H. mantegazzianum* plants are widely spaced and, with only a coarsely branched root system, make the soil less resistant to erosion.

RESTRICTION OF ACCESS

Dense stands of *H. mantegazzianum* restrict access, particularly on river banks. Restriction arises from the physical presence of tall overhanging leaves and stems and from the deterrent effect of the risk of injury following human contact.

ROADSIDE OBSTRUCTION

Apart from the unsightly appearance of *H. mantegazzianum* as it matures and yellows in midsummer, the huge overhanging plants can cause obstructions to drivers on roadsides.

INJURIOUS SAP

One of the greatest disadvantages of *H. mantegazzianum* is the poisonous sap, which causes injury to human skin exposed to sunlight. Children and those with sensitive skins are at particular risk. Contact with the leaf and stem bristles can be sufficient to produce a reaction. The number of injuries caused by *H. mantegazzianum* has not, as yet, been quantified, but a local survey has been undertaken on the River Ayr.

CROP DISEASE HOST

H. mantegazzianum provides an alternative host for fungi (*Sclerotinia* sp.) which cause diseases of crops, e.g. oilseed rape (Gray and Noble, 1965).

EFFECTS ON LIVESTOCK

Photosensitization injury to animals has been recorded (Pyšek, 1991), though in Britain cattle, sheep, goats and pigs can normally graze *H. mantegazzianum* without harm.

METHODS OF CONTROL

CHEMICAL

Few herbicides are effective against *H. mantegazzianum*. The most recent recommendations are summarized in Bingham (1989). Glyphosate is the safest and most generally used and is the only effective product cleared for use near water. However, care is required to avoid damage to neighbouring vegetation. Imazapyr, which is persistent in the soil, can be used on non-cropped land. Triclopyr is useful in grassland or non-cropped land, but drift onto other broadleaved species must be avoided.

NON-CHEMICAL

Cutting

Dense *H. mantegazzianum* growth can be reduced by cutting above ground level, but the plants will recover with rapid basal regrowth. This could be a useful pretreatment to summer herbicide treatment where the original growth has become too large.

Chopping

Cutting or chopping *H. mantegazzianum* plants at the root 3–5 cm below ground level is an effective control, particularly at the flowering stage.

Grazing

Cattle or pigs readily graze *H. mantegazzianum* and will eliminate it in the vegetative phase.

STRATEGY OF CONTROL

The control measures above, if properly applied, can be effective in killing individual plants and may ultimately lead to eradication, providing new seeding is prevented. However, local control becomes ineffective if fresh seed supplies continue to arrive from outside sources. In river catchments especially, failure to control flowering and seeding at upstream sites renders long-term control downstream impossible. Individual landowners have often been deterred from undertaking thorough eradication measures because of continued re-infestation from sources upstream. Thus a co-ordinated strategy within a river catchment is required. The normal recommendation is to work downstream from the uppermost infestation (Williamson and Forbes, 1982), but in some cases the opposite strategy has been followed. Gordon District Council (Grampian Region in Scotland) has worked upstream, since vegetative growth begins earlier near the sea. Unless *H. mantegazzianum* reaches massive and widespread proportions so as to constitute a public nuisance, local authorities and other bodies do not often consider it of sufficient importance to merit a thorough and co-ordinated approach to control. At this late stage, effective control then becomes very difficult and expensive, in contrast to that possible with more prompt action at an earlier stage of invasion.

CONTROL EXPERIENCES

Control measures have been adopted in Scotland by individual landowners and some public authorities. Individuals have carried out intermittent cutting of vegetative and flowering plants, with occasional use of herbicides. Local and regional authorities have controlled *H. mantegazzianum* principally by spraying with glyphosate on land (such as parks and footpaths) for which they are responsible. The degree of control practised annually varies considerably from district to district. *H. mantegazzianum* in hedgerows, roadsides and refuse tips often remains untreated. The effectiveness of control in individual areas is often limited by the lack of control on adjacent land. However, there have been several examples of eradication of giant hogweed by the control of small pockets of invasion.

BIOLOGICAL OBSERVATIONS

The distribution of *H. mantegazzianum* on the River Ayr (Tiley & Philp, 1992) consisted of more than 100 infestations, each over 10 m^2 in area. The upper limits on the river coincided with the sites of large country houses, though not all suitable habitats downstream were colonized. Local sites showed gradual spread in the direction of the prevailing wind.

There is little information on the dormancy of *H. mantegazzianum* seeds in the UK, but seeds have remained viable for up to 15 years in Sweden (Lundström, 1989). Field observations in Scotland indicate massive germination both in the autumn shortly after dispersal and in the following spring. Laboratory germination tests indicate that seed viability can be as low as 5%. Seeds did not germinate in the dark. Seedling emergence or survival is much reduced under the canopy of established plants. Colonization of new sites is often associated with high river-level marks from the previous winter.

FLOWERING

Flowering stems are produced from 2–4 year-old plants, i.e. those which have endured a minimum of two winters. After flowering and fruiting, the whole plant dies. This also occurs if the plant is chopped below the junction of root and stem so that all axillary buds are removed. Where axillary buds remain, fresh flowering shoots develop and further perenniality may be induced. Cut flowering stems often have sufficient reserves to allow setting and maturation of seed heads, and to produce at least a proportion of viable seeds. This can be prevented by cutting the stem beneath each inflorescence.

HARMFUL EFFECTS OF *HERACLEUM MANTEGAZZIANUM* SAP

The sap of *H. mantegazzianum*, which is abundant in its fleshy petioles, stems and roots, contains furocoumarins. When activated by ultraviolet light, these substances interact with the human skin inducing photosensitization or photodermatitis. This produces symptoms of mild–severe dermatitis, erythema (reddening), inflammation and slight–severe blistering. Symptoms are often painful and unsightly and may require skin grafts. Damage can be permanent with melanization and the symptoms can recur in later years on exposure to sunlight. The furocoumarins are sufficiently strong under ultraviolet light to produce mutations in bacteria (Clarke, 1975) and the potential harm to human skin should not be underestimated. It is recommended that children and others with sensitive skin should avoid all contact with any part of the plant, including the copious surface bristles.

Cases of photosensitization of domestic animals (cattle, sheep and poultry) have been reported from furocoumarins in other plant species (Ivie, 1978) and there is a possibility that similar symptoms could arise from the ingestion of large amounts of *H. mantegazzianum*.

DISCUSSION

The risk of *H. mantegazzianum* causing serious human injury and its potential harmful effects on indigenous vegetation and public access justify a policy of control with an ultimate aim of eradication, at least locally. Faced with a massive forest-like growth of *H. mantegazzianum* in midsummer, this task might seem insurmountable. However, even the densest stands of *H. mantegazzianum* contain only a limited number of adult flowering plants, distributed among an understorey of vegetative plants which will mature to flowering in 1–3 years. *H. mantegazzianum* is a biennial–perennial monocarpic plant, requiring a minimum of two growing seasons to flower and depending on seed supplies for perpetuation.

There is thus an opportunity of breaking the cycle of renewal by the systematic removal of all flowering plants for a number of seasons. Control of vegetative plants and seedlings will additionally reduce numbers of potential flowering plants in future years. This, however, is less important than the complete prevention of seeding, which, if practised for a number of years, will "flush out" *H. mantegazzianum* from an area. The longevity of seeds in the soil seed bank is unknown and vigilance against sporadic establishment would be required for several years. Observations indicate abundant seed germination in the year following dispersal, but further studies on dormancy and the factors affecting germination are required.

Obviously, imports of fresh seed by water or wind into a cleared area must be prevented. Infestations of *H. mantegazzianum* are not proscribed by the Weeds Act (1954) though the deliberate establishment of *H. mantegazzianum* in the wild is illegal (Wildlife and Countryside Act 1981). A co-ordinated programme is therefore necessary within a river catchment or locality to ensure effective control of *H. mantegazzianum*. Herbicide control using glyphosate is easiest in the early spring when the leaves are small. Increased amounts of chemical are required later in the season and further information on timing and quantities is desirable. Lundström (1989) found spraying the lower leaf surface more effective. Chopping the root below ground level is also an effective, though laborious, method of killing the plant.

ACKNOWLEDGEMENTS

The survey of *H. mantegazzianum* on the River Ayr was supported by the Cumnock and Doon Valley and Kyle and Carrick District Councils. The Scottish Agricultural College receives financial support from the Scottish Office Agriculture and Fisheries Department.

REFERENCES

Bingham, I.J. (1989). *Giant Hogweed: the Problem and its Control*. Leaflet, Scottish Agricultural College, Aberdeen.
Biological Records Centre, 1993, Unpublished records from the Institute for Terrestrial Ecology, Monks Wood, UK.
Clarke, C.H. (1975). Giant hogweed sap: another environmental mutagen. *Mutation Research*, **31**, 63–64.
Clegg, L.M. and Grace, J. (1974). The distribution of *Heracleum mantegazzianum* (Somm. & Levier) near Edinburgh. *Transactions of the Botanical Society of Edinburgh*, **42**, 233–229.
Gray, E.G. and Noble, M. (1965). *Sclerotinia* disease. *Scottish Agriculture*, **44**, 265–267.
Ivie, G.W. (1978). Toxicological significance of plant furocoumarins. In R.F. Keeler, K.R. van Kampen and L.F. James (Eds), *Effects of Poisonous Plants on Livestock*, pp. 475–485. New York: Academic Press.
Lundström, H. (1984). Giant hogweed, *Heracleum mantegazzianum*: a threat to the Swedish countryside. *Weeds and Weed Control, 25th Swedish Weed Conference*, Uppsala, Vol. 1, pp. 191–200.
Lundström, H. (1989). New experiences of the fight against the giant hogweed *Heracleum mantegazzianum*. *Weeds and Weed Control, 30th Swedish Crop Protection Conference*, Uppsala, Vol. 2, 51–58.
McClintock, D. (1975). In C.A. Stace (Ed.) *Hybridisation and the Flora of the British Isles*. London: Academic Press.
Pyšek, P. (1991). *Heracleum mantegazzianum* in the Czech Republic—dynamics of spreading from the historical perspective. *Folia Geobotanica et Phytotaxonomica*, **26**, 439–454.

Tiley, G.E.D. and Philp, B. (1992). Strategy for the control of giant hogweed (*Heracleum mantegazzianum*) on the River Ayr in Scotland. *Vegetation Management in Forestry, Amenity and Conservation Areas. Aspects of Applied Biology*, **29**, 463–466.

Weeds Act, 1954. London: HMSO.

Wildlife and Countryside Act, 1981. London: HMSO.

Williamson, J.A. and Forbes, J.C. (1982). Giant hogweed (*Heracleum mantegazzianum*): its spread and control with glyphosate in amenity areas. *Weeds, Proceedings of the 1982 British Crop Protection Conference*, pp. 967–972.

Wyse Jackson, M. (1989). Observations on the Irish distribution of a plant with serious public health implications: giant hogweed (*Heracleum mantegazzianum* Sommier and Levier). *Bulletin of the Irish Biogeographical Society*, **12**, 94–112.

11 Control and Management of *Heracleum mantegazzianum* (Giant Hogweed)

FELICITE S. DODD,[1] LOUISE C. DE WAAL,[1] P. MAX WADE[1] and GORDON E. D. TILEY[2]
[1] *International Centre of Landscape Ecology, Loughborough University, UK*
[2] *Scottish Agricultural College, Auchincruive, UK*

INTRODUCTION

Heracleum mantegazzianum (giant hogweed) Sommier and Levier is a member of the Umbellifer family (Umbelliferae). Previously it has been referred to as *H. giganteum* Hort. non Fisch, *H. villosum* Hort. (Burke, 1943), *H. asperum*, Siberian cow-parsnip (Nelson, 1991) and cartwheel flower (Coombes, 1985). It is native to the Caucasus and was introduced into English botanical gardens in the late 1800s (Briggs, 1979). *H. mantegazzianum* was promoted by nurserymen as an ornamental plant and was subsequently actively planted in both private and public gardens and parks. Since its introduction it has spread throughout the British Isles, extending from the south coast of England to the north coast of Scotland (Clegg and Grace, 1974) and to Ireland. The species colonizes not only riparian habitats (Pyšek and Prach, 1994) but also agricultural land, road and railway embankments, urban habitats and disused areas such as waste land, demolition sites and abandoned fields (Pyšek, 1994; Williamson and Forbes, 1982). *H. mantegazzianum* can survive on a wide range of substrates, but is frequently found on calcium-rich, potassium-rich (Neiland, 1986), and disturbed soils, preferring a pH range of 6.5–8 (Clegg and Grace, 1974). It also grows at a wide range of altitudes and has been observed by the authors in Switzerland up to 2000 m. In its native area, the west of the Caucasus, *H. mantegazzianum* occurs in meadows near the tree line, along the margins of forest openings, clearings in the upper forest zone (Pyšek, 1991) and along the fringes of mountain streams (Wyse Jackson, 1989).

   H. mantegazzianum is a monocarpic, biennial or perennial herb, growing both from a basal tap root and from seeds. The hollow stem of the flowering

Ecology and Management of Invasive Riverside Plants
Edited by L. C. de Waal, L. E. Child, P. M. Wade and J. H. Brock
© 1994 John Wiley & Sons Ltd

plant grows up to 5 m tall with a diameter of 10 cm or more. The stem is furrowed-ribbed and green with dark reddish-purple spots. *H. mantegazzianum* flowers in June–July and sets seeds in August at an age of 2–3 years, after which the parent plant usually dies back (Kees and Krumrey, 1983; Schuldes and Kübler, 1990; Schwabe and Kratochwil, 1991). Occasionally, the tap root can produce additional crowns the year after flowering, especially if the stem is damaged (Morton, 1978). The white flowers are borne on large umbels, the terminal umbels being hermaphrodite and self compatible while some of the lower satellite umbels are usually male (Tutin, 1980). Tiley and Philp (1994) estimated 60 000 flowers on one large plant, which means a potential for 120 000 seeds per plant to be produced after flowering. In early autumn the non-flowering plants die back leaving a fleshy tap root, which overwinters for up to 4 years and develops increasingly larger shoots every year in the spring until it is ready to flower (Williamson and Forbes, 1982).

The seeds produced form an extensive seed bank in the immediate area of the parent plant. Morton (1978) found that seeds kept dry at room temperature were still viable after 7 years. Lundström (1989) states that there are data suggesting that seed viability of 15 years is possible, but cites no specific references. The seeds are dispersed over only short distances by wind, but this can often be sufficient to reach water, the other important means of natural dispersal. The seeds are reported to float for up to 3 days before they become waterlogged and sink. With a hypothetical river surface velocity of 0.1 m/s a seed could thus be transported by water up to a distance of approximately 10 km (Clegg and Grace, 1974). Human activities have also contributed to dispersal. The seed heads are considered attractive for flower arranging and seeds may be dropped during transport, especially if carried on the tops of vehicles. Subsequent disposal of the seed heads can lead to the development of new colonies of *H. mantegazzianum*, e.g. at rubbish dumps and along river banks and road and railway verges (Lundström, 1984).

In 1925 it was recommended for planting in shrubberies (Anon., 1925) as it is eagerly visited by bees and other insects, though it is referred to as a second-rate bee plant by Howes (1979).

TOXICITY

The sap of *H. mantegazzianum* is phototoxic, which is one of the main and compelling reasons for control. The sap of the leaves and stems contains a number of furocoumarins, which are linear, tricyclic compounds related to psoralen (Hipkin, 1991). The sap exudes from the bristles on the stem and the petioles and from broken or cut plants (Williamson and Forbes, 1982). When the sap comes into contact with skin that is then exposed to ultraviolet light, usually in the form of sunlight, the furocoumarins are activated to phototoxic derivatives (Camm *et al.*, 1976). If not immediately washed off, these can cause skin irritation and burning, swelling and severe, painful blistering approximately 15–20 hours after the original contact. The blisters are often composite, very large and watery. Skin grafts may be required and the damaged skin heals very slowly, leaving residual pigmentation, which, in some cases, develops to recurrent dermatitis for several years after the original contact (Drever and Hunter, 1970). The highest content of furocoumarins has been found in the leaves in June (Pira *et al.*, 1989) and therefore phytophotodermatitis is more severe in spring and early summer when the sap exudes freely from broken plants and sunshine is more intense (Morton, 1978) than in the later life stages of the plant (Ministry of Agriculture, Fisheries and Food, 1988). After flowering, the concentrations of furocoumarins are highest in the fruit, intermediate in the leaf and minimal in the stem (Pira *et al.*, 1989). Plants growing in open and sunny areas with high light intensities are likely to have higher furocoumarin concentrations than plants growing in more shaded areas (Berenbaum, 1981).

A straightforward treatment for the dermatitis is not known to be available. The National Poisons Information Service (personal communication, 1992) makes the following recommendations to medical practitioners: wash skin with soap and water and if necessary treat as a thermal burn. Antihistamines may be given if necessary. The affected area should be kept out of sunlight for 72 hours, for example by covering it up. Frohne and Pfänder (1981) found that no specific treatment healed the dermatitis. Morton (1978) recommends washing the infected area with copious quantities of soap and water and then applying a corticosteroid gel or lotion to relieve the irritation. Hegi (1931) recommends treatment of the irritated skin with lysol to aid recovery.

Stands of *H. mantegazzianum* growing in amenity areas present an obvious hazard to members of the public. Contractors working on the control of the species are specially at risk and should have adequate protective clothing. Children may be attracted to the plant by its large size and hollow stems, which are frequently used as "telescopes" and blowpipes, with disastrous effects.

The plant appears to be less hazardous to animals (Tiley and Philp, 1994). However, a case of suspected poisoning of a goat by *H. mantegazzianum* (Andrews *et al.*, 1985) and foot and beak vesication with subsequent deformities in a brood of ducklings (Harwood, 1985) have been recorded.

ENVIRONMENTAL PROBLEMS

In addition to its phototoxicity, *H. mantegazzianum* poses serious prob-lems as an aggressive competitor because of its size and rapid and prolific vegetative growth. The giant leaves produce dense shade, preventing other species, including its own seedlings, from becoming established and thereby seriously reducing diversity of native plants (Vogt Andersen, 1994; Williamson and Forbes, 1982). A further problem arises when the vigorous growth of *H.*

mantegazzianum dies back at the end of the growing season, leaving large areas of bare ground. This can lead to the risk of soil erosion, especially on steep sites and river banks exposed to winter floods (Williamson and Forbes, 1982). Furthermore, dense stands of *H. mantegazzianum* restrict public access to river banks and amenity areas in summer (Lundström, 1984). In Ireland the plant has become a major problem on fishing rivers such as the Shannon (Caffrey, 1994). It may also limit visibility at the sides of roads and railways (Lundström, 1984). Other problems may arise from the fact that *H. mantegazzianum* is a host for the carrot fly (*Psila rosae*) and the plant pathogen *Sclerotinia sclerotiorum* both of which attack a number of arable and horticultural crops (Neiland, 1986).

Hybrids between *H. mantegazzianum* and *H. sphondylium* occur when the two grow together, the hybrid adopting *H. mantegazzianum* characteristics could increase the problems already posed by *H. mantegazzianum* (Stewart and Grace, 1984).

CONTROL

There is no legal requirement to control *H. mantegazzianum* in any European country. In Britain it is listed in *Poisonous Plants and Fungi* (Ministry of Agriculture, Fisheries, and Food, 1988), where control measures are advocated and it is "an offence to plant or otherwise cause to grow *H. mantegazzianum* in the wild" (Wildlife and Countryside Act 1981, (Section 4, Schedule 9 (Part 2)).

One of the prime requirements for the control of an invasive species such as *H. mantegazzianum* is preventing its further spread. The dispersal of *H. mantegazzianum* is almost entirely by seeds, which are produced annually in very large numbers. Therefore, it is necessary to prevent the plant from flowering and setting seed. Once seeding and widespread dispersal have taken place, the extensive seed bank and the possible long-term seed viability in the soil is an additional problem. A control programme for *H. mantegazzianum* would therefore need provision for monitoring for at least 7 years after the initial control measure to check for reinfestation from dormant seeds and the subsequent spot control. Fortunately, the large size of the plant facilitates post-treatment inspection. It is essential to take precautions to avoid the removal of soil from areas where *H. mantegazzianum* is or was known to be present, because of the residual and persistent seed bank. Where removal of contaminated soil is necessary, seedling emergence can be prevented by burying the soil to a minimum depth of 50 cm and covering it with clean soil (Lundström, 1989).

Co-operation from garden centres and nurserymen should be actively sought to halt the sale of *H. mantegazzianum* seeds and plants for use in gardens. Fortunately, the majority of garden centres now no longer market this plant.

CURRENT CONTROL RECOMMENDATIONS

Current control measures for *H. mantegazzianum* are determined by the particular habitat in which the plant is to be managed and the size and stage of growth of the plant. A variety of methods are available, including the use of herbicides, grazing animals and manual methods such as cutting, digging and ploughing and possibly biological control (Table 11.1).

The photosensitizing properties of the sap of *H. mantegazzianum* necessitates that any person practising the control of this species must wear adequate protective clothing especially during manual control measures. The protective clothing must be waterproof; rubber boots, rubber gloves and a PVC coverall are advisable as well as a face visor (Briggs, 1979). Operators should be careful to avoid rubbing their faces or other unprotected parts of their body with contaminated gloves. All equipment and protective clothing should be washed in water immediately after use.

Table 11.1. Methods for controlling *Heracleum mantegazzianum* in various habitats

	Habitat*	
Control method	Riparian	Non-riparian
Non-chemical		
Cutting	√	√
Pulling	√	√
Grazing	√	√
Hoeing	√	√
Digging	√	√
Ploughing	√	√
Chemical		
Glyphosate, overall	√	√
Glyphosate, spot	√	√
Imazapyr	–	√
Triclopyr	–	√

*In amenity areas, areas with mixed vegetation, low-density and/or areas associated with high nature conservation value, e.g. SSSIs, nature reserves, nature trails, sites important at a parish, district or county level, a non-chemical treatment is preferred. Where chemical treatment is necessary, carefully controlled spot application using a sprayer hood, sponge, weed wiper or paint brush is recommended.

Herbicidal control

Legislation in the UK on the use of pesticides is fully covered in *The UK Pesticide Guide 1992* (Ivens, 1992). The Food and Environment Protection Act 1985 stipulates that only operators with a recognized Certificate of Competence with the relevant modules issued by the National Proficiency Tests Council can apply pesticides. Users of pesticides must comply with the conditions of approval stated on the product label. It is an offence to use non-approved products or to use approved products in a manner which does not comply with the specific conditions of approval. The Control of Substances Hazardous to Health regulations (COSHH) 1988 must also be followed (Ivens, 1992). These require that the risks associated with the use of a pesticide be assessed before it is used and appropriate measures taken to control the risk. Detailed guidance concerning both of these legislations is given in a Code of Practice for the safe use of pesticides on farms and holdings (Ministry of Agriculture, Fisheries and Food and Health and Safety Commission, 1990). Extra precautions need to be taken when applying herbicides in riparian habitats (Ministry of Agriculture, Fisheries, and Food, 1985). If any work is undertaken within 10 m of a river bank, approval of the National Rivers Authority is needed and land drainage consent may also be required. Note that permission from the landowner must always be obtained.

Glyphosate

This is the only herbicide effective against *H. mantegazzianum* which is approved by the Control of Pesticide Regulations, 1986, for use in riparian habitats in the UK (Ivens, 1992). Glyphosate can be applied in a variety of ways. For small stands of *H. mantegazzianum* or isolated plants mixed amongst other species, spot treatment is possible. The main advantage of spot treatment is that it reduces the damage to adjacent vegetation, which can then develop to provide a complete cover suppressing *H. mantegazzianum* seedlings in the later years of the control programme. Spot treatment can be carried out using a knapsack sprayer to apply glyphosate accurately, e.g. Roundup® Pro at 5 litres/ha (2.4 kg a.i./ha as isopropylamine salt).

The solution can be mixed with a proprietary wallpaper paste to a consistency to hang wallpaper and then applied by brush to the two largest leaves (Williamson and Forbes, 1982), though this is not an approved method in the UK. Lundström (1989) and Lundström and Darby (1994) report on the use of a sponge on a long handle to apply glyphosate to the leaf rosettes. To spot-treat plants over 1.5 m tall, a leaf turning device can be used to lift up the leaves and a sponge used to wipe the solution onto the underside of the leaves (Lundström, 1989). Liverpool City Council have treated plants by cutting them in spring and filling the hollow stem with glyphosate, although this method was expensive, it was effective (Sampson, 1990).

Weed wipers or ropewick applicators which were developed for the selective control of tall weeds in crops offer an alternative method of spot control of *H. mantegazzianum*. Most habitats would not allow the use of tractor- or motor-cycle-mounted weed wipers, but hand-held models are available. A 1:2 Roundup® Pro (equivalent to 360g glyphosate/l) aqueous solution is recommended, which should be applied by stroking the wiper in two directions over the leaf blade surface. This method is similar to the sponge method and is suitable for isolated plants growing among sensitive vegetation. *H. mantegazzianum* plants should be treated when the leaves are still small and rigid, but have grown above the level of surrounding plants. Older *H. mantegazzianum* leaves are too large and dissected and also too pliable for the weed wiper technique.

For large stands of *H. mantegazzianum*, spraying can be carried out using glyphosate, e.g. Roundup® Pro applied at 5 litres/ha (2.4 kg a.i./ha as isopropylamine salt). Williamson and Forbes (1982) used a knapsack sprayer, fitted with a fan nozzle at a pressure of 100 kPa. The authors report good control using a knapsack sprayer fitted with a very-low-volume nozzle and a water volume of 80 litres/ha. The first application by any method should be made in March/April, when the rosettes sprouting from the tap roots are approximately 10 cm tall. A second application can be made before the end of May, when *H. mantegazzianum* seedlings which have germinated after the first treatment will be affected. If spraying is delayed until the plants have grown too large or too tall, dense stands of *H. mantegazzianum* become difficult and potentially dangerous for spray operators to work in. The dense foliage will also protect smaller *H. mantegazzianum* plants from the herbicide and these are subsequently able to continue growing (Williamson and Forbes, 1982). Large plants should be cut back and the regenerating regrowth subsequently sprayed.

Glyphosate is non-persistent in the soil, but is also non-selective, so other vegetation may be affected. Re-establishment of native vegetation in treated areas may be necessary in the control programme (Williamson and Forbes, 1982). Shrubs and trees can be safely planted 7 days after application of glyphosate.

Triclopyr

Davies and Richards (1985) achieved good results using triclopyr, a selective and moderately resistant herbicide, e.g. Garlon 2E at 6 litres/ha (1.4 kg a.i./ha as butosyethyl ester) and a high water volume (400 litres/ha) which left a good residual grass cover. A single treatment in early May achieved 100% kill of *H. mantegazzianum*. A wide range of other species rapidly colonized

the ground following the triclopyr treatment, which helped to prevent reinfestation with *H. mantegazzianum* in the following year. For spot treatment,
10 ml of triclopyr in 1 litre of water is recommended. Triclopyr is not
approved for use in or near water in the UK (Ministry of Agriculture, Fisheries and Food, 1985) and therefore it is unsuitable for use in riparian
habitats and where there is risk of run off into a water course. The area
cannot be replanted with trees within 3 weeks of application.

Imazapyr

Imazapyr, e.g. Arsenal 50, is a non-selective, residual herbicide, which also
controls *H. mantegazzianum*, though it is not approved for use in or near
water (Ministry of Agriculture, Fisheries and Food, 1985). This herbicide can
be applied at 15 litres/ha (750 g a.i./ha as isopropyl amine salt) and a water
volume of 450 litres/ha using a knapsack sprayer. Applications should be
made in spring or early summer before the plants become too large. Arsenal
50 is absorbed by the plant within 30 min, which reduces the risk of rain
washing off the herbicide after treatment. Its residual activity ensures control
of germinating seedlings for several months after application, but it also
delays the planting of replacement vegetation. (Department of Agriculture
for Northern Ireland and Department of the Environment for Northern
Ireland, 1990)

Hexazinone

Lundström (1989) reports on the use of a device which introduces Hexazinone tablets into either the stem or a notch of a leaf axil. This is known as
the AB FIC injection method and is being used by some authorities in
Sweden. Hexazinone, a triazinone herbicide as Velpar liquid is no longer
available in the UK.

2,4,5-T

The herbicide 2,4,5-T had been found effective in controlling *H. mantegazzianum* (Kees and Krumrey, 1983, Rubow, 1979). However, this herbicide
is no longer approved for use in Europe. Products containing triclopyr are
an effective substitute on sites away from water (see above).

As mentioned before, an important factor in achieving successful control
with herbicides is early application when the plant is still small. There is an
indication that the plant is more sensitive to herbicide treatment at this early
stage of development and it is easier to apply spot treatment which leaves
other vegetation to persist and requires less chemicals.

When spraying, care should be taken to minimize damage to non-target plants and therefore spot treatment is preferred wherever possible. However, when using glyphosate as a spray, damage to the underlying and surrounding vegetation is inevitable unless using a weed wiper, paste or roughing glove. Dry weather conditions for at least 6 hours and preferably 24 hours after spraying are desirable for the greatest herbicidal effect, otherwise respraying will be necessary. The leaf turning method of applying the herbicide to the underside of the *H. mantegazzianum* leaves makes the effect of rain shortly after application less crucial and it also uses less herbicide (Lundström and Darby, 1994). Special precautions should be taken to minimize the effect of spray drift of the non-selective herbicides glyphosate and imazapyr. Spraying is not advis-able in wind at speeds greater than Force 2 on the Beaufort scale (>3.2–6.5 km/h) measured at a height of 10 m or at speeds of Force 0 (<2 km/h), especially on warm sunny days, when vapour drift is likely to occur (Agricultural Training Board, 1990).

Cutting

Cutting is used as a method of clearing the vigorous top growth of *H. mantegazzianum*. If this is done frequently it will progressively weaken the plant's reserves, leading to reduced growth. The tap root reserves, however, are considerable in all plants other than seedlings. It can therefore take up to several years to kill non-flowering vegetative plants (Schuldes and Kübler, 1991). Very frequent cutting would be required for an appreciable degree of control.

Cutting the mature flowering stems below ground level results in death of the plant since there are no axillary buds on the tap root and much of the root reserves have been exhausted in flowering stem production. Cutting above ground level will allow the basal axillary buds to produce new, but smaller, flowering stems which are capable of seed production. Additional perenniality of the plant for another season may also be induced (Tiley and Philp, 1994). It is essential that the flowering stems are cut before the plant has set seed, to avoid increasing the number of seeds in the seed bank and to avoid seed dispersal either naturally or by moving the cut plant material with flower or seed heads. Cutting should therefore be timed at the full flowering stage; though laborious, this is a very effective control method providing that it is done at the critical stage between flowering and seed set (Schuldes and Kübler, 1991). Delay after this may result in the development of mature fruits from plant reserves within the severed stem (Tiley and Philp, 1994).

The life cycle of *H. mantegazzianum* terminates naturally at flowering and seed production and survival depend on fresh seed supplies. Thus, systematic control of the flowering stage of *H. mantegazzianum* over a number of years will eventually flush out the residual population, assuming that the seed bank has a low viability (Tiley & Philp, 1994). Once the plant has died, cutting must not be carried out, because the ripe seeds will easily dislodge and become scattered.

All *H. mantegazzianum* biomass is best removed from pathways and access points and allowed to decompose in piles. The fleshy cut foliage normally dries and decays rapidly during the summer months. Mature flowering stems are more persistent, especially late in the season when considerable woodiness allows overwinter persistence *in situ*. Flower heads falling into water soon decay, though if the seeds are mature these will float and be dispersed. Wherever flower heads are present, care must be taken to cover them during transport so that seeds are not shed *en route*. The seeds may then be destroyed by burning or burying at a depth of a least 50 cm (Lundström, 1984).

The sap in cut green plants remains actively phototoxic until the plant decays and is thus still hazardous. However, it is difficult to burn cut *H. mantegazzianum* plants, and moving them to an incinerator after seeding is not desirable.

Pulling

Pulling up the young plants early in the year (April–May), using gloves and taking care to avoid breaking the plant, can be used as a possible control method for isolated small plants (Briggs, 1979). Pulling is not suitable for more mature plants as the tap root is too large and the petioles too fleshy. If the plant breaks, the tap root will regenerate a new leaf rosette within a week (Lundström, 1989).

Digging

Digging is an alternative to cutting the plant, which could be an advantage if the tap root is completely removed or sufficiently damaged to prevent regrowth, though chopping the root with a spade or hoe is normally sufficient (Bingham, 1989). Lundström (1989) recommends digging individual specimens early in the growing season to prevent flowering and therefore seed production. However, this is laborious and suitable only for occasional isolated plants.

Ploughing

Seedlings and young plants spreading into agricultural land are easily killed by ploughing. Unfortunately, ploughing is not normally possible in most situations where *H. mantegazzianum* occurs (Bingham, 1989).

Grazing

Cattle, sheep, goats and pigs graze *H. mantegazzianum* generally with no apparent ill effects. However, as mentioned above, a case of suspected poisoning of a goat by *H. mantegazzianum* (Andrews *et al.*, 1985) and foot and beak vesication with subsequent deformities in a brood of ducklings (Harwood, 1985) have been recorded. Grazing will eliminate the plant in the vegetative phase (Tiley and Philp, 1994) and therefore it can be a successful method of control. A study in Denmark showed that *H. mantegazzianum* was controlled efficiently by sheep grazing followed by an increase in floristic diversity (Vogt Andersen, 1994). In Sweden, sheep have been seen grazing stands of *H. mantegazzianum* (Lundström, 1989). A beneficial side-effect of grazing is that trampling by the animals causes substantial damage to the plants and tap roots and this may prevent them from regrowing (Morton, 1978).

Successful control of *H. mantegazzianum* can be achieved by any one or a combination of the above-mentioned methods. These measures of control should certainly be applied before the plant becomes too tall and before it sets seed. Once the controlled site is cleared it should be checked each spring for at least 7 years and any resurgent plants treated. Where control of dense stands is undertaken, the re-establishment of a suitable vegetation cover will help to reduce soil erosion and provide competition against the establishment of *H. mantegazzianum* seedling (Davies and Richards, 1985, Williamson and Forbes, 1982).

CO-ORDINATED CONTROL

H. mantegazzianum is found along linear habitats, such as rivers, streams, canals, railways and roads, and non-linear habitats, such as waste ground, demolition sites, abandoned fields, private gardens and parks. Where a control programme includes a watercourse it is important to start the control upstream, as seeds of *H. mantegazzianum* can easily be carried by water, otherwise cleared sites downstream can rapidly be re-infested. Seeds are also wind borne providing continuous sources of local infestation, e.g. in the draught caused by trains and lorries. Effective control should be based on a co-ordinated approach to achieve control in a whole area of infestation, regardless of ownership of the land.

In Scotland a recent questionnaire survey (G. Tiley, personal communication) indicated that, with a greater interest in countryside access, local organizations are showing increasing concern at the spread of *H. mantegazzianum*. However, the level of perception of *H. mantegazzianum* as a problem weed is very variable. Concern has been expressed by the public, anglers and occasionally by farmers. The farmers fear that *H. mantegazzia-num* may be a source of *Sclerotinia* infection for oilseed rape crops (Gray and Noble, 1965) and are also worried about the cost of *H. mantegazzianum* control. Although there have been high levels of expenditure on conventional *H. mantegazzianum* control, e.g. up to £15 000 in 1989/90 by Moray District Council (Sampson, 1994), no completely successful control programme has yet been reported in the UK.

Current control measures are based on local, often sporadic, attempts with varying degrees of zeal and commitment, ranging from those by individuals, farmers, and anglers, to more organized schemes by local authorities. The main methods of control practised are cutting and the use of glyphosate and triclopyr (Table 11.1). Plans for more formal, wider-based control programmes are being established in north-east, central and southern Scotland (Tiley, in press).

It is vital to eradicate the species in amenity areas and in areas open to the public, because of the health hazard of *H. mantegazzianum*. As mentioned previously, this will require a long-term control programme which may last up to at least 7 years and must ensure that all *H. mantegazzianum* in the area is treated when the plants are still small. Meanwhile, the public should be made aware of the phototoxicity of the species.

LONG-TERM STRATEGY

Herbivores/pathogens

Biological control could be considered as an appropriate alternative, though little is known about potential biocontrol organisms feeding or growing on *H. mantegazzianum* in the Caucasus. The International Institute of Biological Control has established links with the All-Union Scientific Research Institute for Plant Protection (in the former USSR), which should facilitate field surveys of *H. mantegazzianum* in the Caucasus, when funding becomes available (Fowler and Schroeder, 1990). Biocontrol is based on the principle that an introduced species arrives without an associated complement of pathogens and pests which normally keep it under control in its native country. A biocontrol programme is long and expensive, taking at least 4–5 years. It involves collecting pests and pathogens from the host's native country followed by a quarantine period to free the potential biocontrol agent from unwanted parasites and diseases. Host specificity trials follow, then release into a controlled environment and subsequently release into the wild. A biocontrol programme is generally a very effective means of control, but it does not normally eradicate a nuisance species.

H. mantegazzianum contains both linear and angular furocoumarins;

the toxicity and complexity of these chemicals interferes with the growth and metabolism of most herbivores. This results in the fauna being dominated by extreme specialists (Berenbaum, 1981), which can be an advantage when trying to isolate suitable predators for screening as biocontrol agents.

Although many native Umbelliferae herbivores have been recorded on *H. mantegazzianum* in the UK, only a limited number of species were found to cause quantifiable, though low damage, during a study by Sampson (1990, 1994). These species include the leaf chewers *Phaedon tumidulus* (Coleoptera), *Epermenia chaerophyllella, Agonopterix heraclearia* and *A. ciliella* (Lepidoptera); the leaf miners *Euleia heraclei* and *Phytomyza spondylii* (Diptera); the sap suckers; *Philaenus spumaris* and *Eupteryx aurata* (Homoptera); and the flower feeder *Depressaria pastinacella* (Lepidoptera). Because of the prolific growth rate of *H. mantegazzianum* it is unlikely that insects could cause enough damage to reduce growth of the species seriously and prevent it from flowering (Sampson, 1990, 1994).

The only observations of pathogens of *H. mantegazzianum* in Great Britain have been *Sclerotina sclerotiorum*, an agricultural disease (Williamson and Forbes, 1982), various aphid-transmitted virus diseases, powdery mildew *Erysiphe heraclei*, an unidentified soft rot in the roots (Sampson, 1994) and *Melanochaeta asteorae* (Fowler *et al.*, 1991). In Latvia, *Ascochyta heraclei* has been recorded (Fowler *et al.*, 1991). However, there are no records of the amount of damage these potential biocontrol agents cause to *H. mantegazzianum* or records of whether they weaken the tap root thus preventing or delaying flowering in the following year.

Genetic manipulation

Hybrids between *H. mantegazzianum* and *H. sphondylium* have occasionally been reported in Ireland (Wyse Jackson, 1989), Scotland and England (Stewart and Grace, 1984). The hybrids are morphologically intermediate between the parents, but most of the seeds are usually sterile (Wyse Jackson, 1989). The hybrids only occur where the two species grow at the same site (Stewart and Grace, 1984). However, the possibility of eliminating *H. mantegazzianum* by hybridizing it with *H. sphondylium* would be impractical and unlikely to succeed, not only because of the large amount of pollen transfer needed, but also because the hybrid adopts *H. mantegazzianum* characteristics (Stewart and Grace, 1984). The latter would exacerbate the problem of phototoxic sap and cause unwanted evolutionary changes in *H. sphondylium* (Stewart and Grace, 1984).

There is clearly a great need for more research into areas of potential herbivores and pathogens, biocontrol agents and genetic manipulation before any form of biological control can be contemplated.

CONCLUSION

H. mantegazzianum is an invasive alien weed with prolific powers of reproduction. Unless it is subjected to some form of management or control, it is
likely to increase and spread, particularly in places of reduced or declining
management. *H. mantegazzianum* can be eradicated if a committed and co-
ordinated control programme, using the correct techniques and strategies, is
embarked upon.

As the plant is perpetuated from seed, a key factor in its control is totally
to prevent it from seeding. Furthermore, as plants require a minimum of 2–4
years to come to flower, there is a corresponding opportunity to apply
control treatments during the vegetative phase. The public needs to be
clearly informed of the hazardous nature of the sap to the skin of humans in
combination with sunlight. Local authorities should be urged to adopt a
carefully planned, long-term strategy which will effectively control or even
eradicate *H. mantegazzianum*.

REFERENCES

Agricultural Training Board (1990). *Working with Pesticides Guide*. The Regulations
and your Responsibilities. Nottingham: Schering Agriculture.

Andrews, A.H., Giles, C.J. and Thomsett, L.R. (1985). Suspected poisoning of a goat
by giant hogweed. *Veterinary Record*, **116**, 205–207.

Anonymous (1925). A new honey plant. *Bee World*. **6**, 154–155.

Berenbaum, M. (1981). Patterns of furanocoumarin distribution and insect herbivory
in the Umbelliferae. Plant chemistry and community structure. *Ecology*, **62**, 1254–
1266.

Bingham, I.J. (1989). *Giant Hogweed: the Problem and its Control*. Leaflet, Scottish
Agricultural College, Aberdeen.

Briggs, M. (1979). Giant hogweed—a poisonous plant. *BSBI News*, **21**, 27–28.

Burke, F. (1943). *Heracleum mantegazzianum* Som. et Lev. in Cheshire. *North
Western Naturalist*, **18**, 216.

Caffrey, J.M. (1994). Spread and management of *Heracleum mantegazzianum* (Giant
hogweed) along Irish river corridors. In L.C. de Waal, L.E. Child, P.M. Wade and
J.H. Brock (Eds) *Ecology and management of invasive riverside plants*, pp. 67–76.
Chichester: Wiley.

Camm. E., Buck, H.W.L. and Mitchell, J.C. (1976). Phytophotodermatitis from *Heracleum mantegazzianum*. *Contact Dermatitis*, **2** 68–72.

Clegg, L. and Grace, J. (1974). The distribution of *Heracleum mantegazzianum*
(Somm. and Levier) near Edinburgh. *Transaction of the Botanical Society of Edinburgh*, **42**, 233–229.

Coombes, A.J. (1985). *The Collingridge Dictionary of Plant Names*. London: Collingridge.

Davies, D.H.K. and Richards, M.C. (1985). Evaluation of herbicides for control of
giant hogweed (*Heracleum mantegazzianum* Sommier and Levier) and vegetation regrowth in treated areas. *Tests of Agrochemicals and Cultivars*, **6** 100–101.

Department of Agriculture for Northern Ireland and Department of the Environment for Northern Ireland (1990). *Giant Hogweed. The Problem and its Control.*

Drever, J.C. and Hunter, J.A.A. (1970). Giant hogweed dermatitis. *Scottish Medical Journal*, **15**, 315–319.

Fowler, S.V. and Schroeder, D. (1990). Biological control of invasive plants in the UK—prospect and possibilities. In J. Palmer (Ed.), *The Biology and Control of Invasive Plants*, pp. 130–137. British Ecological Society. University of Wales, Cardiff.

Fowler, S.V., Holden, A.N.G. and Schroeder, D. (1991). The possibilities for classical biological control of weeds on industrial and amenity land in the UK using introduced insect herbivores or plant pathogens. *Proceedings of the Brighton Crop Protection Conference—Weeds 1991.* **3**, 1173–1180.

Frohne, D. and Pfänder, H.J. (1981). Doldengewächse als Giftpflazen. *Deutscher Apotheker Zeitung*, **121**, 2269–2274.

Gray, E.G. and Noble. M. (1965). *Sclerotina* disease. *Scottish Agriculture*, **44**, 265–267.

Harwood, D.G. (1985). Giant hogweed and duckling. *Veterinary Record*, March 16, 300.

Hegi, G. (1931). *Illustriete Flora von Mitteleuropa*, 5/2, 1422–1427.

Hipkin, C.R. (1991). Phytophotodermatitis, *BSBI News*, **59**, 7–8.

Howes, F.N. (1979). *Plants and Beekeeping.* London: Faber & Faber.

Ivens, G.W. (Ed.) (1992). *The UK Pesticide Guide 1992.* Wallingford: CAB International and the British Crop Protection Council.

Kees, H. and Krumrey, G. (1983). *Heracleum mantegazzianum*—Zier—Staude, Unkraut und "Gifpflanze". *Gesunde Pflanzen*, **4**.

Lundström, H. (1984). Giant hogweed, *Heracleum mantegazzianum*, a threat to the Swedish countryside. *Weeds and Weed Control, 25th Swedish Weed Conference*, Uppsala **1**, pp. 191–200.

Lundström, H. (1989). New experiences of the fight against the giant hogweed, *Heracleum mantegazzianum. Weeds and Weed Control, 30th Swedish Crop Protection Conference,* Uppsala, **2**, pp. 51–58.

Lundström, H. and Darby, E. (1994). The *Heracleum mantegazzianum* (giant hogweed) problem in Sweden: suggestions for its management and control. In L.C. de Waal, L.E. Child, P.M. Wade and J.H. Brock (Eds), *Ecology and Management of Invasive Riverside Plants*, pp. 93–100 Chichester: Wiley.

Ministry of Agriculture, Fisheries, and Food (1985). *Guidelines for the Use of Herbicides on Weeds in or near Watercourses and Lakes.* Booklet B2078. London: HMSO.

Ministry of Agriculture, Fisheries and Food (1988). *Poisonous Plants and Fungi.* London: HMSO.

Ministry of Agriculture, Fisheries and Food, and Health and Safety Commission (1990). *Pesticides: Code of Practice for the Safe Use of Pesticides on Farms and Holdings.* London: HMSO.

Morton, J.K. (1978). Distribution of giant cow parsnip (*Heracleum mantegazzianum*) in Canada. *Canadian Field-Naturalist*, **92**(2), 182–185.

Neiland, M.R.M. (1986). *The distribution and ecology of giant hogweed* (H. mantegazzianum) *on the River Allan, and its control in Scotland.* BSc dissertation, University of Stirling.

Nelson, E.C. (1991). Small ad for giant hogweed. *BSBI News*, **57**, 26–27.

Pira, E., Romano, C., Sulotto, F., Pavan, I. and Monaco, E. (1989). *Heracleum mantegazzianum* growth phases and furocoumarin content. *Contact Dermatitis*, **21**, 300–303.

Pyšek, P. (1991). *Heracleum mantegazzianum* in the Czech Republic: dynamics of spreading from the historical perspective. *Folia Geobotanica et Phytotaxonomica*, **26**, 439–454.

Pyšek, P. (1994). Ecological aspects of invasion by *Heracleum mantegazzianum* in the Czech Republic. In L.C. de Waal, L.E. Child, P.M. Wade and J.H. Brock (Eds), *Ecology and Management of Invasive Riverside Plants*, pp. 439–454. Chichester: Wiley.

Pyšek, P. and Prach, K. (1994). How important are rivers for supporting plant invasions? In L.C. de Waal, L.E. Child, P.M. Wade and J.H. Brock (Eds), *Ecology and Management of Invasive Riverside Plants*, pp. 19–26. Chichester: Wiley.

Rubow, T. (1979). Bekaempelse af Kaempe-bjørnelko (*Heracleum mantegazzianum*). Meddelelse **81**, (1497), 1–4, *Statens Planteavlsforsøg*: Flakkebjerg.

Sampson, C. (1990). *Towards biological control of Heracleum mantegazzianum*. MSc thesis, Imperial College, University of London.

Sampson, C. (1994). Cost and impact of current control methods used against *Heracleum mantegazzianum* (giant hogweed) and the case for instigating a biological control programme. In L.C. de Waal, L.E. Child, P.M. Wade and J.H. Brock (Eds), *Ecology and Management of Invasive Riverside Plants*, pp. 55–65. Chichester: Wiley.

Schuldes, H. and Kübler, R. (1990). Okologie und Vergesell-Schaftung von *Solidago canadensis et gigantea, Reynoutria japonica et sachalinense, Impatiens glandulifera, Helianthus tuberosus, Heracleum mantegazzianum*. Ihre Verbreitung in Baden-Württemberg sowie Notwendigkeit und Möglichkeiten ihrer Bekämpfung. Baden-Württemberg: Ministeriums für Umwelt.

Schuldes, H. and Kübler, R. (1991). Neophyten als Problempflanzen im Naturschutz. *Arbeitsblätter zum Naturschutz* **12**, 1–16. Baden-Württemberg: Landesanstalt für Umweltschutz.

Schwabe, A. and Kratochwil, A. (1991). Gewässer-begleitende Neophyten und ihre Beurteilung aus Naturschutz Sicht unter besonderer Berücksichtigung Südwestdeutschlands. *NNA Berichte*, Vol. 4/1 (Special issue).

Stewart, F. and Grace, J. (1984). An experimental study of hybridization between *Heracleum mantegazzianum* Somm. and Lev. and *H. sphondylium* L. subsp. *sphondylium* (Umbelliferae). *Watsonia*, **15**, 73–83.

Tiley, G.E.D. (in press) *Control of Giant hogweed*. Technical note. Edinburgh: Scottish Agricultural College.

Tiley, G.E.D. and Philp, B. (1994). *Heracleum mantegazzianum* (giant hogweed) and its control in Scotland. In L.C. de Waal, L.E. Child, P.M. Wade and J.H. Brock (Eds), *Ecology and Management of Invasive Riverside Plants*, pp. 101–109. Chichester: Wiley.

Tutin, T.G. (1980). *Umbellifers of the British Isles*. BSBI Handbook No. 2. London: Botanical Society of the British Isles.

Wildlife and Countryside Act 1981. London: HMSO.

Williamson, J.A. and Forbes, J.C. (1982). Giant hogweed (*Heracleum mantegazzianum*): its spread and control with glyphosate in amenity areas. *Weeds, Proceedings of the 1982 British Crop Protection Conference*, pp. 967–972.

Vogt Andersen, U. (1994). Sheep grazing as a method of controlling *Heracleum mantegazzianum*. In L.C. de Waal, L.E. Child, P.M. Wade and J.H. Brock (Eds), *Ecology and Management of Invasive Riverside Plants*, pp. 77–91. Chichester: Wiley.

Wyse Jackson, M. (1989). Observations on the Irish distribution of a plant with serious public health implications: giant hogweed (*Heracleum mantegazzianum* Sommier and Levier). *Bulletin of the Irish Biogeographical Society*, **12**, 94–112.

12 Seasonal Dynamics of *Impatiens glandulifera* in Two Riparian Habitats in Central England

KAREL PRACH*
International Centre of Landscape Ecology, Loughborough University, UK

INTRODUCTION

Impatiens glandulifera is an introduced species to Europe which continues to expand predominantly in riparian habitats (Koenies and Glavac, 1979; Pyšek and Prach, 1994; Trewick and Wade, 1986) and is predicted to expand further (Beerling, 1994). This expansion is especially due to the dispersal of seeds by water currents (Lhotska and Kopecky, 1966) and to the occurrence of habitats along streams which are convenient for the establishment of the species. It is remarkable that this annual species is able to withstand competition by robust, competitively strong perennials, such as stinging nettle (*Urtica dioica*) often dominant in riparian sites, which are usually highly productive (Grime *et al.*, 1988). Because of this competitive environment, a reduction of *I. glandulifera* populations is predicted at various spatial and temporal scales during the growing season. The aim of the present study, undertaken in 1991, was to quantify the reduction of populations during the season under intensive interspecific competition. Predictability of the population reduction was considered. Another intention was to give arguments for timing of artificial eradication of the species.

MATERIALS AND METHODS

Populations of *Impatiens glandulifera* were regularly observed from April until September 1991 at two riparian localities in Leicestershire, central England: (a) Loughborough, along Blackbrook 0.5 km north-east of the

---

Permanent address: Botanical Institute of the Czech Academy of Sciences, Trebon, CZ-379 82 Czech Republic

Ecology and Management of Invasive Riverside Plants
Edited by L. C. de Waal, L. E. Child, P. M. Wade and J. H. Brock
© 1994 John Wiley & Sons Ltd

village of Shepshed (National Grid Reference SK48/20); and (b) Leicester, in the nature reserve of Narborough Bog on the left bank of the River Soar SSW of the town (National Grid Reference SP54/97 and 54/98).

Six, and five 1 m^2 plots, respectively, were fixed in the first half of April 1991. The pattern of *I. glandulifera* seedlings was mapped in all the plots, which enabled repeated identification of the individuals. Numbers of *Urtica dioica* shoots were counted in the plots and total cover, excluding *I. glandulifera*, was estimated by eye. In two plots at each locality, the height of *I. glandulifera* individuals was measured at intervals of 2 weeks and later in the season at monthly intervals. On the same dates, the height of *U. dioica* was measured in the close vicinity (up to 5 cm) of *I. glandulifera* individuals. The initial numbers of individuals measured in detail were 104 for Blackbrook and 100 for Narborough Bog.

Relations between surviving *I. glandulifera* and various population and community characteristics in the plots were evaluated using common methods of statistical analysis. Relative height of *I. glandulifera* individuals was defined as height of *I. glandulifera* subdivided by the maximum height of *U. dioica* growing up to 5 cm away from each *I. glandulifera* individual. The influence of this characteristic on survival of *I. glandulifera* was tested by the χ^2 test.

The initial occurrence of the seedlings and the final distribution of fruiting plants was mapped in both localities. This is shown for Narborough Bog in Figure 12.1.

RESULTS AND DISCUSSION

The maximum density of *I. glandulifera* was observed at Narborough Bog: 70 plants m^2. Beerling (1990) in a study of three *I. glandulifera* populations in two South Wales locations recorded initial densities of 70, 140 and 284 seedlings/m^2.

A substantial reduction in population size was evident in both localities comparing the areas occupied by seedlings and by adults of *I. glandulifera*. The distribution of both categories is presented in Figure 12.1 for Narborough Bog. The course of the reduction of the populations is shown for each sample plot in Figure 12.2. The highest mortality of individuals was observed in the second half of May and the first half of June. This period can be considered critical for the development of the populations. The population reduction in this period was more pronounced in the Narborough Bog population. Beerling (1990), for his three populations, observed mortality between March and July to be 28, 56 and 60%, respectively, resulting in stands of 50–70 adult plants m^2. This mortality of *I. glandulifera* seedlings was density dependent. There are probably great differences in the intensity and timing

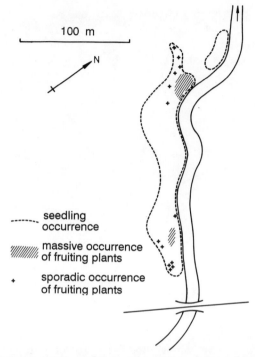

Figure 12.1 Areas occupied by seedlings and adults of *Impatiens glandulifera* in the Narborough Bog nature reserve, England; April and September 1991

of such a reduction (see also Perrins *et al.*, 1990, who observed prolonged reduction until the end of summer). However, the individuals which survived until the second half of June had a high probability of reaching maturity.

The relative height of *I. glandulifera* individuals was the best criterion of whether an individual survived or not. If the relative plant height dropped below a half after 15 May, the probability of survival was low. The χ^2 value was 41.1 (critical value 7.9 for P = 0.005, data for the Narborough Bog population only). The time since May was used in this calculation because before this date the relation between the height of *I. glandulifera* and *U. dioica* was not negative (Table 12.1).

Table 12.1 presents the relationships between the height of *I. glandulifera* and the height of *U. dioica* in current or previous dates using correlation coefficients. The positive effect of *U. dioica* on the growth of *I. glandulifera* in early season became negative in the second half of May (columns 2 and 3). At the end of the season, the effect was again positive, when there was already no or low competitive exclusion. The taller, but thinner, individuals of *I. glandulifera* in the dense cover of *U. dioica* evidently collapsed more easily during the period of rapid growth than the stronger, though smaller,

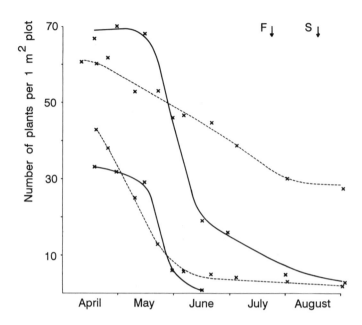

Figure 12.2 Decrease in number of individuals of *Impatiens glandulifera* in 1-m² plots during the 1991 season in Narborough Bog (——) and Black Brook (- - - -) England. Start of flowering (F) and of seed release (S) are indicated

Table 12.1. Correlations between heights of *Impatients glandulifera* and *Urtica dioica* in sampling plots of 1 m² in Narborough Bog

Date	1 *I. glandulifera* current and previous date	2 *I. glandulifera* vs. *U. dioica* current date	3 *I. glandulifera* vs. *U. dioica* previous date	4 *U. dioica* current and previous date
17 April	—	0.631	—	—
30 April	0.763	0.471	0.386	0.748
14 May	0.636	0.192	0.122	0.810
29 May	0.302	0.032	−0.032	0.881
15 June	−0.303	−0.527	−0.377	0.559
28 June	0.855	−0.431	−0.409	0.567
31 July	0.481	0.652	0.558	−0.145
1 September	0.97	not enough data		0.481

individuals (see the negative correlation in middle June in column 1). In general, the correlations between the height in the current and the previous dates are not strong during the whole season in either species (columns 1 and 4). This implies the low predictability and high role of randomness in the population development. *I. glandulifera* was able to exploit even small random openings in the dense *U. dioica* cover caused, for example, by wind action. The population development of both species was affected especially in some plots by the expansion of *Galium aparine*, a creeper which caused the collapse of many individuals of *I. glandulifera* and *U. dioica* at the height of summer (see the coefficients at the end of July in columns 1 and 4). This can be considered as a random biotic disturbance.

There is evidence, from the results, that predicting the fate of any particular individual using the variables measured in this study was difficult early in the season. Over the whole season, various external factors can influence the population dynamics: floods, trampling and wind. These factors interfere with inter- and intraspecific competition and can mask the competitive effects. Table 12.2 summarizes the tested relationships between surviving individuals of *I. glandulifera* and various community and population characteristics.

CONCLUSIONS

The results suggest that no measured criterion of plant growth enabled predictions to be made about the reduction of population size in *I. glandulifera* according to the situation early in the season. However, despite the low predictability of the fate of particular individuals, the remarkable reduction of a whole population during a season can be expected in competitive environments typical of riparian sites. The only criterion with good predictive cap-

Table 12.2. Correlations between number of surviving individuals of *Impatiens glandulifera* and various community and population characteristics, on the basis of observations in 1 m² plots

	No. of survivors of *I. glandulifera*
Initial density of *I. glandulifera*	NS
Heights of *I. glandulifera* in early season	NS
Initial density of *Urtica dioica*	NS
No. of shoots of *U. dioica* in close vicinity of *I. glandulifera*	NS
Initial height of *U. dioica*	NS
Total cover of other species	NS
Relative height of *I. glandulifera* after 15 May	Highly significant

ability was the relative height of *I. glandulifera* individuals later in the season. This criterion integrates various causes, but ultimately expresses the competitive effect of surrounding vegetation.

Thinking about artificial eradication of *Impatiens glandulifera*, it can be concluded that: (a) cutting or pulling before flowering is optimal (Beerling, 1990; Gunn, 1986); (b) herbicide application should be made before flowering and is not necessary earlier than mid-June, because before this date substantial reductions of *I. glandulifera* populations can be expected to occur naturally both in number of individuals and in the area occupied by a population. This fits well with the results of Beerling (1990), who, in assessing the efficacy of 2,4-D in controlling *I. glandulifera*, concluded that application before the end of June is essential if the herbicide is to prevent viable seed being set as well as to ensure the destruction of the plants.

ACKNOWLEDGEMENTS

I thank Derek Lovejoy Partnership and the International Centre of Landscape Ecology, University of Loughborough for sponsorship of the research. I thank Dr P. M. Wade for organizing my stay and the English correction of this paper, and Dr Wade, G. Colonello, Karla Vackova and my wife Eva for their help in the field.

REFERENCES

Beerling, D.J. (1990). *The ecology and control of Japanese knotweed* (Reynoutria japonica) *and Himalayan balsam* (Impatiens glandulifera) *on river banks in South Wales*. PhD thesis, University of Wales, Cardiff.

Beerling, D.J. (1994). Predicting the response of the introduced species *Fallopia japonica* and *Impatiens glandulifera* to global climatic change. In L.C. de Waal, L.E. Child, P.M. Wade and J.H. Brock (Eds), *Ecology and Management of Invasive Riverside Plants*, pp. 135–139. Chichester: Wiley.

Grime, J.P., Hodgson, J.G. and Hunt, R. (1988). *Comparative Plant Ecology. A Functional Approach*. London: Unwin Hyman.

Gunn, I.D.M. (1986). *Biology and control of Japanese knotweed* (*Reynoutria japonica*) *and Himalayan balsam* (*Impatiens glandulifera*) *on river banks*. MSc thesis, UWIST, Cardiff.

Koenies, H. and Glavac, V. (1979). The ability of *I. glandulifera* to compete on river banks of the River Fulda near Kassel, West Germany. *Philippia*, **4**, 47–49.

Lhotska, M. and Kopecky, K. (1966). Zur Verbreitungsbiologie und Phytozönologie von *Impatiens glandulifera* Royle an den Flussystemen der Svitava, Svratka und oberen Odra. *Preslia*, **38**, 376–385.

Perrins, J., Fitter, A. and Williamson, M. (1990). What makes *Impatiens glandulifera* invasive? In J. Palmer (Ed.), *The Biology and Control of Invasive Plants*, pp. 8–33, British Ecological Society, University of Wales, Cardiff.

Pyšek, P. and Prach, K. (1994). How important are rivers for supporting plant invasions? In L.C. de Waal, L.E. Child, P.M. Wade and J.H. Brock (Eds), *Ecology and Management of Invasive Riverside Plants*, pp. 19–26. Chichester: Wiley.

Trewick, S. and Wade, P.M. (1986). The distribution and dispersal of two alien species of *Impatiens*, waterway weeds in the British Isles. *Proceedings 7th International European Weed Research Society/Association of Applied Biologists Symposium on Aquatic Weeds*, pp. 351–356 Loughborough.

13 Predicting the Response of the Introduced Species *Fallopia japonica* and *Impatiens glandulifera* to Global Climatic Change

DAVID J. BEERLING

Department of Animal and Plant Sciences, P.O. Box 601, University of Sheffield, Sheffield, S10 2UQ, UK

INTRODUCTION

The distribution limits of plant taxa have long been correlated by plant geographers with climatic variables (Iversen, 1944). However, such correlations provide no indication of the physiological mechanisms involved in limiting plant distributions. Woodward (1988) provided a mechanistic approach based on plant survival at low temperatures and the length of the growing season required by different types of vegetation to complete their life cycle. This analysis has been used by Beerling (1993) for *Fallopia japonica* (Houtt.) Ronse Decraene and *Impatiens glandulifera* (Royle), two introduced weed species widespread throughout north-western Europe (Di Castri *et al.*, 1990).

Beerling (1993) produced maps showing the spread of *F. japonica* and *I. glandulifera* under an increase of 1.5 and 4.5°C in surface–air temperature. These values are the minimum and maximum increases predicted to occur by General Circulation Models (GCMs) as a resulting of a doubling in the atmospheric CO_2 concentration (Mitchell *et al.*, 1990). In this paper, the same approach has been adopted to produce maps showing the northward spread of both species for a mean temperature rise of 2.5°C, which represents the "best guess" of the Intergovernmental Panel on Climate Change (Houghton *et al.*, 1992). This type of predictive approach gives information on changes in the distribution of individual species based on a model derived from explicit physiological considerations. The approach represents a "halfway house" solution to the problem of predicting changes in plant distribution to global change in that it is neither fully mechanistic or correla-

Ecology and Management of Invasive Riverside Plants
Edited by L. C. de Waal, L. E. Child, P. M. Wade and J. H. Brock
© 1994 John Wiley & Sons Ltd

tive. Best estimates will be achieved through mechanistic process-based models (Melillo et al., 1993) because these incorporate the direct effects of increased CO_2 concentrations on plant physiological processes. The "quick fix" solution represented by correlative models (Prentice et al., 1992) produces enticing maps but these cannot include how relationships between plant distribution and climatic variables (e.g. soil water availability) may change under increased concentrations of atmospheric CO_2.

METHODS

Full details of the method are given by Beerling (1993). Briefly, the method involves establishing (i) the northern European distribution of the plant species from published data, (ii) records of absolute minimum temperatures and the heat sums (used as a measure of the growing season) for climate stations covering northern Europe (data from Müller, 1982) and (iii) climate correlations, by comparing presence and absence of the plant species with the geographical location of the climate stations. To incorporate the effects of a global rise in temperature, the absolute minimum temperatures and growing season lengths, in day-degrees, were recalculated for a 2.5°C rise. This was done by simply adding the average degree rise predicted by the GCMs to the present absolute minimum temperatures and mean daily temperatures. A similar approach has been used to predict global changes in vegetation structure for a doubling of CO_2 concentration (Woodward, 1992). These new values were then compared with the threshold values established by the climate correlations to determine whether a species would be capable of surviving.

CLIMATE CHANGE AND THE DISTRIBUTION OF *F. JAPONICA* AND *I. GLANDULIFERA*

Current projections by GCMs of temperature and soil moisture alterations as a result of increases in the concentration of greenhouse gases will have many effects on the distribution of plants. Some of the most important are (i) an extended growing season in northern regions, (ii) species with a predominantly lowland distribution which will expand to higher altitudes and (iii) species with northern distribution limits which will advance northwards (Hendry and Grime, 1990).

Figure 13.1a and b show the extended northern limits of the distribution of both alien species in north-west Europe. These maps show only the *potential* expansion of species distributions (i.e. where the modified climate has become suitable for the growth of either species according to the predictions

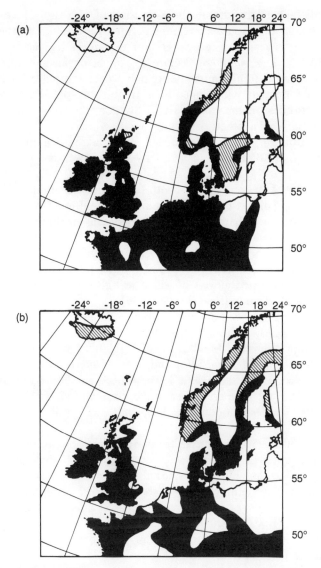

Figure 13.1 Present (■) and predicted (▨) extension of the northern distribution limits of (a) *Fallopia japonica* and (b) *Impatients glandulifera* based on a global surface–air temperature increase of 2.5°C

of the climate correlations). In practice, it may well be very different from the *realized* distributions. Such differences may arise through growth traits affecting the threshold values determined from the climate correlations. For *F. japonica*, the map (Figure 13.1a) shows a spread around southern Sweden and towards higher latitudes on the west coast of Norway. The expansion in Sweden is confined to southern regions because the climate on the east coast has a growing season far too short and minimum temperatures are well below $-30.2°C$. *I. glandulifera* (Figure 13.1b), being an annual, is not constrained by absolute minimum winter temperatures and has a lower predicted heat sum requirement. Consequently it is able to spread northwards into very high latitudes on the east coast of Sweden, the west coast of Norway and even to parts of northern Finland.

These distribution maps are produced after making a number of assumptions (Beerling, 1993). These can be briefly summarized as

(i)   a blanket $2.5°C$ rise ignores both latitudinal variations in temperature that are predicted by the GCMs and seasonal temperature trends;

(ii) GCMs predict that the difference between maximum and minimum yearly temperatures will increase markedly, resulting in an increased frequency of high-temperature events (Wigley, 1985);

(iii) the competitive interactions between other plant species are not incorporated, the distributions of which will also be changing at individualistic rates of migration (Huntley, 1991);

(iv) no attempt has been made to forecast changes at the southern limit of either species, although it is likely that these will occur under a changing climate (Melillo *et al.*, 1990). Factors controlling the southern limit of *F. japonica* and *I. glandulifera* are unknown, but for other species southern and lower altitudinal limits are likely to be controlled by temperature-sensitive competition with southerly distributed species (Woodward, 1988) and water availability.

In conclusion, the maps produced are derived from physiological consideration of plant processes in relation to temperature and may be regarded as "tools" for generating hypotheses testable by experiments. Firmer predictions, based on the method outlined above, require experimental investigations into how the length of the growing season affects the growth of these species and the critical evaluation of the effects of low temperatures on *F. japonica* rhizome and shoot survival. Current work along these lines is in progress at the University of Sheffield.

ACKNOWLEDGEMENTS

I am extremely grateful to Mr D.R. Ascroft for supplying the base maps of north-west Europe.

REFERENCES

Beerling, D.J. (1993) The impact of temperature on the northern distribution limits of the introduced species *Fallopia japonica* and *Impatiens glandulifera*. *Journal of Biogeography*, **20**, 45–53.

Di Castri, F., Hansen, A.J. and Debussche, M. (Eds) (1990). *Biological Invasions in Europe and the Mediterranean Basin*, Dordrecht: Kluwer.

Hendry, G.A.F. and Grime, J.P. (1990). Effects on plants: natural vegetation In M.G.R. Cannell and M.D. Hooper (Eds), *The Greenhouse Effect and Terrestrial Ecosystems of the UK*, pp. 27–31. Institute of Terrestrial Ecology Research Publication No 4. London: HMSO.

Houghton, J.T., Callander, B.A. and Varney, S.K. (1992). *Climate Change 1992: The Supplementary Report to the IPCC Scientific Assessement*. Cambridge: Cambridge University Press.

Huntley, B. (1991). How plants respond to climate change: migration rates, individualism and the consequences for plant communities. *Annals of Botany (Supplement)*, **67**, 15–22.

Iversen, J. (1944). *Viscum, Hedera* and *Ilex*, as climatic indicators. *Geologisk Frenings Frhandlingar*, **66**, 463–483.

Melillo, J.M., Callaghan, T.V., Woodward, F.I., Salati, E. and Sinha, S.K. (1990). Effects on ecosystems. In J.T. Houghton, G.J. Jenkins and J.J. Ephraums (Eds), *Climate Change: The IPCC Scientific Assessment*, pp. 283–310. Cambridge: Cambridge University Press.

Melillo, J.M., McGuire, A.D., Kicklighter, D.W., Moore, B., Vorosmarty, C.J. and Schloss, A.L. (1993). Global climate change and terrestrial net productivity. *Nature*, **363**, 234–240.

Mitchell, J.F.B., Manabe, S., Tokioka, T. and Meleshko, V. (1990). Equilibrium and climate change and its implications for the future. In J.T. Houghton, G.J. Jenkins and J.J. Ephraums (Eds), *Climate Change: The IPCC Scientific Assessment*, pp. 131–172. Cambridge: Cambridge University Press.

Müller, M.J. (1982). *Selected Climatic Variables for a Global Set of Standard Stations for Vegetation Science*. The Hague: Dr W. Junk Publishers.

Prentice, I.C., Cramer, W., Harrison, S.P., Leemans, R., Monserud, R.A. and Soloman, A.M. (1992). A global biome model based on plant physiology and dominance, soil properties and climate. *Journal of Biogeography*, **19**, 117–134.

Woodward, F.I. (1988). Temperature and the distribution of plant species. In F.I. Woodward and S.P. Long (Eds), *Plants and Temperature*, Symposium of the Society for Experimental Biology. **42**, pp. 59–75. Cambridge: Company of Biologist.

Woodward, F.I. (1992). A review of the effects of climate on vegetation: ranges, competition and composition. In R.L. Peters and T. Lovejoy (Eds), *Global Warming and Biological Diversity*. New Haven: Yale University Press,

Wigley, T.M.L. (1985). Climatology: impact of extreme events. *Nature*, **316**, 106–107.

14 Reproductive Biology and Fertility of *Fallopia japonica* (Japanese Knotweed) and its Hybrids in the British Isles

JOHN P. BAILEY

Botany Department University of Leicester, UK

INTRODUCTION

In Europe we are used to treating *Fallopia japonica* as a problem that needs solving. This has not always been the case; an early sales list (von Siebold, 1856) gives a number of uses in addition to the obvious horticultural one. Good forage for livestock, stabilization of sand dunes, nectar for bees, tonic principles in the rhizome and even the attractive dead stems could be used to make matches. Even in modern times, reference has been made to the plant's value as a nectar source and for dune stabilization (Locandro, 1978). Attempts have been made to establish its potential as a biomass producer crop (Callaghan *et al.*, 1984). This paper aims to take a more disinterested view of the plant and its close relatives and their performance in the British Isles.

Fallopia japonica is native to large areas of China, Korea and Japan, the closely related *F. sachalinensis* has a more northerly distribution, sympatric with *F. japonica* in parts of Japan, but extending on its own, north into the Kurile and Sachalin islands. These plants belong to the Polygonaceae, or rhubarb family, and may be found under a number of names in the literature, any one of which is valid depending on views of the taxonomy of the group. Thus, it is *Polygonum cuspidatum* based on splitting *Polygonum* L. *sensu lato* into genera; *Reynoutria japonica* if *Reynoutria* and *Fallopia* are distinct genera; and *Fallopia japonica* based on the recent morphological and biosystematic evidence that points to the amalgamation of the two genera under *Fallopia*.

The genus *Fallopia* is divided into (i), section *Reynoutria*, containing the erect rhizomatous perennials *F. japonica* and *F. sachalinensis* (ii) section

Ecology and Management of Invasive Riverside Plants
Edited by L. C. de Waal, L. E. Child, P. M. Wade and J. H. Brock
© 1994 John Wiley & Sons Ltd

Sarmentosae, the climbing perennials *F. baldschuanica* and *F. multiflora*; and (iii) section *Fallopia*, the climbing annuals *F. convolvulus* and *F. dumetorum*.

There are three giant knotweeds naturalized in the British Isles. Firstly, *F. sachalinensis*: this is by far the largest plant of the three and is easily distinguished by its much larger leaves with cordate bases. This taxon, although strongly rhizomatous, does not occupy anything like the range of *F. japonica* and generally appears to be much less invasive than it. Next there is a dwarf version, *F. japonica* var. *compacta*: this is sometimes grown in gardens, but is rarely found naturalized in this country, although, when it is, it can occupy quite large areas (e.g. North Ledaig, Scotland). *F. japonica* var. *japonica* needs little introduction in terms of its tenacious and invasive habits, though it seems much more at home in the west of the country. It was originally introduced as a garden plant, where its exotic appearance, ease of growth and good display of flowers must initially have charmed the Victorian gardener.

It is worthwhile spending some time looking at the history of the plants in Britain as this may have some bearing on the peculiar population structure found in this country. Its date of introduction to the British Isles is often given as 1825, although this is highly unlikely, for, although the plant was originally described by Houttuyn in 1777, it was probably only from dried material. It was then, to all intents and purposes, lost, as, not only was Houttuyn's book little studied by European botanists, but he put the plant erroneously in the class Decandria Trigyna, which meant that it was separated from the other polygonaceous plants. Von Siebold brought some back from his travels in Japan and independently named it *Polygonum cuspidatum* in 1846. The discovery that this and *Reynoutria japonica* were the same plant was not made until the first quarter of the twentieth century. It is certain that, by 1848, von Siebold was selling from his nursery in Leiden one mother plant and 25 strong plants all for the then large sum of 500 francs. This ties in well with Hooker's (1880b) recollection that it had been cultivated at Kew for a quarter of a century and that it had originally been sent from Holland. This may have been the only introduction of *F. japonica* to the British Isles and all plants here may be of clonal origin, though this would require work in allozymes or DNA restrictions fragment length polymorphisms to confirm it. This would probably be a worthwhile venture, since if it is all genetically identical this could have important implications regarding the use of biological control agents. Examination of a range of specimens from North America indicates that a wider genetic base is to be found in these populations.

Published counts record *F. japonica* with $2n = 44$ and $2n = 88$, *F. japonica* var. *compacta* with $2n = 44$, and *F. sachalinensis* with $2n = 44$ (Bolkhouskikh, 1969). Results at Leicester indicated that the standard *F. japonica* was only present at the octoploid level ($2n = 88$) (Bailey and Stace, 1992). In addition, a number of clones were found with the previously unknown number of $2n = 66$; since these plants were morphologically intermediate between *F. japonica* and *F. sachalinensis* (some having been even mistakenly identified as *F. sachalinensis*), a hybrid origin was suspected. This was ultimately confirmed by a programme of artificial hybridization. Knowledge of the morphology of the hybrid plants considerably honed down our perception of what characterized *F. japonica* in the British Isles. This in turn led to a cytological examination of a number of section *Reynoutria* plants naturalized in this country.

SEX EXPRESSION

The earliest descriptions of *F. japonica* are not very helpful, since the presence of vestigial anthers in the male-sterile plants led to their being termed hermaphrodite. The illustration in Houttuyn (1777) is not detailed enough to distinguish the sex of the plant depicted, though the type specimen from Geneva from which the drawing was presumably made is certainly male-sterile. The first clear illustration of *F. japonica* is that in de Vriese (1849) and is clearly male-sterile. This is of particular interest since the plant came from von Siebold's nursery at Leiden, the most probable source of the initial European introduction, and still probably the most commonly found clone in this country.

Hooker (1880a) described *Reynoutria* as dioecious, and in the case of *F. japonica* var. *compacta* he gave a detailed description of male-fertile and male-sterile flowers. *F. japonica* (Hooker, 1880b) was described as dioecious, but no mention was made of male-fertile plants in Britain; *F. sachalinensis* (1881) was listed as "? polygamous". In all three cases it is the male-sterile plant that is illustrated. Ohwi (1965), in the *Flora of Japan*, and Webb (1964), in *Flora Europaea*, both listed section *Reynoutria* taxa as dioecious. Conolly (1977), on the other hand, suggested that in *F. sachalinensis* male-fertile, male-sterile and hermaphrodite individuals may be found, recalling the polygamous condition noted by Hooker. Conolly also reported that *F. sachalinensis* plants from Amroth, Wales (Specimen no. P68) had male-fertile, male-sterile and hermaphrodite flowers all on a single inflorescence. The observation at Leicester of apparently good seeds on a male-fertile plant of *F. japonica* var. *compacta* also suggested that the sex expression of these taxa might be more complex than straight dioecy. Conolly (1977) also commented on the rarity of male-fertile plants of *F. japonica* and the relative imbalance of male to female clones in *F. sachalinensis*. Bailey and Conolly (1985) found a positive correlation between male-sterility and the octoploid chromosome level in *F. japonica*.

The introduction of cytological data to this problem in *F. japonica* had an immediate, and rather unexpected, outcome. What Conolly (1977) had taken to be the rare male-fertile *F. japonica* plants were now revealed to be hybrids

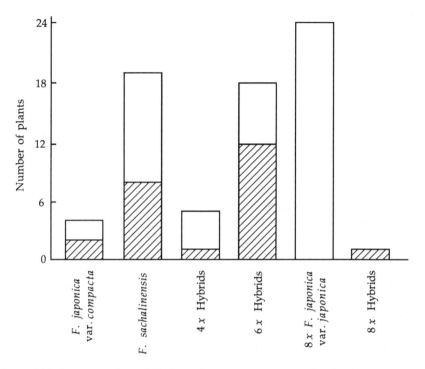

Figure 14.1 Sex expression of *Fallopia Reynoutria* taxa, growing in the British Isles: (□) male sterile. (▨) male fertile

between *F. japonica* and *F. sachalinensis*. Every clone of *F. japonica* var. *japonica* examined in the British Isles by me has been male-sterile. Figure 14.1 shows the distribution of sex expression in the British populations that have been cytologically examined so far. This is not, however, a random survey since it includes virtually every male-fertile plant that I have been able to examine. In the country as a whole, the male-sterile *F. sachalinensis* is much more common than is indicated in the graph; the octoploid *F. japonica* is represented only by male-sterile plants, but even so this graph is not truly representative of the vast predominance of this clone in Britain. An example of the low frequency of male-fertile section *Reynoutria* plants may be gained from the fact that there are no known male-fertile plants growing in the wild in Leicestershire in contrast to hundreds of what, on morphological grounds, may be attributed to the male-sterile octoploid category. In *F. japonica* var. *compacta*, the sexes are more evenly balanced, though four plants can hardly be called a representative sample.

Whilst the male-sterile plants are easily characterized by their small included anthers, the male-fertile plants sometimes produce seed; this obviously implies that some clones are both male- and female-fertile. Male and female organs were measured in 19 clones of section *Reynoutria* plants; only newly opened flowers were chosen and dissected flower parts were measured under a stereo microscope with an eyepiece graticule. These plants could be divided into three groups on the basis of these measurements. Group one constitutes the male-steriles and is characterized by a gynoecium >1.1 mm/mg, a well-developed style, a stigma >0.3 mm long, with small empty anthers on short filaments. The second group may be termed female-sterile since the plants have short, poorly developed gynoecia lacking stigmatal development, and large well-filled anthers borne on long exserted filaments. The third group is intermediate, possessing large ovaries, well-developed stigmas and large filled anthers borne on long filaments. This group is morphologically hermaphrodite, but the question of whether its members can function as hermaphrodites is addressed later.

The *F. sachalinensis* plants examined were either male-sterile or hermaphrodite; this pattern of sex expression is known as gynodioecy and is thought by some to represent an intermediate stage in the evolution of dioecy from hermaphroditism. The *F. japonica* var. *compacta* plants examined were either male-sterile or female-sterile. However, the ability of the occasional flower on a female-sterile plant to set seed suggests that ovary development is not entirely suppressed in all flowers, and, following the usage of Stevens (1988), it is proposed to term them subdioecious. In *F. japonica* var. *japonica*, which probably occurs in gynodioecious populations in its native regions, only male-sterile plants are found in the British Isles, a finding that has important implications regarding propagation via sexual reproduction.

REPRODUCTIVE BIOLOGY

To ensure that we are dealing with sexually reproducing taxa, it is worth considering the ecology and pollination biology of these plants in their native habitats. The little published research on these aspects refers to the position in Japan.

Maruta (1983) in her study of *F. japonica* establishment on Mount Fuji, where at 2500 m above sea level it grows as a pioneer species, found recruitment from seed to be the norm for such populations. Tanaka (1966) found that both male-fertile and male-sterile stands were pollinated by flies, honey bees and wasps. From this it is clear that these are normal insect-pollinated sexually reproducing taxa and that there are other causes of the low seed set that is usually reported for these plants in Britain (Conolly, 1977). Accordingly, a study of pollen fertility, crossability, seed-set and seed viability was undertaken.

Two assessments of pollen fertility were made: staining with Müntzing's acetocarmine, and in-vitro germination. The latter was used because pollen staining only picks out the grains without cytoplasm and those whose cytoplasm is grossly deformed, and is not a very reliable indicator of pollen viability. Since the pollen is trinucleate when shed, it will not germinate in the absence of stigmas. In-vitro pollen germination assessments were carried out using Gamborgs B5 tissue culture medium (without hormones), 0.01% boric acid and 15 or 20% sucrose. This was dispensed into watch-glasses 2 cm in diameter containing section *Reynoutria* stigmas; a disc of cellophane was floated on top of this and fresh pollen tapped out onto the cellophane. After 1 or 2 h the cellophane was mounted on a microscope slide and the percentage of germinated pollen was counted (see Table 14.1). In general, the ratio between pollen staining and pollen germination was about 3:1. Notable exceptions are *F. baldschuanica* and the hybrid *F. japonica* var. *japonica* × *F. japonica* var. *compacta*, which had a germination rate of 0.65% against a stainability of 17.5%. This taxon in particular and the hexaploids in general had very irregular meiosis.

Table 14.1. In-vitro pollen germination in *Fallopia*

Taxon		Specimen no.	% Pollen germination	% Pollen stainability
F. baldschuanica		P174	5.49	49.1
F. japonica var. *compacta*		P99a	36.1	98.7
F. sachalinensis		P68	15.85	
		P55	29.8	
		P62	20.7	
	Mean		22.1	61
F. japonica var. *compacta*		P13	3.8	
x *F. sachalinensis* (4x)		P79c	9.13	
		P78a	11.1	
	Mean		8.0	17.5
F. japonica x *F. sachalinensis* (6x)		P75d	0.95	
		P32	12.3	
		P119	0	
	Mean		6.63	25
F. japonica x *F. japonica*		P76a	0.59	
var. *compacta*		P76b	0.72	
	Mean		0.65	17.5
F. japonica x *F. sachalinensis*		P50	27.32	
8 x		P51B	15.7	
	Mean		21.5	68

Having demonstrated that at least some fertile pollen is produced by section *Reynoutria* taxa and their hybrids, pollen–stigma interactions in this group of taxa were examined by placing newly opened flowers in water agar in a Petri dish and pollinating them with the appropriate pollen. After 24 or 48 h the gynoecia were fixed, stained using the aniline blue method (Chu Chou and Harberd, 1970) and examined using a fluorescence microscope for germination and germ-tube growth (Table 14.2). Stigmas of *F. japonica* were clearly compatible with the pollen of various hybrids in the section *Reynoutria*. The much greater pollen germination and penetration in the tetraploid and octoploid hybrids than in the hexaploid hybrids clearly mirrors the results of the meiotic analysis. Artificial pollination in the field showed that the pollen of *F. sachalinensis* and *F. japonica* var. *compacta* also germinated readily on *F. japonica* stigmas and produced viable hybrid seed. These results indicate that *F. japonica* in the British Isles is capable of seed production when presented with the pollen of the other species or hybrids in the section *Reynoutria* naturalized in the countryside.

The hermaphrodite plants such as male-fertile *F. sachalinensis* and the various hybrids are not generally capable of self-fertilization (Table 14.3). Other taxa included in this table are the native annual *F. dumetorum* and the commonly grown garden plant *F. baldschuanica* (Russian vine). *F. dumetorum* shows a very high degree of pollen penetration, with no trace of any incompatibility reaction. *F. baldschuanica*, on the other hand, showed good to very good pollen germination and penetration, but a very strong self-incompatibility reaction, the tubes being stopped in their tracks at the base of the stigma; this obviously accounts for the very poor seed-set on these plants. In contrast, there was little germination or penetration of selfed section *Reynoutria* stigmas and a hint of an incompatibility response in some of the crosses. The outcome of this in the British Isles, where all *F. japonica* var. *japonica* is male-sterile (though potentially fertile), is that pollination can lead only to the production of hybrid progeny; this taxon cannot reproduce sexually in this country.

HYBRIDS AND HYBRIDIZATION

It had been known for some time that male-fertile section *Reynoutria* taxa were extremely uncommon in Britain and comprised only *F. sachalinensis*, a few hybrids and even fewer plants of *F. japonica* var. *compacta*. In spite of this, in years without early autumn frosts, small amounts of viable seed were found on *F. japonica* plants many miles from the nearest source of section *Reynoutria* pollen. Seed and parental rhizomes were collected from 20 localities in Britain (see Table 14.4). Eleven out of 12 collections of seed from octoploid male-sterile *F. japonica* had 54 chromosomes; these plants turned out to be hybrids with *F. baldschuanica* (Bailey, 1988a). The other collection

Table 14.2. In-vivo pollen germination *Fallopia* section *Reynoutria* taxa

Stigma	Specimen no.	Pollen	Specimen no.	No. flowers	Pollen adhesion	Pollen germination	Pollen penetration
F. japonica	P179	*F. sachalinensis* x *F. japonica* var. *compacta* (4x)	P79c	11	++	++	++
F. japonica	P179		P78a	12	++	+++	+
F. japonica	P12		P78a	4	+++	+++	+
F. japonica var. *compacta*		*F. japonica* x *F. japonica* var. *compacta* (6x)	P76b	6	++	++	±
F. japonica	P179		P76a	14	+	+	++
F. japonica	P179		P76b	11	+	++	++
F. japonica	P12		P76a	8	+	+	±
F. japonica	P12	*F. japonica* x *F. sachalinensis* (6x)	P119	8	±	±	±
F. japonica	P179		P119	11	++	±	±
F. japonica var. *compacta*			P32	5	+	−	−
F. japonica	P179		P32	12	±	−	−
F. japonica	P179		P75d	13	++	±	±
F. japonica var. *compacta*			P75d	5	+	±	−
F. japonica	P179	*F. japonica* x *F. sachalinensis* (8x)	P51B	16	+++	+++	+++
F. japonica	P12		P51B	6	++	++	++
F. japonica var. *compacta*			P50	6	+++	+++	+++
F. japonica	P179		P50	14	++	++	++

Table 14.3. Pollen germination and growth on selfed male-fertile *Fallopia* taxa

Taxon	Specimen no.	No. stigmas examined	Pollen			Self-incompatibility
			attachment	germination	penetration	
F. dumetorum	P177	10	+++	+++	+++	–
F. baldschuanica	P174	30	+ to ++	+ to ++	+ to +++	
	P163	25	++ to ++++	+ to +++	+++	+++
F. sachalinensis	P55	10	+ to ++	–	–	–
	P62	20	±	±+	±±	
	P68	14	+	+	±±	±
F. japonica var. compacta	P173	33	–	–	–	–
	P99c	7	+	+	±	±
F. japonica 4x	P114	7	±	–	–	–
F. japonica var. comp x *F. sachalinensis*	P78a	5	++	+	–	–
F. japonica x *F. sachalinensis* 8x	P50	10	±	–	–	–
	P51B	20	±	±	±	–

Table 14.4 Chromosome numbers of seedlings from wild seed of *Fallopia* section *Reynoutria* taxa

Seedling chromosome number (2n)	Female parent *F. japonica* var. *compacta* 2n = 44		*F. sachalinensis* 2n = 44		*F. japonica* var. *japonica* 2n = 88	
	No. seed examined	No. locations	No. seed examined	No. locations	No. seed examined	No. locations
32			13	3		
44	4	1	13	3		
54					32	11
66			1	1	5	1

had 2n = 66 and, owing to the presence in the neighbourhood of a male-fertile *F. sachalinensis* plant, was found to be an *F. japonica* × *F. sachalinensis* hybrid. At the three locations of male-sterile *F. sachalinesis* examined, all the seedlings had 2n = 32 and were, once again, the progeny of *F. baldschuanica* pollen. Very few seeds were found on hermaphrodite plants of *F. sachalinensis* and these had 2n = 44 and were true *F. sachalinensis*. In view of the vast number of flowers that had not set seed in these considerable stands, the few seeds that were produced probably represent the rare breakdown of the incompatibility system. At one of these locations, one plant that was morphologically *F. sachalinensis* was hexaploid (2n = 66); this is thought to have arisen from an unreduced gamete. Similarly, in the large stands of male-fertile *F. japonica* var. *compacta* naturalized in Scotland, very little seed was produced, but that also bred true.

The hybrid between *F. japonica* and *F. sachalinensis* (*F.* × *bohemica*) is not uncommon in the British Isles. More than 20 stands have been examined cytologically, but many more could be added to this list, based solely on morphological characters. Surrey, in particular has been well examined for such plants. This hybrid has often been mistaken for *F. japonica* and is similarly very invasive; details of how to distinguish the two are given in Bailey (1988b). The tetraploid and octoploid hybrids of this combination are also important as sources of fertile pollen (unlike the more commonly found hexaploid plants), though male-fertile and male-sterile clones need to be virtually adjacent in order to produce significant amounts of seed.

SEED PRODUCTION

These plants are not ideal candidates for the student of reproductive biology, since they need to be quite large before they will flower, and their rhizomatous habit makes them most unwelcome at botanic gardens. Their late flowering can also cause problems, as in fact happened in 1986 when a cold late summer and early autumn caused the flowers often to drop without opening, effectively terminating a programme of controlled pollination and observations of seed-set. The problem of where to grow them was solved by rather a novel means at Leicester, when some large tiled redundant fish-tanks were filled with soil. These made ideal *Reynoutria* containment vessels and came complete with water supply. The autumn of 1987 provided a unique opportunity to estimate the seed production of a large collection, grown in comparable conditions, of mature cytologically known accessions in the presence of large amounts of compatible pollen.

The number of flowers on a single well-developed stem was estimated. Later in the season, stems were carefully harvested and the seed produced was counted, by hand in small samples, larger samples being estimated by weight. In spite of the very high number of flowers (up to 191 000), seed-set, with two notable exceptions, was <8% (Table 14.5). Even so, many of these plants appeared to be covered in seed, a sight not usually found in Britain. All the accessions in Table 14.5 are grown in our research beds, except for the last two *F. japonica* accessions, P183 and P184. A comparison of the data for these and the two *F. japonica* plants in the research plots is most instructive. Firstly, the two "wild" clones produced bigger stems with more flowers, probably as a result of not being restricted to a bay with other *Fallopia* plants. Secondly, there was between a 10- and 40-fold difference in percentage seed set between plants grown in the presence of suitable pollen and those isolated from it. Since seed had previously been examined from these "wild" stands, and found to be hybrid with *F. baldschuanica*, we can make a comparison between the two. I am not necessarily suggesting that *F. japonica* is less responsive to pollination by *F. baldschuanica* than by section *Reynoutria* pollen, merely that the sources of *F. baldschuanica* were further from the wild *F. japonica* than was the case with the section *Reynoutria* pollen and the cultivated *F. japonica* plants. Needless to say, the quantities of seed found on the "wild" *F. japonica* stands is quite high considering that it is hybrid between an octoploid with $2n = 88$ and a diploid with $2n = 20$.

The second part of this research was into the effect of sex-expression and ploidy on seed production. With regards to sex expression, the only valid comparison that we can see is between the hermaphrodite and male-sterile clones of *F. sachalinensis* and *F. japonica* var. *compacta*, (*F. japonica* var. *japonica* being only known from male-sterile plants in Britain). In *F. sachalinensis*, the hermaphrodite P55 produced fewer flowers than the male-sterile P115 (Table 14.5), though in such small samples it is not possible to be confident about this. The male-sterile plant was, however, much more successful as a female parent than was the hermaphrodite, although the latter bore an appreciable amount of seed. This is not the case in the wild in Wales, where

Table 14.5. Sex expression, flower production and seed set in *Fallopia* section *Reynoutria* taxa

Taxon	Specimen no.	Sex	Chromosome (2n)	No. flowers/stem	No. Seed set/stem	% Seed set	Cultivated (C) or Wild (W)
F. japonica var. *compacta*	P2a	Male-sterile	44	6176	516	8.4	C
F. sachalinensis	P55	Hermaphrodite	44	56560	2780	4.9	C
	P115	Male-sterile	44	100072	11323	11.3	C
F. sachalinensis x	P13	Hermaphrodite	44	24990	141	0.56	C
F. japonica var. *compacta*	P79c	Male-fertile	44	39778	5	0.01	C
	P78a	Hermaphrodite	44	52416	357	0.68	C
	P79a	Male-sterile	44	18754	6282	33.5	C
F. japonica x *F. sachalinensis*	P75b	Hermaphrodite	66	17685	6	0.03	C
	P75d	Hermaphrodite	66	78195	5	0.01	C
	P32	Hermaphrodite	66	169623	142	0.05	C
	P75c	Male-sterile	66	119195	790	0.07	C
	P31	Male-sterile	66	78909	248	0.31	C
F. japonica x *F. japonica* var. *compacta*	P76b	Male-fertile	66	21896	28	0.13	C
	P51B	Hermaphrodite	88	73798	607	0.82	C
F. japonica	P12	Male-sterile	88	113709	2800	2.46	C
	P179	Male-sterile	88	95045	6152	6.47	C
	P183	Male-sterile	(88)	191552	442	0.23	W
	P184	Male-sterile	(88)	191892	283	0.15	W

Chromosome numbers in brackets () have not yet been counted

the extensive stands of hermaphrodite *F. sachalinensis* at Amroth produced less than a handful of seed: a similar situation was found in the smaller stand at Brithdir (Caerynwch, Merioneth.).

None of the hexaploid (6*x*) plants have regular meiosis, but the 4*x* and 8*x* taxa all have good regular meiosis (Bailey and Stace, 1992). Overall, the hexaploids show extremely low seed set, the 6*x* hermaphrodite hybrid plants being at a double disadvantage, since their initial low fertility (due to irregular meiosis) is compounded by the inherently lower fecundity of the hermaphrodite plants.

VIABILITY OF SEED AND THE ESTABLISHMENT OF SEEDLINGS

In an examination of the role of seed-set in the spread of knotweeds, it must of course be established that such seed as is produced is actually viable. Accordingly, samples of seed were collected from "wild" sites around Britain. Justice (1941) recommends an after-ripening period at room temperature or a period of cold treatments. These seeds were usually given one week at 4°C in the dark and then transferred to 15°C and continuous light. Seeds with only a small amount of endosperm often succumbed to fungal attack at this stage. Table 14.6 gives the results for germination tests on seed collected in the wild in Britain from section *Reynoutria* species. The small numbers of seed involved reflect the difficulty in finding good seed on giant

Table 14.6. Germination rates of British wild-collected seed of *Fallopia* section *Reynoutria* taxa

Taxon	Locality	No. seeds	% Germination
F. japonica var. *compacta*	North Ledaig, Main Argyll	10	70
F. sachalinensis	Cheshunt, Herts.	30	56
F. japonica	Sileby, Leics.	45	46
	Criccieth, Caerns.	17	100
	Barmouth, Merioneth.	7	100
	Petersfield, S. Hants.	13	76
	Llangynadle, Caerns.	2	0
	Boston Lodge, Merioneth.	20	55
	Pwllheli, Caerns.	14	64
	Tyn Coed, Merioneth.	23	35
	Ironbridge, Salop.	11	45
	Pentrefelin, Caerns.	14	36
	Brithdir, Merioneth.	43	88
	Itchen Abbas, N. Hants.	17	94
	Ynys, Merioneth.	2	100
	Leicester, Leics.	21	71

knotweeds in Britain, notably in the remoter areas, where there is less likely to be any Russian vine. These germination rates are extremely good, particularly when you consider that all but the North Ledaig *F. japonica* var. *compacta* and the Brithdir *F. japonica* were pollinated by *F. baldschuanica*. British seed is ready to germinate when shed (Table 14.7).

As is only to be expected, much lower germination rates were found with seed from hybrid section *Reynoutria* taxa, whether in the wild or in the beds at Leicester (Table 14.8). As part of a separate investigation, seed was successfully germinated by embryo culture, the plants were grown on and the chromosomes were counted. Of eight hybrids examined, only two gave rise to euploid progeny, one tetraploid and one octoploid *F. japonica* x *F. sachalinensis*. Seed from hexaploid hybrids of the same combination gave aneuploid ranges between $2n = 48$ and 57, and $2n = 75$ to 77. The other tetraploid hybrids had been pollinated by *F. baldschuanica* and had $2n = 32$. Although no specific tests of longevity of the seed were made, one such sample from a tetraploid giant knotweed pollinated by a Russian vine had a very high germination rate after being stored at room temperature in the laboratory for more than 4 years.

Since seed was collected from places as far afield as Scotland, Wales, Hampshire and London, as well as Leicester, it is clear that production of viable seed on British *Reynoutria* plants is by no means an isolated phenomenon. This is in contrast with Conolly's (1977) findings that seed production was a rare event. This may well be related to changes in pollinator behaviour, for in the late 1970s and early 1980s hive bees were not usually seen visiting *Fallopia* plants, flies and the dipteran bee-mimics being the usual visitors. However, hive bees now commonly visit *Fallopia* plants, and it is suggested that the changing behaviour of hive bees in using the abundant nectar produced by Russian vine and section *Reynoutria* taxa is responsible for the appreciable amount of seed now found on section *Reynoutria* plants in the countryside.

Having shown that seed can be produced by British giant knotweed populations and that such seed is viable, the role of seedling establishment will now be considered. There are no known reports of section *Reynoutria* seedlings in the wild in Britain; and observations of seedings in the collection at Leicester are somewhat anecdotal.

In May 1985, a number of section *Reynoutria* seedlings were observed growing under a plant *F. japonica* in the experimental plots. Not wishing them to grow amongst the other plants, they were removed. In the same year, three more seedlings were found, looking every bit the aggressive pioneer, growing in the gutter and in between the paving slabs. They were not found the following year so it is not known whether they fell victim to the weather or to the ministrations of the gardening staff. These plants were probably *F. japonica* × *F. sachalinensis* hybrids. The requisite for section

Table 14.7. Seed storage period and germination rates of *Fallopia japonica*

Taxon *Fallopia* var.	Location	Vice-county	Wild (W) or cultivated (C)	Sample size	Storage period	% Germination
japonica	Sileby A	Leics.	W	22	5 months	77
japonica	Criccieth	Caerns.	W	17	5 months	100
japonica	Barmouth	Merioneth.	W	7	5 months	100
japonica	Sileby B	Leics.	W	23	5 months	17
japonica	Petersfield	S. Hants.	W	4	5 months	75
japonica	Boston Lodge	Merioneth.	W	20	17 months	55
japonica	Pwllheli	Caerns.	W	14	5 months	64
†*compacta*	Bendeloch	Argyll	W	10	4 months	70
japonica	Race Course	Leics.	C	72	1 month	53
†*japonica*	Llangynadle	Caerns.	W	20	2 days	40
†*japonica*	Markfield	Leics.	W	20	0 days	25
†*japonica*	Leicester	Leics.	W	20	0 days	45

On wet filter pulp at 15°C and continuous light, except those marked by, †, which were incubated at 20°C in 12-hr days; germination monitored for one month.

Table 14.8. Seed viability of hybrid Japanese knotweeds

Hybrid	Specimen no.	Wild (W) or cultivated (C)	Ploidy	% Germination
F. japonica var. *compacta* × *F. sachalinensis (artificial hybrid)*	P78a	C	$4x$	20
F. japonica × *F. sachalinensis*	P30	C	$6x$	15
	P29	C	$6x$	0
	P32	C	$6x$	0
	P31	C	$6x$	37
	P31	C	$6x$	38
	P52	W	$6x$	0
	P129	W	$6x$	6
	P130	W	$6x$	28
	P51	W	$8x$	0

Reynoutria seed production is the presence of a male-sterile plant with an adjacent male-fertile plant. This occurs at Caerynwch Hall (Merioneth), where in the large gardens are found *F. japonica* (male-sterile) and an hermaphrodite *F. sachalinensis*, along with a number of clones of *F. japonica* × *F. sachalinensis* hybrids. There is only circumstantial evidence that these hexaploid hybrids were established spontaneously, since the gardener could have germinated some of the hybrid seed produced there by *F. japonica*. Wild-collected seed of the parentage *F. japonica* × *F. baldschuanica* was overwintered outdoors at Leicester in the winter of 1985/86 and germinated naturally and freely in April and May 1986. Probably the best case of establishment of a section *Reynoutria* seed in the wild is the *F. japonica* × *F. baldschuanica* hybrid found growing in an abandoned railway goods yard in Haringay, London (Bailey, 1988a). Whilst it is certain that a hot summer and good autumn are required for the production of seed and a cold first winter is no bar to the ultimate germination of such seed, one can only speculate upon what conditions the first-year seedlings require in order to survive their first winter. Locandro (1978) observed that in May 1969 in the USA a number of seedlings from an *F. japonica* had germinated in the wild, but that 5 weeks later all were dead. His continued observations since that time suggest that establishment of plants from seed does not occur in his part of the country.

THE SPREAD OF *F. JAPONICA* IN THE BRITISH ISLES

Since *F. japonica* cannot reproduce itself sexually in the British Isles because of the absence of male-fertile clones, its spread must be by vegetative means. Conolly (1977) considered the main spread of the plant to be asexual, by mechanical fragmentation and dispersal of the rhizomes, usually the result of building or road-making schemes. She also suggested that floating stems may be able to establish new colonies downstream. A documented example of spread across sea-water has since been reported (H. McAllister, personal communication). He observed that westerly winds had carried fragments of *F. japonica* var. *japonica* from the extensive coastal stands at Tighnabruaich on the adjacent mainland peninsula to a point a few hundred metres west of Buttock Point on the north west coast of the Island of Bute. The single shoot observed growing through the winter drift in August 1987 was, by November 1989, a well-established stand. In these examples of vegetative spread by water there exists the possibility of propagation without rhizome. In suitable conditions, cut stems are capable of producing adventitious root growth in a matter of days, axillary shoot production could then quickly follow if favourable conditions were maintained.

CONCLUSIONS

We have here an interesting case of the effects of the introduction of alien species with a very limited genetic base. So limited, in fact, that in *F. japonica* var. *japonica* only the male-sterile plant is introduced. Lacking pollen of its own species it is usually pollinated by the related taxon *F. baldschuanica*, which is also an introduction, and normally non-sympatric with *F. japonica* in nature. Apart from the occasional seed produced by male-fertile plants of *F. japonica* var. *compacta* and *F. sachalinensis*, the vast majority of seed produced by giant knotweeds in Britain is of hybrid origin, usually with *F. baldschuanica*. Since only one hybrid of this constitution has ever been found in the wild, and hybrids between *F. japonica* and *F. sachalinensis* are hexaploid with very low fertility, the role of seed production in the spread of *F. japonica* is not merely minimal, as had been suspected, but totally irrelevant. Without the presence of male-fertile octoploid *F. japonica* plants, octoploid *F. japonica* seed cannot be produced in Britain. In fact, we must consider ourselves fortunate that we do not have octoploid male-fertile *F. japonica* here, since this would make the control of *F. japonica* even more difficult.

ACKNOWLEDGEMENTS

I am indebted to Ann Conolly for her invaluable assistance and encouragement, to Professor Clive Stace for his good advice, to SERC for an instant award and to Dorothy Emmett for typing the manuscript.

REFERENCES

Bailey, J.P. (1988a). Putative *R. japonica* Houtt. × *F. baldschuanica* (Regel) Holub hybrids discovered in Britain. *Watsonia*, **17**, 163–164.

Bailey, J.P. (1988b). *Reynoutria*. In T.G. Rich and M.D.B. Rich *Plant Crib*. (Compilers). London: BSBI Monitoring Scheme.

Bailey, J.P. and Conolly, A.P. (1985). Chromosome numbers of some alien *Reynoutria* species in the British Isles. *Watsonia*, **15**, 270–271.

Bailey, J.P. and Stace, C.A. (1992). Chromosome number, morphology, pairing and DNA values of species and hybrids in the genus *Fallopia* (Polygonaceae) *Plant Systematics and Evolution*, **180**, 29–52.

Bolkhovskikh, Z., Grif, V., Matrejeva, T. and Zakharyeva, O. (1969). *Chromosome numbers of flowering plants*. Leningrad: Academy of Sciences, USSR.

Callaghan, T.V., Scott, R., Lawson, G.J. and Mainwaring, A.M. (1984). *An Experimental Assessment of Native and Naturalised Species of Plants as Renewable Energy Sources in Great Britain. III Japanese knotweed (Reynoutria japonica)*. Institute of Terrestrial Ecology (Natural Environment Research Council) Merlwood, Cumbria.

Chu Chou, M. and Harberd, D.J. (1970). Note on visual distinction of fluorescent callose of pollen tubes and sieve tubes in stylar tissue of *Brassica* and its allies. *Euphytica*, **19**, 379–381.

Conolly, A.P. (1977). The distribution and history in the British Isles of some alien species of *Polygonum* and *Reynoutria*. *Watsonia*, **11**, 291–311.

de Vriese, W.H. (1849). *Polygonum cuspidatum* (including Plate). *Jaarboek Koninklÿk Nederlandsche Maatschappÿ Aanmoediging*. Tuinbouw 30–32.

Hooker, J.D. (1880a). *Polygonum compactum*. *Botanical Magazine*, **106**, Tab. 6476.

Hooker, J.D. (1880b). *Polygonum cuspidatum*. *Botanical Magazine*, **106**, Tab. 6503.

Hooker, J.D. (1881). *Polygonum sachalinense*. *Botanical Magazine*, **107**, Tab. 6540.

Houttuyn, F. (1777). *Natuurlyke Historie* **8**. Amsterdam: De Kruiden.

Justice, O.L. (1941). *A Study of Dormancy in Seeds of* Polygonum. Memoir 235, Cornell University Agriculture Experimental Station, Ithaca, New York.

Locandro, R.R. (1978). Japanese bamboo. *Weeds Today*, **9**, 21–22.

Maruta, E. (1983). Growth and survival of current-year seedlings of *Polygonum cuspidatum* at the upper distribution limit on Mt. Fuji. *Oecologia*, **60**, 316–320.

Ohwi, J. (1965). *Flora of Japan*. Washington DC: Smithsonian Institute.

Stevens, D.P. (1988). On the gynodioecious polymorphism in *Saxifraga granulata* L. (Saxifragaceae). *Biological Journal of the Linnean Society* **35**, 15–28.

Tanaka, H. (1966). The insect visitors of *Polygonum cuspidatum* Sieb. et Zucc. *Collecting and Breeding*, **28**, 141–143.

von Siebold, P.F. (1856). *Catalogue Raisonn. Prix-courant des Plantes et Graines du Japon Cultivées dans l'éstablishment de von Siebold and Comp. à Leide*n Leiden and Bohn (Henry and Cohen).

Webb, D.A. (1964). In T.G. Tutin, V.H. Heywood, N.A. Burges, D.H. Moore, S.M. Walters and D.A. Webb (Eds), *Flora Europaea* Vol. **1**. Cambridge: Cambridge University Press.

15 *Fallopia japonica* (Japanese Knotweed) in Wales

JOHN P. PALMER
Richards, Moorehead and Laing Ltd, Ruthin, UK

INTRODUCTION

Fallopia japonica was introduced to the UK in 1825 both as a garden plant and as a fodder plant (Connolly, 1977). A member of the dock family, Polygonaceae, it is a vigorously growing herbaceous perennial with broad leaves forming dense thickets. Stands of *F. japonica* range from isolated plants to clumps covering 500 m^2.

In Britain *F. japonica* reproduces asexually spreading by vigorous rhizome (underground stem) growth into previously 'uncolonized' areas. Small pieces of rhizome moved in soil transport or by water can regenerate into new plants. *F. japonica* is a successful pioneer and has become a persistent and noxious weed. Inclusion of *F. japonica* in the Wildlife and Countryside Act 1981 (Schedule 9, Section 14) makes it illegal to introduce the plant knowingly into the wild.

F. japonica quickly becomes established on bare ground by rapid vegetative growth. In Japan its typical habitat is recent volcanic lava, which it invades within 20 years of volcanic activity. It is reported there to be replaced by other herb species after 50 years or so (Yoshioka, 1974).

In Britain it is a primary colonizer of unmanaged derelict or disturbed land and has been particularly effective at colonizing the banks of downstream reaches of urban rivers. In recent years *F. japonica* has become perceived as more of a problem in unmanaged or semi-intensively managed vegetation such as roadside verges, railway embankments, recreation areas, parks, gardens and graveyards. It has become widespread in South Wales. For this reason the Welsh Development Agency commissioned a study of the status of *F. japonica* and its control in Wales. This paper summarizes the findings of that study (Richards, Moorehead and Laing Ltd, 1990).

Ecology and Management of Invasive Riverside Plants
Edited by L. C. de Waal, L. E. Child, P. M. Wade and J. H. Brock
© 1994 John Wiley & Sons Ltd

METHODS

The study had four components:

(1) A review of the available information on the ecology and control of *F. japonica*.
(2) A survey of the distribution of *F. japonica* in mid-Wales and specific studies of soil chemistry, biomass, species associations, rhizome initiation and growth.
(3) A questionnaire sent to local authorities, National Park authorities, public and private utilities, water authorities, wildlife conservation bodies, farmers' unions and herbicide manufacturers. The questionnaire asked for information on:

    (i)   the general distribution of *F. japonica* in each area,
    (ii) the type of habitats in which *F. japonica* occurs,
    (iii) the damage caused,
    (iv) attempts to control *F. japonica*,
    (v) success of control measures and
    (vi) the cost of control measures and problems associated with them.

(4) Field visits arranged to a variety of sites, identified from questionnaire returns and letters, which included *F. japonica*.

RESULTS AND DISCUSSION

SURVEY OF *F. JAPONICA* IN MID-WALES

Soil chemistry

Soil chemical analysis of 17 stands of *F. japonica* in mid-Wales showed there to be no correlation between stand vigour and size and the soil parameters measured. The data illustrated that *F. japonica* was capable of growing vigorously in soils of pH 4–8 and of a wide range of organic matter contents and other parameters (Table 15.1).

Biomass

Biomass studies concurred with previous findings such as those of Callaghan *et al.* (1984) that annual accumulations could be up to 12 tonnes/ha. In many stands, shoots and leaves were slow to decompose over winter and many shoots remained upright for almost 12 months. These shoots with accumulated leaf litter provided a sheltered environment for new shoots.

Table 15.1. Results of analysis of soil samples from 17 stands of *Fallopia japonica* in mid-Wales

	pH	Organic matter (%)	Potassium	Sodium	Magnesium	Calcium	Phosphorus
Maximum	8.5	24.6	98.04	21.18	98.42	813.60	93.8
Average	6.3	9.62	35.05	10.06	33.66	329.95	39.87
Minimum	4.2	2.3	13.78	2.72	10.98	20.48	7.5

Species association

F. japonica casts a dense shade and there is often little in the way of ground flora associated with it, particularly in summer. However, some spring herbs are able to survive in some situations, and in newly invasive stands a wider range of species is found. Table 15.2 shows the components of the ground flora in 17 stand in mid-Wales. Of these, the herbs *Allium ursinum, Hedera helix, Ranunculus ficaria* and *Urtica dioica* and the three mosses are all shade tolerant.

QUESTIONNAIRE RETURNS

Distribution of *F. japonica* in Wales

F. japonica is present in every district of Wales although its extent varies considerably (Figure 15.1). It is most common in the industrialized districts

Table 15.2. Plant species associated with 17 newly invasive stands of *Fallopia japonica* in mid-Wales

Species	Common name
Eurynchium praelongum	⎫
Thuidium tamariscinum	⎬ Mosses
Atrichum spp.	⎭
Festuca ovina	Sheep's fescue
Agrostis capillaris	Common bent
Ranunculus ficaria	Lesser celandine
Campanula rotundifolia	Harebell
Galium aparine	Cleavers
Allium ursinum	Ramsons
Epilobium montanum	Broadleaved willow herb
Urtica dioica	Common nettle
Rumex obtusifolius	Broadleaved dock
Hedera helix	Ivy

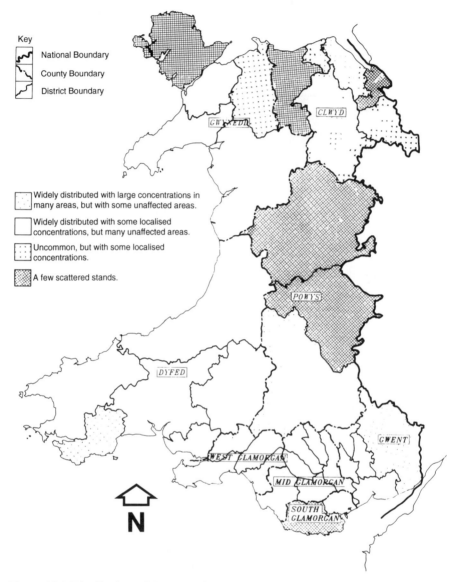

Figure 15.1 Distribution of Japanese knotweed (*Fallopia japonica*) in Wales in 1989 (Reproduced from Richards, Moorehead and Laing Ltd, 1990 by permission of the Welsh Development Agency)

of South Wales, where there are large areas along rivers and railway lines and on derelict land. However, even in these districts, *F. japonica* is absent from substantial tracts of land, especially in the uplands, valley sides and other localized areas which have not been affected by industry or urbanization. In more rural districts, *F. japonica* is generally less common although localized concentrations exist, particularly along roads, railways and rivers and on derelict land. In these situations *F. japonica* has often been brought to a site by dumping of waste which includes rhizomes. In the industrialized South, *F. japonica* has also been spread by tipping, but the large-scale movement of soil which has occurred in these areas has probably been a more important factor. The movement of soil over many years on derelict land and around urban and industrial areas is one of the main factors that has enabled *F. japonica* to become so common in South Wales. Conversely, in the North Wales district of Ynys Mon, which has seen little industrialization in the twentieth century, *F. japonica* is uncommon.

The present distribution of *F. japonica* reflects to an extent its date of introduction to different parts of Wales. South Wales was one of the first places in the British Isles in which *F. japonica* was recorded as growing wild. By the beginning of the twentieth century it was probably present throughout the counties of Glamorgan and in parts of Dyfed (Figure 15.1). By the 1930s it was becoming established in Gwent and may have been moving into parts of North Wales. Certainly by the 1940s it was present in much of Gwynedd, Clwyd and Powys. By the start of the 1950s the only districts where *F. japonica* may not have been present were Ynys Mon, Preseli, South Pembrokeshire and Montgomery and these areas were probably colonized by the end of the decade or during the 1960s.

Whilst *F. japonica* may have been long established in many parts of Wales this does not mean that it has been a problem for the same length of time. Isolated clumps can cause damage, but it is only when *F. japonica* becomes more frequent in a district that it may be perceived as a problem. In many of the districts in South Wales, *F. japonica* has already become sufficiently common to be a serious and widespread problem. In others its increasing spread means that it could reach this stage soon.

Damage caused by *F. japonica*

F. japonica was recorded in questionnaire returns as causing a wide range of problems (Table 15.3).

The damage to structures caused by *F. japonica* was regarded as an occasional or rare problem and no serious damage to buildings was identified. The damage caused to tarmac paving and concrete, particularly pavements along roads to car parks, was recorded as a serious problem in urban areas in Wales. *F. japonica* often spreads into these areas from roadside verges and amenity grasslands. Its presence in these locations is in itself a problem, as it can suppress the growth of sown grass and planted trees, eventually causing their death. In addition to it being costly to eradicate the *F. japonica* and replant the trees, herbs or grass, the dominance of *F. japonica* can prevent

Table 15.3 The number of local authorities (21) in Wales reporting damage of different types caused by *Fallopia japonica*

	Widespread	Occasional	Rare
Damage to structures	0	3	4
Damage to river banks and protection works	12	6	1
Damage to tarmac, paving and kerbs	7	14	2
Loss of valuable wildlife habitat	6	15	6
Invasion of sown vegetation, such as roadside verges and amenity areas	7	19	5
Others (including graveyards, gardens, woodland and grazing land)	3	3	3

the proper use of amenity vegetation. This is particularly so in children's play areas, cemeteries and small picnic areas. A number of Welsh organizations reported that such damage was a widespread problem.

From rural roadside or riverside locations, *F. japonica* often spreads into surrounding hedges, fields and woods, taking over areas which may be of value to wildlife, including woods, the margins of wetlands and areas of grassland. This is a widespread problem in Wales.

The damage caused to the landscape by *F. japonica* was a more difficult problem to quantity. Many organizations regarded it as unsightly, particularly in winter in amenity grassland and other urban locations. A few felt that it was attractive and improved the appearance of area of derelict land. The perception of attractiveness or unsightliness of *F. japonica* perhaps depends on personal taste and on the location. In Gwynedd and probably in other attractive areas of Wales and England its frequent presence along roads, which in itself may not be unattractive, is a problem because the plant may obscure spectacular scenery for the motorist.

Perception of *F. japonica* as a problem by District Councils

During the course of the study it became clear that the perception by some District Councils of the problems caused by *F. japonica* in their own area varied considerably from the problem outlined in other sources of information. For example, some councils in the South Wales valleys did not regard *F. japonica* as a problem, yet other sources of information and our own work showed that these valleys were some of the most heavily infested areas in Wales, with a considerable amount of damage caused by *F. japonica*. The perception by District Councils of the problem was important as it tended to reflect the effort they put into controlling *F. japonica*. Hence, if they regarded it as a serious problem, they spent some time and money in attempting to control the plant, whilst if they did not regard it as a problem they did little to control it.

Of the 24 District Councils that responded to the questionnaire, the majority considered *F. japonica* to be an occasional or rare problem; about a sixth regarded the plant as a widespread problem, whilst the same number felt that it was not a problem.

It is surprising that some District Councils of South Wales do not regard *F. japonica* as a problem, considering the extent to which it is found in those districts. The plant has, of course, been long established in these areas and has been part of the scenery since childhood for most people. A further clue to the reason for this perception is that some of these authorities are only just beginning to attempt environmental improvements to areas such as parks, playing areas and public open spaces, and many of the problems caused by *F. japonica* are not appreciated until these kinds of projects are attempted.

In Wales many of the organizations which responded to the questionnaire appeared to be aware that *F. japonica* had been present in their areas for a considerable length of time (Table 15.4). Two of the 15 that responded to this section of the questionnaire thought that *F. japonica* had been present since the nineteenth century and 10 thought that the plant had been present prior to 1970.

The damage caused by *F. japonica* was regarded as more recent, only two suggesting that the plant was a problem before the 1960s. Indeed, the majority of the organizations suggested that *F. japonica* had become a problem during the 1970s and 1980s. This coincides with not only increased earthmoving activity but also a greater awareness of derelict land and its wildlife importance and the great explosion in non-intensively managed "amenity" land.

Benefits of *F. japonica*

Some questionnaire respondents identified benefits due to *F. japonica*. These are listed with comments:

(1) *F. japonica* stands provide a suitable microenvironment for spring herbs on derelict land. In Wales there is little evidence of a ground flora of significant value developing under *F. japonica*. Officers of bodies such as the Nature Conservancy Council (now English Nature) regard *F. japonica* as a threat to wildlife.

(2) Along riverbanks *F. japonica* stands provide resting-up places for otters and cover for some birds. *F. japonica* is not better than other tall riverside plants in this respect. Otters are not found in the industrialized areas of South Wales where *F. japonica* is concentrated.

(3) *F. japonica* is of value to bees and invertebrates late in the season in

Table 15.4. Perceptions by the various Welsh organizations of the length of time *Fallopia japonica* had been present and/or been a problem in their area (by County)

Organization	Approximate date *F. japonica* first arrived in the area	Approximate date *F. japonica* first became a nuisance
Clwyd		
Alyn & Deeside DC	—	1985
Colwyn BC	—	1983/84
Denbigh BSBI Recorder	Frequent by 1960	—
Dyfed		
Dinefwr BC	—	1940s or 1950s
Llanelli BC	1950	—
South Pembrokeshire DC	1975	1980
Ceredigion BSBI Recorder	Frequent by 1935	—
Pembrokeshire BSBI Recorder	—	1973
National Trust: Stackpole	1980 or earlier	—
National Trust: North Pembrokeshire	1950s or earlier	—
Gwent		
Blaenau Gwent BC	1970	1974
BSBI Recorder for Gwent	Probably since 1957	—
Gwynedd		
Arfon DC	—	1985
Snowdonia National Park	—	Mid-1970s at least
Mid Glamorgan		
Mid Glamorgan CC	—	1968
Cynon Valley BC	1950	—
Swansea Groundwork Trust	—	1960 or earlier
Merthyr Groundwork Trust	—	1960
Powys		
Powys CC	1960 or earlier	—
Brecknock Wildlife Trust	1975	1982
South Glamorgan		
Vale of Glamorgan BC	1969	1969
Cardiff City Council	—	1960 or earlier
Glamorgan Heritage Coast	1980	—
West Glamorgan		
Lliw Valley BC	1890 or earlier	—
West Glamorgan CC	1896 or earlier	1940
National Trust: Gower	—	1985

BC, Borough Council; DC, District Council; CC, County Council; C, City Council.

urban areas. It is certainly true that flies, bees and wasps are attracted to *F. japonica* late in the season. A reason for this is that it flowers later than most plants. Whether *F. japonica* is of significant benefit to bees has not been demonstrated—most *F. japonica* plants do not produce pollen in the UK so it could only be of use as a nectar source.

If it is of significance in nectar supply it can only be of a very local nature.

(4) *F. japonica* can provide protection to river banks. It can, but this benefit is outweighed by the disadvantage of its spread down water-courses to other areas and the damage it can cause to river bank protection works.

(5) *F. japonica* is useful as a quick-establishing plant in some ameneity planting. This has not been found so in Wales, where *F. japonica* quickly dominates other vegetation and is then very difficult to eradicate.

CONTROL OF *F. JAPONICA* IN WALES

Existing stands

Attempts to control existing *F. japonica* stands in Wales have included:

(i)   digging up plants and rhizomes,
(ii) cutting,
(iii) use of selective herbicices,
(iv) use of non-selective herbicides and
(v)   combinations of (i) and (iv).

Grazing has been effective in controlling invasion into pasture in some instances, but has not been used as a specific control method. However, observations suggest that grazing or mowing of pastures infested with *F. japonica* during May to July, when the plant is growing most vigorously, helps to prevent its spread.

No other control methods have been identified from other parts of the UK or in overseas literature searches.

Major conclusions on the success of the five methods of control are:

(i) Digging up plants and rhizomes is labour intensive and fails to control or eradicate without the use of other control methods. No successful instances of this method were identified except where all the soil was also removed. This method tends to be impractical in all but the smallest stands and has a tendency to spread the plant further because parts of rhizomes break off and regrow around the site of the original stand.

(ii) Cutting is also labour intensive. No instances of eradication of *F. japonica* have been identified using this method alone, although in some cases this has been nearly achieved. The method requires considerable persistence and if this is practised control can be achieved.

(iii) The use of selective herbicides has met with some success in situations where the loss of broadleaved species is not considered a problem and grass can quickly establish when *F. japonica* dies. Table 15.5 shows the herbicides (selective and non-selective) and their use by authorities returning questionnaires, in controlling *F. japonica*. The most widely used selective herbicide has been picloram, which is persistent and is not approved for use near watercourses. Because of its persistence, picloram cannot be used where broadleaved plants or trees and shrubs are to be planted within 2 years of spraying. Its use is therefore restricted and it is perhaps best used in situations such as those grave-yards which are not of wildlife value and are located some distance away from watercourses. Another selective herbicide which has been used by a number of authorities is triclopyr. This was used in con-junction with 2,4-D+ dicamba and the vegetation was sprayed in May. However, this was reported as being less successful in control-ling *F. japonica* than picloram. As with picloram, triclopyr cannot be used near watercourses. For eradication, all the evidence suggests that repeat spraying is necessary.

(iv) The use of non-selective herbicides has also met with some success. Of all the herbicides noted in questionnaire returns, the translocated, non-selective herbicide glyphosate was the most widely used. It is approved for use near watercourses and is one of the safest herbicides available, since it is of low mammalian toxicity (LD_{50} rat = 5400 mg/kg) and is rapidly deactivated in soil. The successful use of glyphosate on *F. japonica* depends on the timing of applications and the most successful control has been achieved with more than one application per season. Repeat applications in following seasons have usually been necessary. Glyphosate has been used, with limited success, on nature reserves. Other non-selective herbicides which have met with some success have been based on imazapyr and sodium chlorate. Both are persistent and unapproved for use near watercourses. They are not suitable for use on vegetation of wildlife value or where establish-ment of vegetation is intended in the near future.

(v) Combinations of treatments have often been used at some sites. No particular combination appears to have been more successful than the use of individual herbicides except where cutting has been used to make *F. japonica* more accessible for herbicide applications. Alter-natively, when applying herbicides, the plants may be sprayed earlier in the season or applied using an extension lance or boom. Successful eradication has been claimed in trials in Ireland using cutting in com-bination with glyphosate herbicide.

Where control has been "successful" it was achieved through perseverance

Table 15.5. Herbicides used and their success in controlling *Fallopia japonica*

Active ingredient	Persistence	Selectivity	Approved under PSPS*		No. of Authorities using it	Effectiveness — Yes	No	Not known or results uncertain
				W†	ES†			
Glyphosate	No	No	Yes	W	9	3	6	0
				ES	19	9	5	5
Asulam	No	Yes	Yes	W	1	—	1	—
				ES	0	—	—	—
2,4-D amine	No	Yes	Yes	W	0	—	—	—
				ES	1	—	1	—
Triclopyr	Yes	Yes	No	W	1	—	—	1
				ES	5	4	—	1
Picloram	Yes	Yes	No	W	6	4	—	2
				ES	2	1	—	1
2,4-D + mecoprop	No	Yes	No	W	0	—	—	—
				ES	1	1	—	—
2,4-D + dicamba	No	Yes	No	W	2	—	2	—
				ES	21	—	—	—
2,4-D + triclopyr + dicamba	Yes	Yes	No	W	0	—	—	—
				ES	2	1	1	—
Triclopyr + dicamba + mecoprop	Yes	Yes	No	W	3	—	3	—
				ES	0	—	—	—
Sodium chlorate	Yes	No	No	W	2	2	—	—
				ES	2	2	—	—
Atrazine + 2,4-D + sodium chlorate	Yes	No	No	W	1	—	1	—
				ES	0	—	—	—
Amitrole + atrazine + diuron	Yes	No	No	W	0	—	—	—
				ES	2	1	—	—
Paraquat	No	No	No	W	1	—	1	—
				ES	1	—	1	—
Bentazone = MCPB	No	Yes	No	ES	1	—	1	—
Monolinuron	No	Yes	No	W	1	—	1	—
Imazapyr	Yes	No	No	ES	1	1	—	—
Fluroxypyr	No	Yes	No	ES	1	1	—	1

*PSPS Pesticide Safety Precaution Scheme
†W Wales; ES England and Scotland

on small areas with no boundaries adjoining land from which *F. japonica* could invade. Extremely few examples of *F. japonica* eradication have been documented in Wales. The problems of multiple or unidentifiable ownerships of land infested with *F. japonica* and the ease with which land can become re-infested, after eradication, through vegetative spread or re-introduction in soil, are as great as the resistance of the plant itself to control methods.

Control of the invasion of uninfested land

If *F. japonica* could be prevented form spreading to new sites, a major step forward would have been taken in dealing with the problems.

Control of the vegetative spread of *F. japonica* can only be achieved by controlling the existing stand of plants. Illegal tipping is prohibited by existing legislation, but is not enforced, whilst the movement of soil infested with rhizomes needs to be limited. Only four local authorities in Wales said they limited the movement of infested soil where possible, but many commented on the practical difficulty of doing so. In England, the London Borough of Havering issues an instruction to staff of the Parks Section of the Public Works Division which contains the following information:

(i)   a statement that it is a criminal offence under the Wildlife and Countryside Act 1981 to plant or otherwise cause *F. japonica* to grow,
(ii) a description of the plant,
(iii) an instruction to notify supervisory staff of the presence of the plant in any area and
(iv) a brief control strategy.

This is obviously an important step towards prevention of the spread of *F. japonica* on the banks of watercourses and of rhizomes and stems falling into watercourses during earthworks on river banks, and could be a model for other local authorities.

CONCLUSIONS

F. japonica is widespread throughout Wales and is most abundant in the industrialized areas of South Wales. The plant is capable of tolerating a wide range of soil chemical and physical conditions. It causes damage to non-intensively managed vegetation, paving, walls and vegetation and is a particular problem on river banks, roadside verges, railway embankments, graveyards, parks and gardens. Both the extent of *F. japonica* infestation and the perception of it as a problem have increased in recent years.

Control attempts have included both non-herbicidal and herbicidal use.

None gives control at the first attempt and unless care is exercised some non-herbicidal methods may result in the further spread of the plant. Few restrictions on the movement of soil infested with *F. japonica* had been applied in Wales at the time of the survey.

Control of *F. japonica* in the future is dependent on education of people involved in the movement of soil and on planned strategies of control. The possibility of biological control should also be investigated.

ACKNOWLEDGEMENTS

This work was carried out under a Welsh Development Agency research contract. Thanks are due to Gwyn Griffiths and Tom Bourne of the Welsh Development Agency for their support and to David Beerling and Ron Edwards of the University of Wales College of Cardiff and environmental science students of the University College Wales, Aberystwyth, who contributed to the study. I also acknowledge the assistance of Patricia Frederick and Nick Thomas, environmental scientists with Richards, Moorehead and Laing Ltd. Lastly, thanks are also due to the many respondents to the questionnaire and for the helpful input from members of the public.

REFERENCES

Callaghan, T.V., Scott, R., Lawson, G.J. and Mainwaring, A.M. (1984) *An Experimental Assessment of Native and Naturalised Species of Plants as Renewable Energy sources in Great Britain. III. Japanese Knotweed Reynoutria japonica.* Institute of Terrestrial Ecology; (Natural Environment Research Council), Merlewood, Cumbria..

Connolly, A.P. (1977). The distribution and history in the British Isles of some alien species of *Polygonum* and *Reynoutria. Watsonia,* **11**, 291–311

Richards, Moorehead and Laing Ltd (1990). *Japanese Knotweed* (Reynoutria japonica) *in Wales.* Report to the Welsh Development Agency, Cardiff.

Wildlife and Countryside Act 1981. London: HMSO.

Yoshioka, K. (1974). Volcanic vegetation. In M. Numata (Ed.), *Flora and Vegetation of Japan* pp. 238–256. Tokyo and New York: Elsevier.

16 Classical Biological Control for Exotic Invasive Weeds in Riparian and Aquatic Habitats—Practice and Prospects

SIMON V. FOWLER and ANTHONY N. G. HOLDEN

International Institute of Biological Control, Silwood Park, Ascot, UK

INTRODUCTION

Classical weed biocontrol involves the introduction of specialized exotic herbivores to reduce the density and impact of a target weed. The target weeds are often, but not exclusively, introduced exotics from other regions of the world. The ecological basis of classical weed biocontrol is that the abundance of many plants in their natural environment is controlled by natural enemies, and that most insect herbivores and many plant pathogens are extremely host specific (Strong *et al.*, 1984).

The first major successes in weed biocontrol were achieved during the early part of the twentieth century against weeds such as *Opuntia* spp. in Australia and *Hypericum perforatum* in the USA (Julien, 1992). Since these early successes, there has been a total of at least 729 weed biocontrol programmes, using invertebrates or fungi, against over 140 weed species world-wide (Julien, 1992). According to one analysis, 39% of programmes have led to substantial control of the target weeds (Julien *et al.*, 1984). This rate of success is not as high as practitioners would like, but should improve with better knowledge and application of ecology, particularly in the choice of target weeds and the selection of agents (Waage, 1990). Several of the major successes have involved aquatic or semi-aquatic weeds (Table 16.1).

Most biological control programmes to-date have involved the introduction of highly specific natural insect enemies of the weed. Recently, host-specific pathogens have been used to control weeds successfully (Templeton and Greaves, 1984).

A common feature to all these weed biocontrol programmes is their exemplary safety record. All programmes now involve careful selection and

Ecology and Management of Invasive Riverside Plants
Edited by L. C. de Waal, L. E. Child, P. M. Wade and J. H. Brock
© 1994 John Wiley & Sons Ltd

Table 16.1. Examples of successful classical biocontrol programmes against aquatic or semi-aquatic weeds (data from Julien, 1992)

Weed species	Common name	Countries where biocontrol successful
Alternanthera philoxeroides	alligator weed	Australia, New Zealand, USA, Thailand.
Pistia stratiodes	water lettuce	Australia, USA, Zimbabwe
Eichhornia crassipes	water hyacinth	India, Australia
Salvinia molesta	water fern	many countries

screening of the insect and fungal agents to ensure their specificity to the target weed. With the correct screening procedures, none of the introduced agents for weed biocontrol has caused further pest problems.

To-date, no weed biocontrol programmes have been completed in the UK, but the Agricultural and Food Research Council has funded a 5-year research programme on the potential biocontrol of *Pteridium aquilinum* (bracken) (Fowler *et al.*, 1989). Britain has, however, benefited from successful biological control programmes against insect pests, notably *Eriosoma lanigerum* (apple woolly aphid) and *Dendroctonus micans* (spruce bark beetle).

In this paper, we concentrate on the classical approach to weed biocontrol because it is appropriate to most of the invasive plant species in riparian and aquatic habitats. In the following section we discuss the advantages and disadvantages of classical weed biocontrol and give some examples of the economics of this form of weed control. We outline the procedures followed in a typical classical weed biocontrol programme. Finally, we report on the current status and prospects for weed biocontrol programmes of invasive plants in the UK, concentrating on the three species, *Fallopia japonica* (Japanese knotweed), *Heracleum mantegazzianum* (giant hogweed) and *Impatiens glandulifera* (Himalayan balsam), for which preliminary investigations have been conducted.

CLASSICAL BIOLOGICAL CONTROL: ADVANTAGES AND DISADVANTAGES

As with any weed control strategy, classical biological control has its advantages and disadvantages. On the negative side, it is slow acting and often involves a reduction in spread or vigour of weeds rather than eradication. Eradication may occur on a local scale, but it is difficult to predict in advance. Consequently it tends to be an inappropriate technique for annual crops or other weed problems where immediate, total control is essential. The host specificity that makes the releases of agents safe to non-target plants means that the control is specific to one or a few weed species, hence it is unsuitable for species-rich complexes of weeds where rapid total control is needed.

On the positive side, once classical biological control agents are successfully established, the control is permanent, requiring little or no further expenditure. Classical weed biocontrol can therefore be extremely cost effective. It is usually totally self perpetuating, requiring no repeated applications—in contrast to mechanical or herbicidal control. The dispersal abilities of agents are usually adequate to locate most patches of the target weed, and if necessary this process can be easily augmented by local transportation. Control can be achieved in areas and types of terrain where conventional methods would be impossible to employ, but, perhaps most importantly, biological control is environmentally very safe with no human or animal health risks, no harmful residues and no harmful effects on the local flora. To summarize, successful biological control of weeds is permanent, extremely cost effective and environmentally acceptable.

CLASSICAL WEED BIOCONTROL: ECONOMICS

To illustrate how cost effective classical biological weed control can be, we have used data from a control programme against the *Salvinia molesta* (water fern) in Sri Lanka (Table 16.2; Doeleman, 1989). Infestations of *S. molesta* reduce the area available for rice cultivation and interfere with activ-

Table 16.2. Annual economic losses caused by *Salvinia molesta* in Sri Lanka, at 1987 rates

		UK £000s
Rice production		249
Fishing and other losses		99
Health costs		134
Current control		147
Environmental costs		?
Less:		
Economic benefits		0
Substitute weeds		49
	Total	579

Data extracted and simplified from Doeleman (1989).

ities such as fishing, with resulting economic losses. Disease vectors such as mosquitos breed more successfully in areas of water infested by the weed, leading to increased incidence of diseases, such as malaria, to which economic costs can be attached (Table 16.2). Current control of the weed uses both mechanical and herbicidal methods which can be costed reasonably simply (Table 16.2). In contrast, environmental problems caused by the weed were deemed impossible to cost (Table 16.2). The weed was considered to have no significant economic benefit (Table 16.2), but it was appreciated that, if control were successful, other aquatic weeds would replace *S. molesta* to at least some extent. Any economic losses caused by weeds replacing *S. molesta* needed to be considered as a negative aspect to the potential control of *S. molesta* (Table 16.2).

To-date this represents one of the best examples of a cost/benefit analysis of classical biocontrol. Unfortunately, many biocontrol programmes have neglected to follow up successful or unsuccessful releases with cost/benefit studies, usually because of abrupt cessation of funding once releases are made.

The biological control programme involved the release of just one agent, the weevil *Cyrtobagous salviniae*. However, much of the basic research had already been conducted in Australia and the agent had a proven track record of success. The programme commenced in 1986 and releases continued until 1989. The costs of the programme are shown in Table 16.3.

The estimated returns from the programme were calculated assuming that the losses in Table 16.2 would be completely alleviated and are presented over an arbitrarily chosen 25-year period. The calculated return ratios indicate that, for each £1 invested, the economic gain was between £36 and £88 over the 25-year period.

A biological control programme initiated for the UK would include the original research costs and need a greater input to cover labour costs. As an example, data for the current International Institute of Biological Control (IIBC) programme agains the Canadian rangeland weed *Euphorbia* spp.

Table 16.3. Costs of the biological control programme against *Salvinia molesta* in Sri Lanka; at 1987 rates

		UK £000s
Research costs		50
Implementation		74.6
	Total	126.4

Data extracted and simplified from Doelman (1989).

Table 16.4. Costs of the UK/Canadian biological control programme against *Euphorbia* spp.; at 1991 rates

Annual costs:	UK £000s
Staff	20
Surveys (year 1 only)	3
Quarantine	6
Chemotaxonomy	3
Other	2
Total	34

(leafy spurge) are given in Table 16.4. The estimated total costs over 5 years amount to approximately £150 000.

This on-going programme, involving field collections in Europe and extensive research in quarantine at IIBC (UK), has been concentrating on several host-specific rust fungi with potential to control this European plant that has achieved serious weed status in Canada.

PROCEDURES IN BIOLOGICAL CONTROL

The initial research necessary for a classical biocontrol programme includes (a) background work to establish whether the weed is an appropriate target for biocontrol, (b) field surveys of the natural enemies attacking the weed in its area of origin and (c) host-specificity testing. Assuming that appropriate potential agents are found and that permission to release is forthcoming, the programme can proceed to the practical aspects of release and monitoring.

BACKGROUND WORK

It is essential to establish the exact taxonomic status of the target weed and for introduced weeds, to determine its probable area of origin. The natural enemies attacking the target weed in the UK should be studied, to ensure that potential agents have not been inadvertently introduced already and to allow the selection of agents that are ecologically distinct from existing native herbivores.

Knowledge of the economic impact of the weed, such as that presented for the *Salvinia* programme in Table 16.2, is required to justify the initiation of a biocontrol programme on a purely cost/benefit basis. For many of the aquatic and riparian weeds in the UK much of the benefit of biocontrol may be environmental, such as improved conservation of native fauna and flora, recreation and flood control. An environmental balance sheet should be constructed for any proposed biocontrol programme. Conflicts of interest may be revealed by any of these studies and need to be resolved. Examples include possible risk to closely related plants of value, positive economic uses for the target weed and the environmental consequences of the reduction of weed infestation.

FIELD SURVEYS

The purpose of field surveys is to discover the best possible biocontrol agents from among the range of insect herbivores and plant pathogens attacking the target weed in its native range (Schroeder and Goeden, 1986). Interest would centre on potential agents that have an impact on the population dynamics of the target weed, attacking critical stages in the life history of the plant and/or causing large-scale damage to the plant. Further information can be obtained from herbarium records and literature searches. Ecological studies on potential agents and the weed in its area of origin increase the likelihood of finding successful agents, as well as providing early information on their field host specificity.

HOST SPECIFICITY TESTING

It is vital that any introduced biocontrol agents are host specific to the target weed and unable to attack other plant species. Fortunately, many insect herbivores and plant pathogens are highly host specific, in some cases restricting their attack to sub-specific genotypes of their host plant. Not surprisingly, the process of host specificity testing is the most time-consuming and expensive part of any weed biocontrol programme. Internationally accepted criteria are used to select plant species for testing (Wapshere, 1989) commonly resulting in a test plant list of over 50 species. These will include plants closely related to the target weed occurring in the UK as natives, crops or ornamentals. Further plant species may be included on the basis of morphological or biochemical similarity to the target weed or occurrence in similar habitats. Plants which normally act as hosts to organisms closely related to the potential biocontrol agent are also included.

Host specificity tests are designed to establish the range of host plants that an agent will be restricted to once released. The procedure varies depending on the type of organism being considered. For pathogens, IIBC employs the whole-leaf clearing and staining technique of Bruzzese and Hasan (1983). This enables microscopic examination of pathogen development within the leaf and assessment of plant:pathogen defence responses, to complement macroscopic observations of plant health. With insect agents, initial testing normally involves simple starvation tests in the laboratory, where the plant-feeding stage of the insect is given the abrupt choice of starving to death or feeding on alternative hosts. Most plant species on the test list are readily eliminated by these simple but rather unnatural, tests. However, when insect herbivores are confined and given no choice of food, they may attack host plants which they never damage in the field. Thus, although these simple tests are a good way to shortlist possible host plants from a long list of plant species to be tested, further more realistic tests are required. With insect herbivores, the next stage may involve laboratory trials where agents are given a choice of plants including their normal host plant. For all potential agents, the final stage of testing may include field trials in the country of origin or attempts to rear the potential agent through its entire life cycle on test plants. The results of all these tests are carefully scrutinized before any application for a release is prepared. Where these procedures have been correctly applied, no examples have been reported of biocontrol agents unexpectedly attacking non-host plant species.

POTENTIAL TARGETS IN THE UK

Any major weeds, but particularly introduced species, could represent potential targets for classical biological control. Here, we concentrate on three weeds: *Fallopia japonica* (Japanese knotweed), *Heracleum mantegazzianum* (giant hogweed) and *Impatiens glandulifera* (Himalayan balsam), for which some preliminary studies have been conducted.

FALLOPIA JAPONICA

The spread of *Fallopia japonica* (Japanese knotweeds) in the UK, since its importation for ornamental use in the last century, has been documented by Conolly (1977). The few natural enemies that have colonized *F. japonica* in the UK were studied by Emery (1983). The environmental impact of the weed and current problems with control measures have been the subject of an environmental consultancy (Palmer, 1990). In Japan, *F. japonica* is a common plant, especially in open ground, verges and even volcanic fumaroles. However, it is not an invasive weed and is regarded as an ordinary component of the native vegetation (M. Miyazaki, personal communication, 1989). Preliminary faunal surveys in 1991 by entomologists at Yamaguchi University resulted in a list of 40 insect species that were collected or reared from *F. japonica* in Yamaguchi and adjacent prefectures. Only tentative identifications are available to date, but most of the insects are herbivores and many belong to insect families that include successful specialist biocontrol agents used against other target weeds in other parts of the world (Table 16.5).

Table 16.5. Tentative identification of some of the 40 insect species collected or reared from *Fallopia japonica* (Japanese knotweed) in 1991 in Japan

40 Insect species (5 orders, 22 families) including:	
Hemiptera	Aphididae (1), Ricaniidae (2) Coreidae (1), Plataspidae (10)
Coleoptera	Scarabaeidae (4), Cerambycidae (1) Chrysomelidae (7), Curculionidae (4)
Lepidoptera	Gracillariidae (1), Tortricidae (3) Lymantriidae (1), Geometridae (1) Noctuidae (1)

In addition to these insect herbivores, an as yet unidentified fungal disease was reported as highly damaging to *F. japonica* at all the sites that were surveyed (K. Yano, personal communication, 1992). Several other pathogens have been identified from *F. japonica* both in Japan and in the UK. One of the Japanese species, the rust *Puccinia polygoni-weyrichii*, is certainly a promising potential biocontrol agent warranting further study (Fowler *et al.*, 1991).

HERACLEUM MANTEGAZZIANUM

Heracleum mantegazzianum was introduced into the UK for ornamental purposes in the nineteenth century and has since become a troublesome weed (Williamson and Forbes, 1982). Preliminary searches of available literature have yielded no information about its insect herbivore fauna in its native range in the Caucasus. Other plants in the Umbelliferae are attacked by a wide range of specialized insect herbivores in the UK, so field surveys of *H. mantegazzianum* in the Caucasus can be expected to be rewarding. Several species of native herbivores have colonized this alien weed in the UK, most of which also attack native hogweed, *H. sphondylium* (Sampson, 1990). Similarly, only two pathogens have been recorded on *H. mantegazzianum*, both also occurring on *H. sphondylium*. A number of other pathogens have host ranges restricted to *Heracleum* spp., most collections having been made from *H. sphondylium*. The collections, mostly from Britain, Europe and the Baltic republics, indicate that a rich mycoflora occurs on *H. sphondylium*. It could be expected that field surveys in the Caucasus would establish that the range of diseases associated with *H. mantegazzianum* is more extensive than indicated from our existing records.

IMPATIENS GLANDULIFERA

Impatiens glandulifera is an invasive annual that is becoming increasingly common in the UK, typically as a weed of water margins (Perrins *et al.*, 1990). Its native range includes northern Pakistan, but literature searches by the PARC/IIBC station at Rawalpindi, Pakistan, have revealed little knowledge of the plant or of any natural enemies (insects or pathogens) attacking it. Likewise, there are no records of pathogens attacking the plant in the herbarium at the International Mycological Institute (Egham, UK). *I. glandulifera* is not a weed in its native environment, explaining this paucity of information on its range and biology. Natural enemies will attack *I. glandulifera* in its native range, but field surveys will be needed to collect and identify these.

To summarize, several of the introduced aquatic and riparian weeds in the UK are potential targets for biological control. Despite the obvious advantages of biological control for long-term and environmentally safe weed suppression, weed biocontrol has yet to be used in the UK. There is a lack of awareness and knowledge of biological weed control in the UK. We hope that articles such as this will improve this situation and, in particular, help to allay concerns over the host specificity of potential releases and the long-term safety of the technique. The major barrier to implementation appears to be lack of an appropriate administrative and funding structure for classical weed biocontrol in the UK.

REFERENCES

Bruzzese, E. and Hasan, S. (1983). A whole leaf cleaning and straining technique for the host specificity studies of rust fungi. *Plant Pathology*, **32**, 335–338.

Conolly, A.P. (1977). The distribution and history in the British Isles of some alien species of *Polygonum* and *Reynoutria*. *Watsonia*, **11**, 291–311.

Doeleman, J.A. (1989). *Biological Control of Salvinia molesta in Sri Lanka: an assessment of costs and benefits. ACIAR Technical Report 12*. Australian Centre for International Agricultural Research, Canberra.

Emery, M.J. (1983). *The ecology of Japanese knotweed (Reynoutria japonica Houtt). Its herbivores and pathogens and their potential as biological control agents*. MSc thesis, University of Wales, Bangor.

Fowler, S.V., Holden, A.N.F. and Schroeder, D. (1991). The possibilities for classical biological control of weeds of industrial and amenity land in the UK using introduced insect herbivores or plant pathogens. *Proceedings of the Brighton Crop Protection Conference, Weeds—1991*, **3**, 1173–1180.

Fowler, S.V., Lawton, J.H. and Speed, C.B. (1989). Biocontrol of bracken, *Pteridium aquilinum*, in the UK.: prospects and progress. *Proceedings of the Brighton Crop Protection Conference, Weeds—1989*, **3**, 997–1004.

Julien, M.H. (1992). *Biological control of weeds. A world catalogue of agents and their target weeds*. 3rd edition. Wallingford: CAB International.

Julien, M.H., Kerr, J.D. and Chan, R.R. (1984). Biological control of weeds: an eva-
luation. *Protection Ecology*, **7**, 3–25.
Palmer, J.P. (1990). Japanese knotweed (*Reynoutria japonica*) in Wales. In J. Palmer
(Ed.), *The Biology and Control of Invasive Plants,* pp. 96–110. British Ecology
Society, University of Wales, Cardiff.
Perrins, J., Fitter, A. and Williamson, M. (1990). What makes *Impatiens glandulifera*
invasive? In J. Palmer (Ed.), *The Biology and Control of Invasive Plants*, pp. 8–34.
British Ecological Society, University of Wales, Cardiff.
Sampson, C. (1990). *Towards biological control of* Heracleum mantegazzianum (*giant
hogweed*), *Umbelliferae*. MSc. thesis, Imperial College, University of London.
Schroeder, D. and Goeden, R.D. (1986). The search for arthropod natural enemies of
introduced weeds for biological control—in theory and practice. *Biocontrol News
and Information*, **7**, 149–155.
Strong, D.R., Lawton, J.H. and Southwood, T.R.E. (1984). *Insects on Plants*. Oxford:
Blackwell Scientific Publications.
Templeton, G.E. and Greaves, M.P. (1984). Biological control of weeds with fungal
pathogens. *Tropical Pest Management*, **30**, 333–338.
Waage, J. (1990). Ecological theory and the selection of biological control agents. In
M. MacKauer, L.E. Ehler and J. Roland (Eds) *Critical Issues in Biological Control.*
pp. 135–157, Andover: Intercept.
Wapshere, A.J. (1989). A testing sequence for reducing rejection of potential biocon-
trol agents for weeds. *Annals of Applied Biology*, **114**, 515–526.
Williamson, J.A. & Forbes, J.C. (1982). Giant hogweed (*Heracleum mantegazzianum*):
its spread and control with glyphosate in amenity areas. *Weeds, Proceedings of the
1982 British Crop Protection Conference*, pp. 967–972.

17 Controlling Invasive Weeds Using Glyphosate

ARNIE STENSONES AND RICHARD P. GARNETT
Monsanto plc., Thames Tower, Leicester, UK

INTRODUCTION

This paper explores techniques using glyphosate for the control of invasive weeds. The weeds considered are all invasive aliens imported for ornamental, or, in the case of *Spartina anglica* (common cord-grass), for land management purposes. *Reynoutria japonica* (Japanese knotweed), *Heracleum mantegazzianum* (giant hogweed), *Impatiens glandulifera* (Himalayan balsam), *Rhododendron ponticum* (rhododendron) and *Spartina anglica* (common cord-grass) have all escaped from the niche that was envisaged for them, establishing themselves in both rural and urban environments, with enough vigour to displace native species, so resulting in monocultural stands of low ecological benefit.

This paper is concerned with the use of glyphosate to kill these weeds effectively. The control techniques described must fit two major considerations: firstly, those of personal and environmental safety and, secondly, that the weed control technique forms part of the total management strategy needed to restore natural plant diversity and native plant habitats.

Most sites where invasive weeds are a problem are in locations where special sensitivities exist. *R. japonica*, *H. mantegazzianum* and *I. glandulifera* often proliferate beside streams, commercially important for their sport fishing and where the potential effect of a control method on invertebrate populations must be taken into account. *R. ponticum* and *S. anglica* are often found on sites which have a high conservation value and where the use of herbicides has to be carefully evaluated.

GLYPHOSATE SAFETY AND PRESCRIPTIONS

An understanding of the safety and environmental profile of glyphosate is a first step in considering the appropriateness of a glyphosate-based weed

Ecology and Management of Invasive Riverside Plants
Edited by L. C. de Waal, L. E. Child, P. M. Wade and J. H. Brock
© 1994 John Wiley & Sons Ltd

control programme as part of a strategy plan for controlling invasive weeds.

In terms of safety to people, glyphosate is recognized as having favourable safety properties (Atkinson, 1985). Glyphosate has a very low acute toxicity and irritation potential. It also has a favourable subchronic and chronic toxicity profile. Repeated low-dose exposure does not produce malformations in offspring, or affect the ability to reproduce. Glyphosate does not cause gene changes, does not produce or induce cancerous formations and has no effect on the nervous system of living creatures. It has no affinity to fatty tissues and is passed unchanged through living creatures which ingest it. Further, it does not accumulate in feeding chains.

As one of the nine products approved in the UK for aquatic use (Ministry of Agriculture, Fisheries and Food, 1985) and one of the seven active ingredients recommended by English Nature to be suitable for use in nature reserves (Cooke, 1986), glyphosate is considered to pose little hazard to wildlife and to have favourable environmental characteristics.

An understanding of its fate in soil and water is important, both in the light of the sensitive situations which many invasive weeds favour and in the light of public and conservation concerns about the downside effects of herbicide use in terms of soil and water fate.

The key features of glyphosate safety relate to its physical fate in breakdown (Tooby, 1985; Torstennson, 1985). Firstly, it binds to soil colloids, or to suspended matter in water and to bottom sediment. This feature immobilizes activity. Secondly, it breaks down rapidly into harmless natural substances. In temperate soil conditions, it has a half-life of 30–60 days. A further important consideration is that glyphosate only acts on green and growing vegetation and is herbicidally inactive in soil.

A 3-year study in British Columbia, by four Canadian government agencies, confirms these points (Feng and Thompson, 1990; Feng et al., 1990); Reynolds, 1989). Of particular concern was the possible leaching of active ingredient into river tributaries and the effect on invertebrate populations and salmon spawning grounds. The findings showed that:

(i)   glyphosate broke down rapidly after spraying,
(ii) neither glyphosate nor its major metabolite persisted in soil or leaf litter and did not leach or run,
(iii) glyphosate had a small, but transient, effect on the small fauna and soil microflora, less than that caused by variations in soil water,
(iv) there were no glyphosate residues in the invertebrate community after treatment,
(v)   there were no glyphosate residues in young salmon after direct glyphosate application.

Overall, the study showed that glyphosate had minimal impact on both forestry and aquatic ecosystems.

VEGETATION MANAGEMENT

REYNOUTRIA JAPONICA

R. japonica was first introduced into the UK as a handsome garden ornamental. Its spread has been either by rhizomes being washed down stream, so gaining bankside dominance, or by landscaping operations in planting schemes or highway work. Roblin's (1988) work has resulted in management strategies which enable optimal kill when the plant reaches a manageable size. The recommendations for treating with glyphosate (as Roundup) are shown in Table 17.1. Because R. japonica has a large root system, experience shows that mature clumps may regrow from a small amount of rhizome material. It is important, therefore, to repeat the programme in early autumn or the following spring to ensure effective treatment of regrowth (Child et al., 1992).

HERACLEUM MANTEGAZZIANUM

H. Mantegazzianum can dominate the native flora and make access to the water difficult for fishermen. It is a prolific seeder and once present can colonize rapidly. Manual control methods are dangerous, since the sap causes light-induced blistering which can be severe enough to require hospitalization. The recommended treatment is shown in Table 17.1. The best time

Table 17.1. Recommended treatments with glyphosate (as Roundup) for four invasive plant species

Species	Common name	When to treat	Dose (l/ha)	Notes
Reynoutria japonica	Japanese knotweed	May	5	When 1 m high
Heracleum mantegazzianum	giant hogweed	April/May	5	Apply when plants small and actively growing Re-treat emerging seedling growth
Impatiens glandulifera	Himalayan balsam	April/May	5	Re-treat seedlings
Rhododendron ponticum	rhododendron		8+	Stump regrowth
		June–Sept	2% Mixture B	
		Nov–March	20% solution	On stumps

to spray is at the rosette stage (Williamson and Forbes, 1982). After a month, the centre of the plant will yellow as a result of glyphosate working at the growing points and the whole plant will then turn yellow and die. To ensure effective long-term control, new plants should be spot-treated to maintain control, so emphasizing the need to monitor treatment and re-treat if needed.

H. mantegazzianum produces a prolific seed bank. A year after treatment, small seedlings will re-establish and must be sprayed out, otherwise problems will come back. Since glyphosate has no residual soil action, natural species will recolonize and become dominant. At this stage, spot-application using a weed-wiper can be useful.

IMPATIENS GLANDULIFERA

I. glandulifera can gain dominance by seeding or spread by water, or, in liking the damp fertile conditions by river banks, balsam can rapidly take hold at the expense of native species. In small quantities it can be controlled by pulling or cutting. Control by spraying with glyphosate is similar to that for *H. mantegazzianum* (see Table 17.1). In situations where bankside control is needed, treatment from a boat can be effective, especially on canals, and the use of lightweight telescopic lances can facilitate application where access is difficult.

RHODODENDRON PONTICUM

Another garden import which has become a major problem is *Rhododendron ponticum*. It is a major problem in the west of Scotland and in Wales and Ireland. Control can be effectively achieved with glyphosate, especially when cutting and stump treatment are co-ordinated to maximize the use of available labour and there is a careful follow-up campaign to deal with regeneration or new seedling emergence (Foley, 1990; Tabbush and Williamson, 1987). Recommended treatment is shown in Table 17.1. Seedlings germinate best in moss cover. These will require treatment to achieve lasting control and then treatment should be integrated into a control programme.

SPARTINA ANGLICA

Spartina anglica was introduced as a biological tool to stabilize or reclaim mud flats. However, today it covers some 10 000 ha of intertidal flats around the UK. Its drawback is that it can rapidly colonize mud flats as a monoculture, so reducing botanical diversity and covering mud flats which are strategically important feeding grounds for migrating ducks and waders. It has a dense, widespread rhizome system, which binds the mud.

Table 17.2. Results of treatments in July with glyphosate for the control of *Spartina anglica* (Garnett *et al.*, 1992)

Treatment	Dose (ga.i./ha)	% Biomass reduction
Glyphosate	1800	59%
Glyphosate + Mixture B	1800	90%
	2% Mixture B	

The results of treatments applied in July 1989, at Lindisfarne (Northumberland), are shown in Table 17.2. *S. anglica* is a tough species and where tides cover the target area the use of Roundup in only 100 litres of water per hectare is a major logistical advantage. Spraying should be done at the neap tide, Mixture B being added to the spray to increase efficacy in the short period when the *S. anglica* is uncovered.

Studies undertaken by Durham University and Portsmouth Polytechnic on the effect on invertebrates of spraying with glyphosate to control *S. anglica* (see Table 17.3) (Garnett *et al.*, 1992) showed that:

(i)   effective *Spartina* control can be achieved,
(ii) the variations in invertebrate populations are greater than the changes caused by spraying,
(iii) the best results were achieved by treatments in July,
(iv) significant improvements in biomass control were achieved by adding Mixture B.

Table 17.3. Effect on invertebrates of spraying with glyphosate to control *Spartina anglica*

Species	Effect on numbers
Hydrobia	There was an apparent decline after spraying owing to different tide conditions at the assessments before and after spraying. There was a trend to a greater reduction after the use of Mixture B. The population recovered within 1 year.
Macoma	Decreased after spraying. Complete recovery within 1 year.
Tubifex	Increased after spraying.
Corophium arenarium	No significant effect
Corophium volutator	Declined immediately after spraying. Complete recovery within 7 weeks.

CONCLUSION

The use of glyphosate is an effective tactic as part of a strategy of invasive weed control. Timing is an important variant in achieving effective results, particularly in selecting a growth stage.

REFERENCES

Atkinson, D. (1985). Toxicological properties of glyphosate—a summary. In E. Grossbard and D. Atkinson (Eds), *The Herbicide Glyphosate* pp. 127–133. London: Butterworths.

Child, L.E., de Waal, L.C., Wade, P.M. and Palmer, J.P. (1992). Control and management of *Reynoutria* species (knotweed). *Aspects of Applied Biology*, **29**, 295–308.

Cooke, A.S. (Ed.) (1986). *The Use of Herbicides on Nature Reserves. Focus on Nature Conservation*, **14**. Peterborough: Nature Conservancy Council.

Feng, J.C. and Thompson, D.G. (1990). Fate of glyphosate in a Canadian Forest Watershed. 2. Persistence in foliage and soils. *Journal of Agricultural Food Chemistry*, **38**, 1118–1125.

Feng, J.C., Thompson, D.G. and Reynolds, P.E. (1990). Fate of glyphosate in a Canadian Forest Watershed. 1. Aquatic residues and off target deposit assessment. *Journal of Agricultural Food Chemistry*, **38**, 1110–1118.

Foley, C. (1990). *Rhododendron ponticum* at Killarney National Park. In J. Palmer (Ed.) *Biology and Control of Invasive Plants* pp. 62–63. British Ecological Society, University of Wales, Cardiff.

Garnett, R.P., Hirons, G. Evans, C., and O'Connor, D. (1992). The control of *Spartina* using glyphosate. *Aspects of Applied Biology*, **29**, 359–364.

Ministry of Agriculture, Fisheries and Food (1985). *Guidelines for the Use of Herbicides on Weeds in or near Watercourses and Lakes*. Booklet B2078. London: HMSO.

Reynolds, P.E. (Ed.) (1989) *Proceedings of the Carnation Creek Workshop*. Forestry Canada/British Columbia Ministry of Forests, Victoria, British Columbia.

Roblin, E. (1988). Chemical control of Japanese knotweed (*Reynoutria japonica*) on river banks in South Wales. *Aspects of Applied Biology*, **16**, 1–7.

Tabbush, P.M. and Williamson, D.R. (1987). *Rhododendron ponticum* as a forest weed. Forestry Commission Bulletin 73. London: HMSO.

Tooby, T.E. (1985). Fate and biological consequences of glyphosate in the aquatic environment. In E. Grossbard and D. Atkinson (Eds), *The Herbicide Glyphosate*. London: Butterworths, pp. 206–217.

Torstennson, L. (1985). Behaviour of glyphosate in soils and its degradation. In E. Grossbard and D. Atkinson (Eds), *The Herbicide Glyphosate*. London: Butterworths, pp. 137–150.

Williamson, J.A. and Forbes, J.C. (1982). Giant hogweed (*Heracleum mantegazzianum*): its spread and control with glyphosate in amenity areas. *Weeds, Proceedings of the 1982 British Crop Protection Conference*, pp. 967–972.

18 Alien Invasive Weeds—an Example of National Rivers Authority Sponsored Research

LIZ ROBLIN
National Rivers Authority, Glan Tawe, Swansea, UK

INTRODUCTION

The National Rivers Authority (NRA) is an environmental protection agency which has responsibilities for inland and coastal waters. The authority was established by the Water Act 1989 and is served by 8 regions in England and Wales (Figure 18.1). It has responsibilities for pollution control, flood defences, water resources, fisheries, conservation, recreation and navigation. The NRA's flood defence maintains some 36 000 km of designated main river and riparian land and manages 800 km of sea walls and embankments to protect people and property against flooding.

Vegetation growing along river banks may be affected by major engineering schemes and macrophytes growing within watercourses may require control to maintain sufficient channel capacity. In some cases soil is imported to sites where earth embankments need to be reinforced or raised to maintain and/or improve flood defences. This soil may contain seed and plant roots not compatible with the existing riparian flora. There is therefore the potential to increase the spread of undesirable species within a river catchment. Some of these species can physically damage new structures and interfere with flood defences or compete with native plants. The NRA is required under section 2(2) of the Water Resources Act 1991 ". . . to such an extent as it considers desirable, generally to promote the conservation . . . of flora . . .". This duty gives the Authority additional responsibilities to conserve native flora and may require the control of invasive species in areas where riparian vegetation is threatened.

Ecology and Management of Invasive Riverside Plants
Edited by L. C. de Waal, L. E. Child, P. M. Wade and J. H. Brock
© 1994 John Wiley & Sons Ltd

HEAD OFFICE
Rivers House
Waterside Drive
Aztec West
Almondsbury
Bristol
BS12 4UD
Tel: (0454) 624400
Fax: (0454) 624409

LONDON OFFICE
Eastbury House
30-34 Albert Embankment
London SE1 7TL
Tel: (071) 8200101
Fax: (071) 8201603

ANGLIAN
Kingfisher House
Goldhay Way
Orton Goldhay
Peterborough PE2 5ZR
Tel: (0733) 371811
Fax: (0733) 231840

NORTHUMBRIA & YORKSHIRE
21 Park Square South
Leeds LS1 2QG
Tel: (0532) 440191
Fax: (0532) 461889
Gosforth Office
Eldon House
Regent Centre
Gosforth
Newcastle Upon Tyne
NE3 3UD
Tel: (091) 2130266
Fax: (091) 2845069

NORTH WEST
Richard Fairclough House
Knutsford Road
Warrington WA4 1HG
Tel: (0925) 53999
Fax: (0925) 415961

SEVERN-TRENT
Sapphire East
550 Streetsbrook Road
Solihull B91 1QT
Tel: (021) 7112324
Fax: (021) 7115824

SOUTHERN
Guildbourne House
Chatsworth Road
Worthing
West Sussex BN11 1LD
Tel: (0903) 820692
Fax: (0903) 821832

SOUTH WESTERN
Manley House
Kestrel Way
Exeter EX2 7LQ
Tel: (0392) 444000
Fax: (0392) 444238
Bridgwater Office
Rivers House
East Quay
Bridgwater
Somerset TA6 4YS
Tel: (0278) 457333
Fax: (0278) 452985

THAMES
Kings Meadow House
Kings Meadow Road
Reading RG1 8DQ
Tel: (0734) 535000
Fax: (0734) 500388

WELSH
Rivers House/Plas-yr-Afon
St Mellons Business Park
St Mellons
Cardiff CF3 0LT
Tel: (0222) 770088
Fax: (0222) 798555

Figure 18.1 Regions of the National Rivers Authority for England and Wales (reproduced by permission of the National Rivers Authority).

ALIEN WEEDS

Alien invasive weeds which have been particularly difficult to control along riverbanks include *Fallopia japonica* (Houtt) Ronse Decraene (Japanese knotweed), *Heracleum mantegazzianum* Sommier & Levier (giant hogweed) and *Impatiens glandulifera* Royle (Himalayan balsam). *Crassula helmsii* (T. Kirk) Cockayne (swamp stonecrop), an aquatic plant, is also cause for concern in some inland waters.

F. japonica has successfully colonized river banks and is now widespread and abundant throughout England and Wales, being particularly abundant in the industrialized valleys of South Wales. It is a perennial plant which grows in dense monocultures with rapid growth in early spring. Plants have been recorded growing at a mean of 3 cm/day at a site in Swansea, Wales, during May 1987 (Roblin, 1988). Extensive thickets, often reaching 3 m in height, impede the inspection of flood embankments and can cause instream blockages when the hollow stems die back in winter. The plant's competitiveness and ability to spread rapidly endangers native species and under Schedule 9 of the Wildlife and Countryside Act 1981, section 14, it is an offence "to plant or otherwise cause to grow in the wild . . ." this listed alien species.

H. mantegazzianum is another introduced species covered by this legislation. The plant, although locally abundant, is not as widespread as *F. japonica*. However, its distribution has increased rapidly perhaps by a factor of forty in the last 50 years. It develops from a rosette of leaves and grows to an impressive height of 4–5 m with leaves over 1 m length. The seeds are dispersed locally by wind, but the main mechanism for long-distance dispersal is by water, near which it is principally found. The problem with this plant is not so much the impact on flood defences, but the danger of direct contact with NRA personnel and the public alike. When touched, chemicals in the sap can produce severe blistering on skin exposed to ultraviolet light (phytophotodermatitis). Once the skin is sensitized, the reaction can re-occur on exposure to light, and pigmentation changes in the skin may be permanent. This reaction is frequently incorrectly diagnosed by the medical profession as being caused by liquid chemicals or polluted waters.

I. glandulifera is increasing along river banks and is reducing conservation value at some sites. It is an annual plant producing a large number of seeds, which may overwinter for several years. The seeds are transported by water and are able to colonize river banks and gravel shoals downstream. Die-back of the plants in autumn leaves the banks exposed, resulting in increased erosion during high winter flows. It is not currently controlled by legislation.

C. helmsii Swamp stonecrop, a native of Australia, has been sold from garden centres as an oxygenator for ponds. It has since become established in the wild, where it has adapted to a range of aquatic habitats. It occurs from 0.7 m above to 3 m below water level and its ability to reproduce rapidly from fragmented plants is a cause for concern. Although not yet abundant, this species needs careful monitoring and control if future management problems are to be avoided.

CONTROL

It was apparent, with the formation of the NRA, that the management of alien weeds varied throughout the regions. At the majority of sites, invasive plants have traditionally been controlled with other bankside vegetation by opportune cutting or regular mowing. Chemical control using herbicides approved for use near watercourses (Ministry of Agriculture, Fisheries and Food, 1985) has been used in some regions. Limited control of *F. japonica* had been achieved using glyphosate and 2,4-D amine (both at 6 litres/ha) in the former Welsh Water Authority (Edmonds, 1986; Flower, 1987; Gunn, 1986) and latterly in several NRA regions, although there was no clear guidance on such control. There was therefore a requirement to identify the needs of the eight regions and to provide guidance on the control and management of invasive species.

RESEARCH AND DEVELOPMENT

A contract, commissioned by the NRA, was subsequently awarded to the International Centre of Landscape Ecology, Loughborough to carry out a 2-year research and development project from March 1991. The overall objectives of the project were: to identify methods for the control of invasive plants; to formulate good management practices which minimize the risk to flood defence and to enhance the conservation and recreation value of river corridors. The project included:

(1) A literature review on the biology, ecology and existing management of the four invasive species.
(2) An evaluation of the most effective methods of control in or near watercourses.
(3) Production of concise guidelines on the control and subsequent management of the target plants. This information will be available not only to NRA staff, but also to the general public and other organizations responsible for weed control.
(4) Establishing control sites to monitor the long-term effects of control.
(5) Investigating the feasibility of using a biological control agent for the control of Japanese knotweed.

The project has already been extended to include an additional species, *Azolla filiculoides* Lam. (water fern), which has been identified as a problem in the South West, Severn-Trent, Northumbria and Yorkshire and Anglian NRA regions. Further details are available from the author.

REFERENCES

Edmonds, A.P. (1986). *The distribution and control of an introduced species*, Reynoutria japonica *in selected rivers in South Wales*. Unpublished report, Welsh Water Authority.

Flower, C.J. (1987). *Biology and control of* Reynoutria japonica *on river banks*. Part 1. Unpublished report, Welsh Water Authority.

Gunn, I.D.M. (1986). *Biology and control of Japanese knotweed* (Reynoutria japonica) *and Himalayan balsam* (Impatiens glandulifera) *on river banks*. Parts 1 and 11. MSc thesis, UWIST, Cardiff.

Ministry of Agriculture, Fisheries and Food (1985). *Guidelines for the Use of Herbicides on Weeds in or near Watercourses and Lakes*. Booklet B2078. London: HMSO.

Roblin, E. (1988). Chemical control of Japanese knotweed (*Reynoutria japonica*) on river banks in South Wales. *Aspects of Applied Biology*, **16**, 201–206.

Water Act 1989. London: HMSO.

Water Resources Act 1991. London: HMSO.

Wildlife and Countryside Act 1981. London: HMSO.

19 A Practical Strategy for the Control of *Fallopia japonica* (Japanese Knotweed) in Swansea and the Surrounding Area, Wales

DEBORAH J. HILL

Swansea City Council Planning Department, Swansea, UK

INTRODUCTION

Japanese knotweed (*Fallopia japonica*) is widespread throughout Wales and is particularly abundant in the industrial areas of South Wales. It is a serious and increasing problem in Swansea and the surrounding area.

F. japonica is present throughout the city, occurring most frequently on derelict, disturbed or reclaimed land, alongside rivers and streams, in church grounds, on roadside verges and beside railways.

Much research has been undertaken on the ecology of *F. japonica* and on chemical methods of control for individual stands (Beerling, 1990; Palmer, 1990; Roblin, 1988). This paper addresses some of the management problems associated with the control of *F. japonica* over a large area. It looks at the limitations of control methods currently being applied by the Swansea City Council and highlights the need for a co-ordinated interagency approach to the control of *F. japonica* in Swansea and adjoining areas.

EXISTING APPROACH TO *F. JAPONICA* CONTROL

Swansea City Council owns large areas of land within the city and *F. japonica* management is necessary on many of these sites. Treatment of *F. japonica* is carried out by the Council's Direct Labour Organization and outside contractors, and normally entails spraying with glyphosate. Priority areas for *F. japonica* control currently include:

(i) land identified for environmental improvement and landscaping as part of the Council's "Greening the City" initiative,

Ecology and Management of Invasive Riverside Plants
Edited by L. C. de Waal, L. E. Child, P. M. Wade and J. H. Brock
© 1994 John Wiley & Sons Ltd

(ii) sites of high nature conservation or amenity value and

(iii) sites where *F. japonica* infestation creates a hazard or is causing damage.

Treatment programmes are normally funded from the Council's own budgets and sometimes from grant-aided budgets for urban greening projects (mainly through the Welsh Development Agency and the Welsh Office Urban Programme).

LIMITATIONS OF THE CURRENT APPROACH

This approach has achieved a certain degree of control in some areas. The annual nature of local authority budget planning and to some extent of grant-aid schemes does, however make it difficult to plan long-term treatment programmes. In recognition of this the Welsh Development Agency has now agreed to a three year funding programme for *F. japonica* treatment.

In addition, this site-specific approach to *F. japonica* treatment fails to address a number of other key factors that affect the control of *F. japonica* throughout the city. These include:

(1) Control of *F. japonica* on land owned by the City Council that is not currently considered a priority for treatment.

(2) Control of *F. japonica* on land not in City Council ownership (much work is currently being carried out, particularly by the National Rivers Authority and West Glamorgan County Council, but there are many areas that are not being treated).

(3) Prevention of the spread of *F. japonica* into areas free of *F. japonica,* e.g. by controlling the movement of *F. japonica* contaminated soil, and/or the movement of *F. japonica* stem and rhizome material.

(4) After-use of treated sites, to reduce the likelihood of re-colonization by *F. japonica.*

(5) Lack of public awareness of the problems caused by *F. japonica* and how to control it.

(6) The need to respond to the numerous and increasing requests for help from members of the public and local groups for information on and practical assistance with *F. japonica* eradication.

(7) The need for improved liaison with other agencies involved in *F. japonica* treatment at a local level.

(8) Concern over the potentially enormous costs and environmental impact of implementing a programme of chemical *F. japonica* control for the whole city.

(9) The need for a consistent approach between local authority areas.

THE NEED FOR A CO-ORDINATED APPROACH

There are many agencies currently involved in research into, or the practical implementation of *F. japonica* control methods, at both a local and a national level. Following initial discussions with officers of the National Rivers Authority in Swansea it was agreed that if any real progress was to be made in controlling the spread of *F. japonica* in the Swansea area a comprehensive, co-ordinated, city-wide approach would be needed. Such an approach would need to involve a wide range of agencies and individuals and to look at as many different aspects of the problem as possible. The need for a planned programme for control has also been highlighted by the Welsh Development Agency (1991).

SWANSEA KNOTWEED WORKING GROUP

As a first step towards achieving a more co-ordinated approach, a Swansea Knotweed Working Group has been set up. Present member organizations include the National Rivers Authority, Swansea City Council, West Glamorgan County Council, the International Centre of Landscape Ecology and Richards, Moorehead and Laing Ltd. In addition, the Countryside Council for Wales, the Prince of Wales' Committee and British Rail have expressed an interest and will be invited to join the group.

The benefits of such a co-ordinated interagency approach are numerous:

(1) Greater knowledge and expertise available to deal with the problem.
(2) Co-ordinated control on sites of varied ownership and management.
(3) More effective use of existing resources for the control of *F. japonica* (human resources and funding).
(4) Increased potential for obtaining grant aid from outside sources.
(5) Continuity and consistency of approach.

The key aim of the Knotweed Working Group is to plan, develop and implement a strategy for the co-ordinated control of *F. japonica* in Swansea. The outline strategy agreed to-date is described below.

OUTLINE STRATEGY FOR THE CONTROL OF *F. JAPONICA* IN SWANSEA

(1) Undertake an initial survey of *F. japonica* distribution throughout the city.
(2) Identify a pilot area to test and monitor the effectiveness of co-ordinated control methods. This will be a three year project and will involve:

    (a) identification of and liaison with all relevant bodies, organizations and landowners within the pilot area,

    (b) agreeing and implementing appropriate control methods

    (c) monitoring the management and control work in pilot areas and

    (d) reviewing and amending the strategy for control.

(3) If successful, extend methods of control tested in the pilot area to other areas of the city.

(4) Raise public awareness of the control methods available, e.g. through the local media, distribution of existing information, establishment of a Japanese knotweed helpline and the preparation of an advice leaflet that is specifically relevant to Swansea.

(5) Investigate ways of controlling the spread of *F. japonica* from site to site, e.g. through control of the movement of soil containing *F. japonica* and provision for the safe disposal of mechanically removed *F. japonica* material.

PROGRESS TO-DATE

The time-scale for implementation of the above strategy is dependent to a large extent on the level of resources available. A survey of *F. japonica* in urban Swansea has now been completed. This work was undertaken by the International Centre of Landscape Ecology with funding from Swansea City Council and the National Rivers Authority. It is intended that the data will be incorporated into the Council's Geographical Information System database. It will provide an important baseline for measuring the rate of spread of *F. japonica*, to identify possible target areas for the proposed pilot project and to monitor the effectiveness of control strategies.

Although some work can be done with existing resources, any real progress on the implementation of items (2) to (5) of the strategy is dependent on additional funding. Approaches are being made to a number of agencies to support this work.

REFERENCES

Beerling, D.J. (1990). The use of non-persistent herbicides, glyphosate and 2, 4-D amine, to control riparian stands of Japanese knotweed (*Reynoutria japonica* Houtt.) *Regulated Rivers, Research and Management*, **5**, 413–417.

Richards, Moorehead and Laing Ltd. (1990). *Japanese Knotweed (Reynoutria japonica) in Wales*. Report to the Welsh Development Agency, Cardiff.

Roblin, E. (1988). Chemical control of Japanese knotweed (*Reynoutria japonica*) on river banks in South Wales. *Aspects of Applied Biology*, **16**, 1–7.

Welsh Development Agency (1991). *Guidelines for the Control of Japanese Knotweed (Reynoutria japonica)*. Cardiff: Welsh Development Agency.

20 Status of *Fallopia japonica* (Japanese Knotweed) in Wales

DAVID J. BEERLING[1] and JOHN P. PALMER[2]

[1]*Department of Animal and Plant Sciences, PO Box 601, University of Sheffield, Sheffield S10 2UQ, UK*
[2]*Richards, Moorehead and Laing Ltd, Ruthin, UK*

INTRODUCTION

The introduction of *Fallopia japonica* (Houtt.) Ronse Decraene (Japanese knotweed) into Britain in the early nineteenth century was followed by a rapid colonization of all areas of the country (Conolly, 1977). *F. japonica* has become particularly abundant in Wales, nuisance growths occurring on river banks, amenity areas, "development land" and in other urban situations. These growths can damage building structures and have heightened the concern of the National Rivers Authority (NRA), local councils and the Welsh Development Agency (WDA). Consequently both the NRA (Welsh Region) and the WDA have funded research into the status of *F. japonica* in Wales.

This chapter has four main aims: (i) to describe the riparian and non-riparian distribution of *F. japonica* in the Principality of Wales, (ii) to examine the type of structures damaged by *F. japonica* and local authority control practices, (iii) to report the results of experimental studies assessing the effectiveness of cutting as a control method and of the viability of rhizome fragments and (iv) to describe a case study at Dolwyddelan, a village within the Snowdonia National Park, North Wales, with a recorded history of the introduction and spread of *F. japonica* (Richards, Moorehead and Laing Ltd, 1990). Based on the results, improved management practices are recommended, designed to contain the spread of *F. japonica* in Wales and other areas of the British Isles more effectively.

Ecology and Management of Invasive Riverside Plants
Edited by L. C. de Waal, L. E. Child, P. M. Wade and J. H. Brock
© 1994 John Wiley & Sons Ltd

DISTRIBUTION

RIPARIAN OCCURRENCE

Distribution data from all major rivers in Wales were collected by bailiffs, within each region of the NRA (Welsh Region). To co-ordinate bailiffs in each division (South Eastern, South Western, and Northern), regional conservation and fisheries officers were requested to provide census forms enabling bailiffs to (a) identify *F. japonica* accurately, (b) provide information on the scale of abundance along 200 m lengths of river bank (absent, present in small amounts, abundant or absent) and (c) provide the location of sites visited (National Grid references). Forms were issued in 1987 and an interim map produced which indicated the rivers requiring further surveys. In 1988, survey forms were re-issued to provide data for rivers not surveyed in 1987 (full details of the survey are given by Beerling (1990a)). By the end of 1988, 643 National Grid references were collected and plotted on a digitised map of Welsh rivers (with average flows >2.5 m^3/s) using a mainframe computer (DEC Vax) and GIMS (Geographical Information and Mapping System) mapping software. The riparian distribution of *F. japonica* (Figure 20.1) was compared with unpublished surveys of several Welsh rivers (Gunn, 1986; Welsh Water Authority, 1986) for verification. Figure 20.1 shows that *F. japonica* was present on many rivers throughout Wales (84% of those surveyed). It was particularly abundant in north-western and south-eastern Wales, but with patchy distribution elsewhere. Its range was notably restricted along the Usk and the upper reaches of the Wye; these two rivers would be especially suited to monitoring the future spread of the plant. The proportions of sites where *F. japonica* was absent, present in small amounts, or abundant were 55.5, 25.2 and 19.3%, respectively.

NON-RIPARIAN OCCURRENCE

In 1989 the environmental consultants Richards, Moorehead and Laing (RML) determined the distribution of *F. japonica* by district in Wales. Questionnaires were sent to local authorities and supplemented with data from surveys in mid-Wales by the University College of Wales, Aberystwyth and other areas by RML staff. Sixty percent of Welsh Counties replied and provided sufficient information, when combined with the other survey data, to produce Figure 20.2, showing the distribution and abundance of *F. japonica* by district. The geographical pattern of abundance (Figure 20.2) reflects a combination of the time since introduction into a district, climatic restrictions and the extent and frequency of earth-moving operations in the area. South Wales was one of the first areas of introduction and consequently *F. japonica* is most abundant there; it was not until the 1930s that

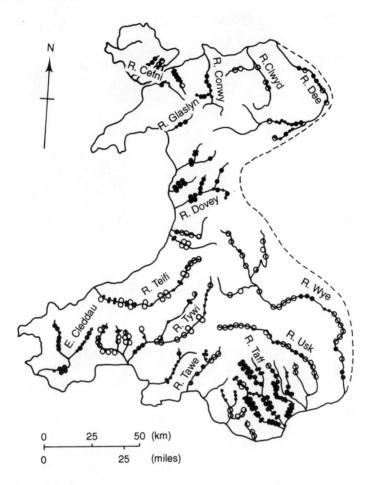

Figure 20.1 Distribution of *Fallopia japonica* in 1988 on rivers within the National Rivers Authority (Welsh Region). Scales of abundance were ● abundant, • present in small amounts ○ known absence. Symbols either side of a river indicate left and right bank distribution, centred symbols indicate unspecified by bailiffs. All abundance values were for 200-m lengths of river bank and are subjective (from Beerling, 1990a)

it became established in North Wales and Gwent. The remaining areas were colonized by the 1960s and here the plant was less abundant. In upland Wales (Brecon, Radnor and Montgomery) *F. japonica* was restricted to localized concentrations, as might be expected for a plant that occurs mainly below 320 m (Beerling *et al.*, in press) and in an area with few major construction schemes, such as road building and flood protection works.

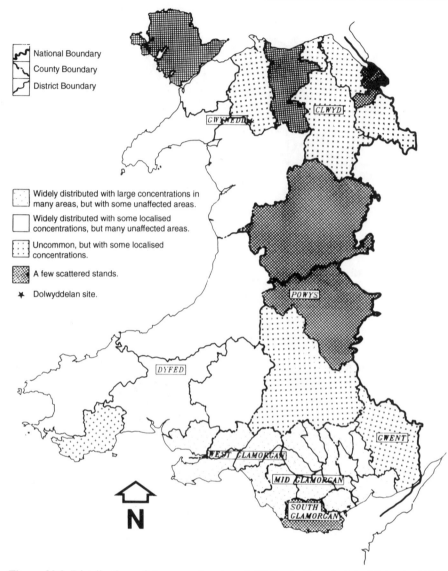

Figure 20.2 Distribution of Japanese knotweed (*Fallopia Japonica*) in Wales in 1989 (reproduced by permission of the Welsh Development Agency). A star indicates the Dolwyddelan site described in the case study

Clearly *F. japonica* is present throughout Wales on river banks and in non-riparian localities. The two distribution maps (Figures 20.1 & 20.2) must, however, be considered together because local availability of the plant on river banks is important when considering the spread of the plant into other areas. Conversely, the geographical distribution of the plant away from watercourses is important when assessing the likely invasion of river banks.

DAMAGED STRUCTURES AND LOCAL AUTHORITY CONTROL PRACTICES

The questionnaire returns provided information on the type of structures damaged by *F. japonica* in Wales and on the location of sites with nuisance growths of the plant. Table 20.1 shows that flood protection schemes suffered the most widespread damage. The open structure of the concrete cellular flood revetment blocks frequently used in such schemes (Lewis and Williams, 1984) makes them susceptible to displacement by *F. japonica* within a few seasons' growth (Beerling, 1991a; Edwards and Howell, 1989). Occasional damage (Table 20.1) occurred when stands of *F. japonica* encroached from waste land onto roads and pavements, penetrating tarmac and displacing paving stones and kerb blocks. Whilst *F. japonica* can physically damage structures, its introduction into new sites should also be avoided on conservation grounds; dense stands rapidly become established and reduce the diversity of both floral (Grime *et al.*, 1988) and invertebrate (Beerling, 1990a; Emery, 1983) species.

To control *F. japonica* and prevent damage to structures, Welsh local authorities used 15 herbicides (three non-persistent) and five manual methods. Glyphosate was the most frequently used herbicide, but achieved only limited success; 52% of authorities reported effective control and 48% regarded it as unsuccessful. Recent comparative trials with glyphosate and 2,4-D amine suggested that the latter was equally effective for reducing the

Table 20.1. Type of structure damaged by *Fallopia japonica* and sites of nuisance stands reported by local authorities in Wales

Type of damage/sites of nuisance stands	Widespread	Occasional	Rare
Damage to flood protection schemes	12	6	1
Damage to tarmac, paving and kerbs	7	17	6
Invasion of sown vegetation (e.g. roadside verges and amenity areas)	7	19	5
Other (including graveyards, gardens, woodland and grazing land)	3	3	3

biomass of *F. japonica* within a single season (Beerling, 1990b). The selective action of 2,4-D amine allowed the persistence of grass swards after treatment, producing an aesthetically pleasing surface relatively resistant to soil erosion—a problem which can arise after treatment with glyphosate (Roblin, 1988). Five methods of manual control all involved cutting plants or the excavation of the underground rhizome system; none was reported to be successful.

EXPERIMENTAL INVESTIGATIONS

EFFECTIVENESS OF CUTTING CLUMPS AS A CONTROL METHOD

The expansion of stands of *F. japonica* on the banks of the River Sirhowy at Cwmfelinfach, near Caerphilly (National Grid Reference ST 188 913) was measured over a 3-year period (1988–90) and the effect of cutting stands down, a practice sometimes carried out by site managers, examined. Figure 20.3 shows that cut stands expanded greatly in radius, compared with uncut stands, suggesting that this practice increased lateral rhizome growth (Beerling, 1990a). Stand expansion (expressed as radial increase) was independent of initial stand size (Figure 20.3). However, the degree of expansion differed in 1989 and 1990. Scott (1988) reported that cutting *F. japonica* stems in late May increased stem density from 40 to 80 per m^2 after 2 weeks. Flailing of *F. japonica* stems was used as a method of control by the National Parks Authority in Snowdonia and the Glamorgan Nature Trust (Gregson, 1981); both were regarded as ineffective and labour intensive.

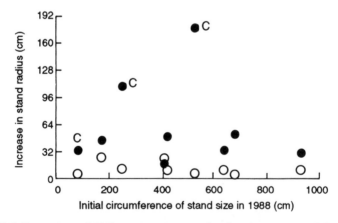

Figure 20.3 Expansion of *Fallopia japonica* stands after 1 year ○ and 2 years ●; C indicates stands cut down after measurement in June 1989 (from Beerling, 1990a)

Further long-term work is needed to assess the effects of cutting on the vigour of *F. japonica*. However, this initial study shows that cutting stands promotes the spread of *F. japonica* and cannot be recommended as a method of control.

VIABILITY OF RHIZOME FRAGMENTS

The viability of fragments of rhizomes and whole corms was investigated in 1988 using a range of sizes, with and without buds, planted in triplicate under natural conditions. The results (Table 20.2) showed that both corms and rhizome fragments >7.8 g (wet weight) were able to produce foliage rapidly within 50 days (Beerling, 1990a). These rhizome fragments were smaller than those used by Callaghan *et al.* (1984) to establish populations of *F. japonica* (mean fresh weight 62.2 g; mean number of buds 4). Clearly, these results have implications for organizations which transport topsoil between sites for land drainage purposes or for use on land reclamation and building sites. These practices will lead to increased abundance and spread of *F. japonica* through (i) maceration of existing rhizome systems into small viable fragments and (ii) the spread of viable fragments onto new areas of land.

DOLWYDDELAN: A CASE STUDY

Dolwyddelan (National Grid reference SH 748 531) is a small village in the Afon Lledr Valley between Betws-y-Coed and Blaenau Ffestiniog which lies within the border of the Snowdonia National Park (Figure 20.2). The area was typical of many rural sites colonized by *F. japonica* in Wales, but unusual in having a known site history. In 1989 all *F. japonica* stands in Dolwyddelan were mapped and for each stand four characteristics were determined: (i) habitat type, (ii) the type of habitat being invaded, (iii) the damage or benefits caused to sites and (iv) the mode of introduction. A total of 69 stands of *F. japonica* was recorded from a variety of habitats, although it was most common along the banks of the Afon Lledr and roadside verges (Table 20.3); 75 and 25% of stands were on private and public land, respectively. Stand sizes ranged from single-stemmed shoots to patches >500 m^2; frequencies of stand sizes were >3 m^2 62%, 3–7 m^2 26%, 8–14 m^2 6% and >14 m^2 6%. A subjective assessment of the invasiveness of each *F. japonica* stand was made by recording the habitat into which the leading edge encroached. Those habitats most at risk from invasion were pasture, river banks and roadside verges (Table 20.3). Nuisance growths of the plant along roadside verges reduced visibility for road users, and visual intrusion of the landscape by tall dense stands was also reported (Table 20.4). The largest

Table 20.2. Growth of *Fallopia japonica* rhizome fragments after 50 days; all values are means of three replicates ± SE

Fragment type	Initial weight of rhizome	Final weight of rhizome	Mean percentage increase	Biomass of above-ground shoots produced after 50 days (dry weight, g)		
	(wet weight, g)			Stems	Leaves	Total
Rhizome no buds	10.2 ± 2.7	16.7 ± 4.2	63.7	1.2 ± 0.2	1.6 ± 0.3	2.8 ± 0.5
Rhizome two buds	13.1 ± 3.9	21.7 ± 7.9	65.6	1.0 ± 0.1	1.4 ± 0.1	2.4 ± 0.2
Rhizome three buds	7.8 ± 1.0	13.2 ± 2.5	69.2	0.71 ± 0.1	1.3 ± 0.1	2.1 ± 0.2
Corm no buds	93.7 ± 26.6	111.3 ± 12.7	18.8	3.7 ± 1.0	1.6 ± 0.2	3.2 ± 0.4
Corm one bud	55.1 ± 8.2	55.4 ± 8.2	0.54	0.55 ± 0.1	0.57 ± 0.1	1.1 ± 0.2
Corm three buds	24.4 ± 4.9	24.4 ± 5.1	0.0	0.55 ± 0.1	0.57 ± 0.1	1.1 ± 0.2

Table 20.3. Location and types of habitat invaded by *Fallopia japonica* in the Dolwyddelan area, North Wales

Habitat	Number of stands	Number of invasive stands
Roadside verge	13	11
River banks and shingle	36	13
Rough pasture	5	30
Gardens	3	5
Abandoned slate quarries	6	5
Woodland	3	1
Miscellaneous	3	2

NB: The number of stands considered invasive was greater than the total number counted (69) in rough pasture and gardens because large stands may occupy more than one habitat.

Table 20.4. Type of damage/benefit and the location of nuisance stands of *Fallopia japonica* at Dolwyddelan ($n = 69$ sites

Damage or benefit	Percentage of total sites
Loss of grazing pasture	34
Damage to flood revetment schemes	4
Damage to structures (buildings and walls)	3
Out-competing planted vegetation (i.e. roadside verges etc.)	9
Reduced car park space	1
Reduced visibility along roads	13
Visually intrusive	13
No damage	12
Stabilizing river bank	2

recorded category of habitat lost in the Dolwyddelan area was grazing pasture (Table 20.4). This was surprising because previous work established that on riparian areas regularly grazed by either sheep or cattle the abundance and occurrence of *F. japonica* was significantly ($P < 0.01$) lower than in ungrazed areas (Beerling, 1991b). The discrepancy with the present results may be attributable to different grazing regimes. Plants grazed throughout the growing season are effectively cropped and reasonable control is achieved. If, however, animals are introduced into fields late in the season *F. japonica* plants become too tall to permit effective cropping by either sheep or cattle, resulting in poor control and a potential loss of grazing pasture.

Table 20.5. Mode of introduction of *Fallopia japonica* into Dolwyddelan

Mode of introduction	Number of stands	Percentage of total
In imported earth to construct flood protection schemes	10	14.5
Vegetative spread along flood-protecting embankment	5	7.3
Rhizome dispersed downstream	19	27.6
In material imported to widen the A470 road	9	13
Vegetative spread along widened verges of the A470 road	2	2.9
In tipped rubbish	9	13
Not known	15	21.7

The 69 stands in Dolwyddelan were assessed, where possible, for their mode of introduction into the area (Table 20.5). The most important anthropogenic mode was the importation of soil contaminated with rhizome fragments for use with the two civil engineering schemes in the area (road widening and the construction of flood revetment works). In 1980 the Welsh Water Authority constructed an embankment along the Afon Lledr to prevent flooding in Dolwyddelan. *F. japonica* stands subsequently became established within it, extending along 57% of the 350 m length. The widening of the A470 road in Dowlyddelan, the second engineering scheme, was carried out during the 1980s. After this operation, linear stands of *F. japonica* were established along 78% of the 160 m length of roadside verge.

This case study in Dolwyddelan illustrates how *F. japonica* may become locally abundant within a short period and its invasiveness in a number of amenity areas—a situation typical of many sites in South Wales. Virtually no attempt to control the plant was made, except where it occurred in private gardens and, in consequence, Dolwyddelan may now suffer an expansion of *F. japonica* distribution comparable to that experienced by some towns in South Wales (e.g. Maesteg and Pontypridd; Conolly, 1977).

DISCUSSION AND MANAGEMENT RECOMMENDATIONS

The survey of local authority management practices and the extent to which *F. japonica* was considered a problematic weed in Wales indicated that a more rigorous and systematic approach was required to contain the spread of the plant effectively. Based on the results presented in this paper and on other studies, the following management recommendations are proposed.

CONTROL

Manual cutting of stands is unlikely to be an effective long-term control measure and there were no reports by local authorities that lasting control was achieved using this method. Chemical control of *F. japonica* is the only practical option in the absence of any biological control organisms and where its use is compatible with existing land uses. Before attempting to control *F. japonica* it is essential that each site should be assessed for location of stands, ease of access for spraying equipment and operators, choice of herbicide, timing of application, funding and follow up treatment. Control of stands on non-riparian land has been achieved using the persistent herbicides picloram or dicamba (Scott and Marrs, 1984). On sites where *F. japonica* grows near watercourses, only herbicides approved under the Pesticide Safety Precaution Scheme can be used (Ministry of Agriculture, Fisheries and Food, 1984). Of those approved under the scheme, the selective non-persistent herbicide 2,4-D amine is especially suitable because it allows persistent grass cover; glyphosate may be appropriate when grass swards are not important (Beerling, 1990a, b). To establish effective control it is essential that arrangements are made for treated areas to be monitored in subsequent seasons and that any regrowth is re-treated. Besides treating large conspicuous stands it is also important to control small isolated populations from which subsequent invasions may occur (Moody and Mack, 1988). Mathematical modelling of alien plant invasions shows that a minimum of 30% of the satellite populations within an area should be destroyed in order to improve the effectiveness of control treatments (Moody and Mack, 1988).

LAND USE

Riparian land use affects the abundance and occurrence of *F. japonica* along river banks (Beerling, 1991b). Where grazing occurs on sites with *F. japonica* present, livestock should be kept on the land throughout the whole growing season. Grazing is an important land use capable of reducing riparian abundance, especially when farmers are prepared to allow stock access to the water's edge.

F. japonica frequently dominates the vegetation on waste ground in Wales, and local authorities reported many cases where dumped rubbish containing rhizome fragments led to new sites of establishment for the plant, particularly on land near or adjacent to gardens. Policies are therefore required to prevent further spread of the plant onto new areas of land by this method of dispersal.

MOVEMENT OF TOPSOIL

Clearly some dispersal of *F. japonica* occurred through the movement of contaminated topsoil and its use on land reclamation and building sites. Long-distance dispersal of *F. japonica* also occurs by the downstream transport of rhizomes by water, particularly when rivers are in spate. To prevent further unnecessary anthropogenic increases in the distribution of *F. japonica*, the movement of topsoil should be controlled, using only soil obtained from sites free of *F. japonica*. In some cases Welsh authorities reported that such restrictions were already enforced, topsoil being inspected for any visible signs of *F. japonica* before being removed. Such restrictions should also apply to the dumping of unwanted topsoil. A theoretical method of decontaminating top soil would be to sieve out any rhizome fragments. Whilst this technique may work for the small quantities of soil used by gardeners, it would clearly be impractical for large-scale topsoil transport used in industry. A more practical alternative would be to establish a programme of education to ensure that operators moving soil can identify the above-ground shoots and foliage of *F. japonica* during the growing season and the dead stems, underground rhizomes and corms during the winter period. In addition, planners, ecologists, surveyors and engineers should be made aware of *F. japonica* and its potential problems.

ACKNOWLEDGMENTS

We thank the National Rivers Authority (Welsh Region) for their help with the river corridor surveys, the Welsh Development Agency for funding, and all those who provided questionnaire returns. This paper was written whilst D. J. Beerling held an SERC Total Technology Studentship at the School of Pure and Applied Biology, University of Wales College of Cardiff.

REFERENCES

Beerling, D.J. (1990a). *The ecology and control of Japanese knotweed* (Reynoutria japonica) *and Himalayan balsam* (Impatiens glandulifera) *on river banks in South Wales*. PhD thesis, University of Wales, Cardiff.

Beerling, D.J. (1990b). The use of non-persistent herbicides, glyphosate and 2,4-D amine, to control riparian stands of Japanese knotweed (*Reynoutria japonica* Houtt.). *Regulated Rivers, Research and Management*, **5**, 413–417.

Beerling, D.J. (1991a). The testing of cellular concrete revetment blocks resistant to growths of *Reynoutria japonica* Houtt. (Japanese knotweed). *Water Research*, **25**, 495–498.

Beerling, D.J. (1991b). The effect of riparian land use on the occurrence and abundance of Japanese knotweed (*Reynoutria japonica* Houtt.) on selected rivers in South Wales. *Biological Conservation*, **55**, 329–337.

Beerling, D.J., Bailey, J.P. and Conolly, A.P. (in press). *Fallopia japonica* (Houtt.) Ronse Decraene, Biological Flora of the British Isles. *Journal of Ecology*.

Callaghan, T.V., Scott, R., Lawson, G.J. and Mainwaring, A.M. (1984). *An Experimental Assessment of Native and Naturalised Species of Plants as Renewable Energy Sources in Great Britain. III. Japanese Knotweed* Reynoutria japonica. Institute of Terrestrial Ecology (NERC), Merlewood, Cumbria.

Conolly, A.P. (1977). The distribution and history in the British Isles of some alien species of *Polygonum* and *Reynoutria*. *Watsonia*, **11**, 291–311.

Edwards, R.W. and Howell, R. (1989). Welsh rivers and reservoirs: management for wildlife conservation. *Regulated Rivers, Research and Management*, **4**, 213–223.

Emery, M.J. (1983). *The ecology of Japanese knotweed, its herbivores and pathogens and their potential as biological control agents*. MSc thesis, University of Wales, Bangor.

Gregson, D. (1981). Control of Japanese knotweed in Glamorgan. *Conservation Officers Bulletin*, **7**, 25–26.

Grime, J.P., Hodgson, J.G. and Hunt, R. (1988). *Comparative Plant Ecology: A Functional Approach*. London: Unwin Hyman.

Gunn, I.D.M. (1986). *Distributional survey of Japanese knotweed*. MSc thesis, UWIST, Cardiff.

Lewis, G. and Williams , G. (1984). *Rivers and Wildlife Handbook: A Guide to Practices which Further Conservation of Wildlife in Rivers*. Sandy, Bedfordshire: RSPB and RSNC.

Moody, M.E. and Mack, R.N. (1988). Controlling the spread of plant invasions: the importance of nascent foci. *Journal of Applied Ecology*, **25**, 1009–1021.

Ministry of Agriculture, Fisheries and Food (1985). *Guidelines for the Use of Herbicides on Weeds in or near Watercourses and Lakes*. Booklet B2078. London: HMSO.

Richards, Moorehead and Laing Ltd (1990). *Japanese Knotweed* (Reynoutria japonica) *in Wales*. Report to the Welsh Development Agency, Cardiff.

Roblin, E. (1988). Chemical control of Japanese knotweed (*Reynoutria japonica*) on river banks in South Wales. *Aspects of Applied Biology*, **16**, 1–7.

Scott, R. (1988). *A Review of Japanese Knotweed Control*. NCC/NERC contract report, Institute of Terrestrial Ecology, Natural Environmental Research Council, Merlewood, Cumbria.

Scott, R. and Marrs, R.H. (1984). Impact of Japanese knotweed and methods of control. *Aspects of Applied Biology*, **56**, 291–296.

Welsh Water Authority (1986). *River Tawe Management Plan*. Scientific Services SW/ 12/86.

Index

Note: Page references in *italics* refer to Figures; those in **bold** refer to Tables

in *Tamarix* control 38
vegetation management 185–7
weed control using 183–8

Hedera helix 71, 161
Heracleum asperum see Heracleum mantegazzianum
Heracleum giganteum see Heracleum mantegazzianum
Heracleum lanatum 63
Heracleum mantegazzianum 19, 243 *see also* giant hogweed
biological control in the UK 174, 180
biological observations 106–7
  harmful effects 107
control and management 55–64, 94–9, 111–24
  along Irish river corridors 67–75
  chopping 105
  control experiences 106
  coordinated 121–2
  current recommendations 115–22
  cutting 74, 105, 119–20
  digging 120
  field survey 59–64
    herbivores found on 60, **61**
    impact of herbivores on 63–4, **63**
    plant diseases 60–1
    recruitment of herbivores onto 61–2
  genetic manipulation 123
  grazing as control method 77–89, 95, 105, 121
    changes in plant communities 81–7, *82*, **83–4,** *85, 86*
    response to cessation of 87, **87**
    study area 78, *79*
    study area before treatment 80–1
    vegetation analyses 78–80, *81*
  herbicidal 72–4, 94, 104, 116–19
  long-term strategy 122–3
  herbivores/pathogens 122–3
  mechanical methods 95
  ploughing 120
  postal survey 56–9
    cost of control 58–9, **58**
    habitats colonized 57
    methods of control 57
    regions affected 57
  pulling 120

in Scotland 121
selective control 95–9, *96–8*
in Sweden 93–100
crop disease host 10
disadvantages of 103–4
distribution 101–2, *102*, 111–12
effect on native flora 103
effects on livestock 104
flowering 106
glyphosate control 55, 57, 70, 72–4, 94, 104, 106, 116–17, 119, 183, 185–6
hybridization 103
invasion and spread 45–53, 67–75, 93–4
  altitude and 50, *51*
  effect of climate on 50–2, *52*
  history 45–6, *47*, 52
  role of recipient habitat 46–50, **48,** *49–50*
rate of spread 103
restriction of access 103–4
river bank erosion 103
roadside obstruction 104
seed dispersal 68
seed viability 223
species description 77–8, 190
toxicity 104, 112–14
Heracleum sphondylium 56, 59, 71, 72, 103, 114, 123, 180
  herbivores found on 60, **61**, 61–2, 63
Heracleum villosum see Heracleum mantegazzianum
herbicides *see under* names
hexakinon
  in *Heracleum mantegazzianum* control 118
hexazinone
  in *Heracleum mantegazzianum* control 118
  in *Tamarix* control 38, 39
Himalayan balsam *see Impatiens glandulifera*
hydrogen peroxide 11
Hypericum perforatum 173

imazapyr
  in *Fallopia japonica* control 168
  in *Heracleum mantegazzianum* control 104, 118, 119
  in *Tamarix* control 38, 39

Index compiled by Annette Musker

SHROPSHIRE LIBRARIES

Please return or renew before the last date stamped below. Renewal may be in person or by telephone, providing it is not required by another user. Please quote details on label below.